Doubts and Decisions
for Living

VOLUME I
The Foundation of Human Thoughts

List of Books by This Author
(As at 2016)

Non fiction

The Nature of Love and Relationships 2011, **2016** 2nd Edition
Doubts and Decisions for Living:
   Volume I: The Foundation of Human Thoughts   **2014**
   Volume II: The Sanctity of Human Spirit   **2014**
   Volume III: The Structure of Human Life   **2014**
Relationship Facts, Trends, and Choices **2016**
The Mysteries of Life, Love, and Happiness **2016**
Relationship Needs, Framework, and Models **2016**
Gender Qualities, Quirks, and Quarrels **2016**
Marriage and Divorce Hardships **2016**

Fiction

Persian Moons 2007, **2016** 2nd Edition
Midnight Gate-opener 2011, **2016** 2nd Edition
My Lousy Life Stories   **2014**

Doubts and Decisions
for Living

VOLUME I
The Foundation of Human Thoughts

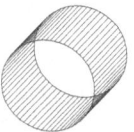

Tom Omidi, Ph.D.

Copyright © 2014 by Tom Omidi

All rights reserved. No part of this book may be reproduced, translated, or transmitted in any form or by any means—graphic, electronic or mechanical, including photocopying, recording, taping or information storage or retrieval systems—without the prior written permission of the publisher or author.

Library and Archives Canada Cataloguing in Publication

Omidi, Tom, 1945-, author
Doubts and decisions for living / Tom Omidi, Ph.D.

Contents: Volume I. The foundation of human thoughts
Volume II. The sanctity of human spirit
Volume III. The structure of human life.

ISBN 978-0-9783666-6-7 (v. 1 : pbk.).
ISBN 978-0-9783666-7-4 (v. 2 : pbk.).
ISBN 978-0-9783666-8-1 (v. 3 : pbk.).

1. Conduct of life. I. Title.
II. Title: Foundation of human thoughts.
III. Title: Sanctity of human spirit.
IV. Title: Structure of human life.

BJ1581.2.O45 2014   170'.44   C2014-903378-8

Cover page design by Tom Omidi

Published by Eros Books,
Vancouver, British Columbia
Canada

contact@erosbooks.net

Printed in the United States of America

For my children

"And you…!?
"Have you yet figured out
 all your reasons for living?"

Table of Contents

	Page
Prologue	1
Introduction	5

PART I: Thoughts and Feelings

Chapter One: Humans' Fundamental Thoughts	21
Reasons for Living	24
Means of a Happy Life	26
Making Our Lives Complete	28
Enjoying Life at Its Fullest	31
Exploring the Inner 'Self'	36
Defining the Essence of Humanness	37
Effecting Change and Improving Social Order	40
Choosing a Path of Wisdom	41
Gaining Our Freedom	44
Living Practically but Not Submissively	50
Nurturing Our Positive Doubts	53
Fighting but Not Fearing Depression	57
Making Major Life Decisions	62
Finding a Reliable Companion	63
Optimizing Our Physical and Mental Health	63
Chapter Two: Perceived and Real Worlds	69
Characteristic of the 'Real World'	70
Characteristic of the 'Perceived World'	70
Perceptions about Our Identity	73
Perceptions about Dependence and Independence	74
Perceptions about Love	75
Perceptions about Religions	75
Perceived and Real Worlds	82
Exploring the Real World	87
A Picture of the Real World	92

Table of Contents (Cont.)

	Page
PART II: Facts and Myths	
Chapter Three: The Essence of Facts	101
The Complexity Level of Our Perceptions	104
Meaning and Implication of Our Perceptions	106
Facts, Myths, and Challenges	109
Establishing a Framework	112
Chapter Four: Main Mental Reconciliations	115
Physical Self, Spiritual 'Self', Humanness	115
Life, Freedom, Valuing Our Doubts	122
Nature, Love, Relationships	125
Physical Growth, Truth, Psychological Growth	129
Social Living, Happiness, Coping and Adaptation	131
Economic Constraints, Chance, Contentment	134
Personal Limitations, Enlightenment, Decisions	138
Personal Needs, Purity, Needs Gratification	141
Perceived Reality, Real Reality, Health	144
Death, Creation/Creator, Spirituality	147
The Nature of Facts, Myths, and Challenges	151
PART III: Happiness and Depression	
Chapter Five: Power and Personality	157
Personality Aspects	159
Addendum: A Comparison of the Id, Ego, and	
Superego with Self, Ego, and Model	164
Chapter Six: 'Self' and Happiness	167
Description of Happiness	168
'Happiness' Attributes	169
The Happiness of 'Model'	173
The Happiness of 'Ego'	178
The Happiness of 'Self'	182
Personality Aspects' Role for Happiness	186

Table of Contents (Cont.)

Page

Chapter Seven: Personality and Depression	189
The Depression of 'Model'	190
The Depression of 'Ego'	192
The Depression of 'Self'	195
The Happiness/Depression Cycles	197
The Formula of Happiness	200

<u>PART IV: Philosophy and Reality</u>

Chapter Eight: Social Conscience and Philosophy	207
Personal Philosophy	208
Our Habits and Life Routines	210
Basic Plans and Ideologies	212
The Ideal Personality	216
The 'Self' Aspect of the Ideal Personality	217
'Model' and 'Ego' Roles for the Ideal Personality	223
Chapter Nine: Thoughts and Wisdom	225
The Fundamental Questions	227
The Main Philosophical Questions	229
The Foundation of Human Thoughts	234
Managing Our Thoughts	236
The Significance of No-thought Experiences	239
Chapter Ten: Thoughts and Sufferings	245
Common Sources of Suffering	249
The Structure of Human Life	255
Life's Major Decisions	258
'Life' and 'Self' Decisions	262
The Substance of 'Life' and 'Self' Decisions	263
The 'Self' and 'Life' Impasse	267

Table of Contents (Cont.)

Page

Chapter Eleven: Actions and Adjustments 271
   1. Social Disorder 272
   2. The Role of Destiny 273
   3. Personal Negligence 275
      The Morality of Our Actions 276
      Awareness and Actions 277
      The Capacity to Adjust and Act 282
      Changes and Adjustments 285
Chapter Twelve: 'Forward Thinking' Philosophy 291
      Phase Three Reference 297
      Phase Two Reference 301
      Phase One reference 305
Epilogue 309

List of Tables and Diagrams

Table 1.1: Humans' Fundamental Thoughts 22
Diagram 2.1: The Path of Awakening—Eros Dimension. . . 85
Table 3.1: Suggested List of Facts, Myths, and Challenges . 113

Prologue

The night my first child was born, thirty years ago, my life changed forever—for better or worse, I would never know. Many lucky (or doomed) parents probably feel the same way when suddenly a huge sense of love and responsibility hits them like a sledgehammer and keeps them anxious for the rest of their lives. At the time, I had a flourishing career in Iran with promising prospects. But, that night, I felt I should do everything in my power to make my kids' future as solid and happy as possible. The first thing to do then was to find a peaceful place for them to grow up in—a better society with more opportunities and freedom. After a few months of struggling with all kinds of doubts, the need for taking some risks became obvious. I left my wife and child behind to travel to the United States in 1981 and apply for immigration to Canada, which appeared to be the best country for my children to live in. Depriving myself from the joy of witnessing my baby start to talk and walk was only one of many sacrifices I had to make to pursue my goal. All along, many other doubts tortured me about my sanity to plan such a difficult and unpredictable future and leave behind everything I loved in my own country, including my parents, family, and friends.

Due to the Iran-Iraq war and the closure of all borders, only government authorities were allowed to leave Iran on official business. And the U.S. consulates had stopped issuing visitor's visas to Iranian citizens due to the hostility between the U.S. and Iran's new regime. Yet I overcame all these obstacles and got our permanent residency papers from the Canadian Consulate in Los Angeles within a year, despite a ban on education-based admissions—due to the recession and high unemployment in Canada. Then my young wife and daughter had to flee Iran through Pakistan border with enormous difficulty and hardship on top of the large sum of money we paid for smuggling them on foot out of Iran. In Vancouver, I looked for a job matching my qualifications for four years and our second child was born too. By then we had spent our lifetime savings. We were on the verge of destitute when I finally found a relatively suitable job. Afterward, life became somewhat easier and our kids grew up away from all the hassles of wars, the educational curriculum of an Islamic regime, and the limited freedom of expression in Iran. Overall, I often believe my decision thirty years ago has been correct.

The above short account of our pains to bring our kids to Canada cannot reflect the true hardship that my wife and I endured to make our kids' future more enriching and to give them an opportunity to live in a better environment. A large book should explain the details of all the challenges and setbacks we faced to finally make this dream come true.

But the main point for mentioning our story—just for settling in Canada—is to stress the agony that most parents willingly bear for their children. Yet, as my kids got older, it seemed that I had an even more taxing task ahead. I felt that my main responsibility as a parent was to answer their questions and guide them during adolescence when all kids face the highest amount of doubts about themselves and life and must make very serious decisions in a short span of time. As a parent, my duty to enlighten them, if I could, appeared ten times more important and difficult than all the hardships of bringing them to Canada and providing them with a comfortable life. Considering the hassles of living in modern societies with inefficient economies, unreliable job markets, phony lifestyles, and materialistic values, it was necessary to prepare my kids to think somewhat independently instead of accepting all those values blindly. I had to tell them what life was all about—if I could. The questions were whether I understood life myself and whether my kids cared about hearing my interpretation of life. The answer to both questions seemed to be a resounding 'no.' I did not know much about life myself, and my children, like all other kids, were not interested in hearing the advice of their old-fashioned parents. Still it seemed imperative to me to somehow complete my responsibility. I had to establish my opinions about the main features of human life and struggles for my own benefit at least. Maybe I could then share my sound conclusions with others, too, especially youths who strive to find themselves and their futures in such debilitating environment. It dawned on me finally that it would be more productive to write a book gradually and systematically instead of offering random ideas here and there. Then maybe my kids and others took the trouble of reading this account of a parent's wisdom leisurely on their own.

Therefore, I started this trilogy fifteen years ago and finished it in three years. Through extensive research and contemplation, a comprehensive book evolved gradually, but I failed to get my kids to read it carefully. The reasons for my failure to raise their interest are noted in the Epilogue. Apparently, we all like to discover our naivety about modern life and society the hard way—after many years of experimentation and disappointments. Perhaps my kids read this book more keenly eventually when their youthful egoism subsides and social artificialities become more apparent to them. Would it be too late by then to sharpen their focus and revamp their lifestyles? Would the points raised in this trilogy be still useful to set their life priorities more realistically and escape life traps?

Not all parents have the time and patience to explore the meaning and effects of the new lifestyles objectively and collectively. Besides, it is hard to draw a general picture of life and its pitfalls in the 21st century. No study in this area can be easy, straight forward, or complete. But I have accepted this task on behalf of many parents who would like to give their children a more realistic view of life outside the misleading social norms.

Happy reading
Tom Omidi, Ph.D.
Vancouver, 2014

Introduction

This trilogy intends to aid young adults who face many questions and doubts about life, but must make timely, smart decisions for their welfare and future. Yet, the discussions are equally useful for us all, especially parents, to assess our life dilemmas. As our unconscious 'inner child' deeply affects our perceptions and relationships at all ages, the messages of this book can kindle our drive for self-awareness. They can help us explore the meaning of life and seek the means of achieving contentment and freedom more naturally. Maybe then, we could give some valuable advice to our kids too.

Thus, this trilogy intends to explore the main characteristics of living, which revolves around humans' inherent ability to think, feel, and act. This requires an evolving Foundation of Human Thoughts (as discussed in Volume I), a divine mentality (and high spirits) for understanding and compassion (as discussed in Volume II), and a supposedly purposeful Structure of Human Life (as discussed in Volume III). In return, a vast amount of excruciating doubts and decisions affect or drive our thoughts, actions, and feelings. In fact, our doubts and decisions reflect our deepest urges to think, feel, and act. They also goad us to develop a refined logic and common sense for grasping the meaning of life and the purpose of our existence. Accordingly, the matter of learning about ourselves and choosing the right path of life highly depends on how well we understand the nature, as well as the consequences, of our doubts and decisions.

Parents' Dilemmas

Every caring, intelligent parent doubts his or her parenting skills. We keep asking ourselves many questions: Have I done right by my children? Have I been a good mentor and role model for them? Have I communicated everything I know about life that may be useful to them for developing their value systems and for making the right decisions? Most importantly: Are my perceptions of life valid enough to share with others?

These and similar doubts perturb every conscientious parent, as we wish to prepare our children for life challenges. Some of us are humble enough to admit that we can never be sure about the meaning of life and the kind of lifestyle that might best give our kids a peaceful future. So, we try to be careful with our advice and definitely not get dogmatic with some of our lousy opinions. Yet, we are concerned about their welfare and happiness in our failing societies. We hope they do not repeat our mistakes. Actually, we subconsciously wish to relive, through our children, the stages of life that have proven to be either blissful or nightmarish for us, which must be somehow corrected now at least for (or through) our children. For example, we may advise our children about their careers or relationships, because we have succeeded or failed in our own decisions.

However, advising our kids is a risky and difficult task nowadays, as no reliable guidelines are available for living in our overly complex, chaotic, and superficial societies. In particular, explaining the meanings of success and happiness is impossible nowadays as we witness the depressing outcome of our supposedly astute search for life's virtues. How can anybody not doubt the validity of his/her interpretations of happiness and success, if s/he is not too arrogant? Only a few wise and selfless parents might know life's secrets. Even then, their ideas would appear absurd and so radically different from the alluring lifestyles that push youth only for more pleasures and greed.

Meanwhile, many parents overindulge their children to enhance their self-image and chances of success in a materialistic environment. Accordingly, kids have become too self-absorbed and spoiled to grasp the intricacies of life or care about their parents' cautions and teachings. Some parents, especially 'mothers,' go even to the odd extreme of adopting their kids' whimsical values and lifestyles just to show their modernity and support. They look quite silly when they behave and speak like their children. They pretend to be happy that at least their kids do not disdain them as often. Something is definitely wrong in a society where adults imitate their children as part of parenting.

Parents' inexperience and mentality nowadays hurt their kids' characters, too, whether they attempt to be a mentor or remain rather passive to let their kids figure out life on their own. Most of us are naïve about life and conditioned by social demands and the upbringing flaws of our own parents. Thus, we damage our children's psyche as well as our relationships with them by the time they reach adolescence.

Nevertheless, we finally learn that we cannot gain our kids' trust or hold enough influence over them. Both social influence and a premature urge for independence goad them not to listen to any advice, anyway. At best, they learn to listen diplomatically without understanding. They quickly find their parents out of touch with the fast-changing world. The wisdom of not only elderly, but any grownup, usually appears funny to them. They take even the slightest age difference as ignorance and obsolescence. So, even if we had something important to share with them, the right conditions never arise, because parents lose their authority too fast nowadays. Only a few lucky, patient, and selfless parents might succeed to build a lax and active relationship with their children and share their viewpoints without getting too pushy and dogmatic.

Youths' Conundrums

On the one hand, youths' drive to doubt their parents' wisdom, like a subtle rebellion, is often a blessing, because most of us have nothing useful to teach our kids, anyway, or do not know how to do it. Their resistance could *potentially* help them become free thinkers and listeners with objective mentalities if the society and media did not confuse them so tenaciously. In fact, both parents and society cause substantial confusion and anxiety for youths with their superficial teachings, tainted perceptions, and phony lifestyles. Peer influence during adolescence also hinders youths' desire to think objectively and independently.

On the other hand, the absence of guidelines or a reliable role model for children, due to cultural collapse in societies, hinders youths' chance for building even a primary foundation of thoughts and developing their own life values and ways. In this passive and senseless environment, our children are helplessly at the mercy of society that has no intention or capacity to teach them life's true meaning and issues. Instead, the effects of the rising financial insecurity and social deprivations for youths only make them more restless, desperate, and radical.

Children's interest in reading is somewhat encouraging as they usually learn more from reading than listening. However, what they read nowadays is often misleading them, too. Unfortunately, very few books exist for helping youths with their doubts and decisions for living, and for developing their foundation of thoughts on a solid ground. Not enough intelligent books are available to help youths understand the sad nature of the world they are inheriting, instead of raising their soppy sentimentalities and high expectations from life. Books must give them enough facts and ideas to think for themselves, instead of filling their minds with trivia, fantasy, and corny conclusions. Books must offer practical techniques and tools for establishing their personal options and choices for living. Youths must grasp the most likely consequences of their major life decisions and doubts before their hasty choices lead to lifelong depression and a sad way of subsistence. These books should reflect only our sincere lessons from life without pushing popular values to justify our own lifestyles. We need books that address major life issues in a simple language for youths, to discourage consumerism and pleasure-seeking mentality. Nonetheless, communicating through books is our last chance to stop their ultimate mental deterioration and the influence of misguiding books, TV, video games, and social media.

Along with some positive attributes our kids may inherit from us, many irreversible psychological defects infect children's mentality. They imagine we hurt them deliberately too. Even when they do not show hostility and anxiety, they often suppress an enormous level of traumas and cynicism about their parents—sometimes rightfully and sometimes due to their misperceptions. Unfortunately, even as adults, they (like the rest of us) seldom find the opportunity to recognize their idiosyncrasies and the means of overcoming them, in particular the ones etched in their unconscious minds during childhood. The outcome is that every generation, in the last century at least, has become less cultured and more doubtful about the authenticity of their lifestyles.

Social and Personal Dilemmas

Humans (especially youths) become too conditioned to think and learn anything useful outside their narrow personal perceptions and beliefs, unless some strong incentives goad them follow a long process of self-awareness. Fortunately, we all question the purpose of our struggles, while we face many complex dilemmas regularly too. We have tried, especially during adolescence and early adulthood, to find someone whose wisdom we could trust to share our thoughts with, but nobody has seemed clever enough. Thus, many of us live in depression most of our lives, because we cannot resolve our doubts about the validity of our lifestyles and we cannot make the right decisions for attaining a peaceful existence.

We have an intricate nature and a delicate soul, but have fully dedicated ourselves to social rules and values that serve neither our nature nor our soul. We are born into tough, mental conditioning environments, and forced to live in an erratic, complex society that nobody seems capable of understanding or directing its course. Overall, the perplexities of human nature and world have created havoc and stress for us all, and we are becoming increasingly disheartened with ourselves, our relationships, and socioeconomic environments. We are becoming more confused about our identity and the way we can, or should, relate to social norms and other individuals. Our relationships are mostly incomplete and often cause tremendous disappointments and sufferings. We feel our psychological dysfunctions and insecurities, but cannot help ourselves or trust anybody to help us. And, of course, our natural growth itself is often threatened by the mere necessity of living under such meagre conditions within contaminated environments.

Social and personal shortfalls are not new developments, but the downfall acceleration is now making us dizzy. Yet we are expected to adapt ourselves to this hectic condition more eagerly in order to survive. We feel obliged to set our life objectives according to some frivolous criteria of success and individualism. We must stay positive and pretend to love the life structure formulated around the interests of conglomerates and capitalism. So, we are burdened with a vast amount of unsettling problems and dilemmas, while our inner conflicts and doubts about our life choices keep piling up. Unfortunately, all these sad clues and sufferings, evident in all aspects of our lives, do not teach us anything either. We do not stop and ask, 'Is the reality of life supposed to be so gloom?'

Even for finding a remedy for our problems and anxieties, we mostly look outwardly and seek refuge in the same kinds of values and relationships that have created our problems in the first place. Consequently, the whole society feels more baffled and helpless every day about its options and identity. The bitterness of some of our experiences, especially our relationships and careers, which we had counted on to bring us happiness and peace, devastates many of us. They just prove quite contrary to what we had expected them to be and do for us.

Nowadays, everybody, especially youth, feels defeated and doubtful about his/her purpose of living or even a simple, truthful definition of life. Without reliable criteria and guidelines, making the right choices is difficult. Yet, we must decide about a large variety of critical and urgent matters every day. Thus, we just make our half-hearted decisions, hope for the best, wrestle with our doubts, and life goes on. Meanwhile, we mostly scorn ourselves for our inability to adapt perfectly to conditions and rules that we have taken as the reality of life.

We are intelligent and curious inherently and thus question the validity of our ideas, struggles, and values rather regularly. Ultimately, we face two conflicting realities: The reality of social living and the reality of our 'being.' These realities reflect the contradictory forces of external demands versus the intrinsic needs of humans. As we are mainly preoccupied by, and attracted to, external values and incentives, we have lost touch with our inner needs and dimensions. We have sacrificed our real identity in hopes of building an artificial personality through social compliance and adaptation. Accordingly, we suffer because we cannot harmonize our two conflicting realities, i.e., external versus internal realities. The question is whether they can ever be reconciled. Most likely, no, because social 'living' has become too demanding and erratic to allow any kind of compromise with our sense of 'being.' This conundrum clearly highlights our dilemmas about living and the crooked structure of life we have laid out mostly in recent decades.

We have many intellectual and instinctual dimensions that work together to build our characters and direct our efforts and visions. We seek philosophical notions, psychological knowledge, interpersonal skills, spiritual guidance, and inner 'self' energy to identify the essence of our being and find solutions for our unresolved questions and problems. We guess (and also doubt) that there must be a more fundamental reality of the universe and a higher dimension of being (perhaps our soul) that is part of our existence in spite of our lack of wisdom to comprehend it readily. We read many books to find some reasonable answers, but most of these books have become too specialized and narrow in scope. They usually tackle each dimension of humans and a related discipline or thought process to suggest solutions. Thus, even when we attempt to grasp our identity, we do not use all our knowledge and energy. We ponder some ideas sporadically without learning the full potential and limitations of humans.

There is an old saying that every individual should have two lives: One to experience and one to live. Many of us believe we would do many aspects of our lives differently if we were given a second chance to start over. After reaching certain age without having had the benefit of a thoughtful and informed decision process, it is often too late for many of us to change ourselves or our lifestyles. However, we can reassess our values and adjust our *ways of thinking,* if our experiences have taught us anything useful. Then we could possibly help our children, too, in their thinking processes perhaps through passive leadership as an honest role model. Instead of being a dogmatic parent and pushing our vague and distorted images of life upon our children, we could try to draw a truer picture of life for ourselves by reflecting upon our experiences and analysing their significance truthfully. The objective is to rebuild our fundamental thoughts according to, i) our honest view of the symbols that make one's life sensible or futile, ii) our interpretations of major life challenges and relationships, iii) our awareness about our debilitating prejudices and hang-ups, and iv) our fresh set of beliefs and convictions, and their reliability for resolving our dilemmas and making decisions. We want to test, and set, our convictions before communicating them to our children. We like to assess and accept the sad truth about life in the 21st century. Only then, our reflections may become a worthy and truthful mirror for our children to look into as well. Maybe we could even get involved in developing a solid set of guidelines for new generations about life's authentic values and essentialities. Alas, the existing socioeconomic forces limit the chances of pursuing this sacred mission—to think freely and open-mindedly, at least during our private contemplations.

Plausible Solutions

This trilogy suggests that we cannot resolve our dilemmas about our lives and identity by studying only a particular dimension of our being, e.g., our psyche, and by using only one discipline, e.g., psychology, to explain it. Rather, we must draw upon all our intellectual and instinctual abilities to explore and reconcile our life purposes within the context of social (dis)orders and pressures. It is not even enough to learn about ourselves; we should also learn how to resist the social and economic conditions that suppress our real needs and reinforce many of our psychological defects, including the ones that our parents have initially inflicted upon us.

Our main goal in life is to not only explore our humanistic dimensions away from social norms and values, but also explain them within the context of socioeconomic facts and expectations. Our challenge is to realize and internalize who we are and what we need to survive within the harsh realities of our perceived world. However, we also wish to justify both our existence and our efforts for social adaptation based on our own rules of true humanness. We strive for living practicality while attaining the aesthetic values of life and being. Can we ever, and how, reach this delicate balance?

Hence, the goal of this trilogy is to address these challenges by exploring the philosophical, psychological, spiritual, practical, ethical, and other main dimensions of human beings and discuss them collectively in a simple language. The intention is to apply all these dimensions for grasping the purpose of our being, building a more fruitful and tranquil life, and somehow adapting to socioeconomic environments as well. We can learn to develop a simple life philosophy that incorporates the realities of our socioeconomic structure, but also directs us toward the path of selfhood. Even when we remain inclined to live within our conventional value systems and decision-making processes, we can still draw on a valid foundation of thoughts to choose a more natural path of life and make our critical decisions wisely. There are some effective ways of establishing the foundation of our thoughts and assessing its validity and strength.

Regardless of our age and the level of social success, many of us continue, intuitively, to seek our ultimate 'self' in hopes of redeeming our dying spirits. While younger, we have difficulty identifying and relating to our true self. We are merely influenced and distracted by social norms and demands, which we believe address our needs the best automatically. Thus, we simply adopt and nurture a load of debilitating ideas and values. Sometimes we may rebel against the rules we find offensive or nuisance, but often we do not have proper values or convictions to replace social norms and teachings. When we grow older, we get too involved with our routine dilemmas to concern ourselves with the seemingly irresolvable question of 'self.' We simply continue to follow the prevalent lifestyles and try to blend in because society would not allow non-conformers to succeed. Some of us have become so rigidly conditioned that cannot even entertain the idea of questioning social norms and value systems; we simply accept them as an integral aspect of the universe—a fact of life—and move on. We never find time or allow our thoughts to wander in unfamiliar territories. We are afraid, or do not know how, to examine our identity and purpose of living. We simply live because we are here. We strive to feed our ego because it gives us a relative sense of superiority and superficial existence. But can this feeling of superiority provide a meaningful and peaceful venue for our being? Can it substitute a real sense of self-fulfillment and purposefulness in life? Most of us would never find out.

We need a framework to help us understand the basics of living and being happy, while meeting the requirements of social conformity for survival too. However, we also need a platform to help us rise above the dark clouds of conformity that obscure our vision of a true 'self'—to get a fresh perspective of who we are.

With regard to the pessimistic tone of some arguments in this trilogy, two points need clarification: **First,** the premise of the book is that we cannot avoid the negative impacts of socioeconomic structure on the way we think and behave. As much as we may try to stay positive and control our idiosyncrasies, endless social pressures stir our defective habits and hinder our intention to find peace and goodness. It is hard to become a truthful person in a society that does not support honesty and justice. **Second,** for finding the inner strength to fight back the negativities of our socioeconomic systems, we must initially acknowledge them as a debilitating reality and get ready to face them head on. We should stop sweeping the reality under the rug and hiding behind positive thinking gimmicks. We must handle negative situations and thoughts regularly as they cause the majority of our doubts and dilemmas. The point is that we cannot overcome our doubts, resolve our problems, and encounter our defects unless we at least grasp the impact of social negativities somehow—instead of ignoring or propagating them so irresponsibly and shamelessly.

At the same time, we need convictions and resilience to enjoy life's limited privileges. For solving any serious problem, we must analyse it, which rekindles hurt feelings and bad experiences. Yet, we must handle these negative thoughts and feelings effectively, rather than trying to justify or stifle them, or get too depressed or agitated to tackle them constructively. In fact, the more we grasp the depth of social negativities as real hurdles for personal growth, the higher would be our chances to go past them by redefining our lives outside their influence. A positive-thinking attitude to hide or ignore our negative thoughts cannot give us the convictions and awareness we require to enhance our real 'self' and overcome our problems. We must smarten up if we wish a better life for future generations.

Book's Structure

We believe our actions must be based on valid choices and deep convictions. We also assume our value systems and beliefs reflect our knowledge of a reliable reality according to logical criteria. We believe human life must be supported by some fundamental thoughts, either our own or other individuals' whom we admire, respect, and accept as authorities. These essential thoughts set and validate our beliefs and life philosophy to follow as a guiding light. Therefore, Volume I of this trilogy explores the foundation of human thoughts.

Besides a solid foundation of thoughts, we require a high-spirited mentality to appreciate the significance of our lives, needs, and thoughts, and then turn them into fruitful actions and tangible outcomes. For this purpose, we try to explore the meaning and characteristics of our spirits that drive the engine of our existence. We try to empower our spirits to face life hardships calmly and find our identity. We also like to explore the meaning and purpose of spirituality that keeps our thoughts and spirits together, free and productive. We hope to learn about, and find, our spirit and spirituality in a personal way, away from all religious and social influences. Volume II covers these topics.

And, of course, going through various stages of life, we can envision a structure of life that everybody follows and hopes to cope with, while this rigid process highly influences the outcome of our major life decisions too. The topics covered in Volume III concentrate on the structure of life and the way we may adapt ourselves to it more effectively by strengthening the foundation of our thoughts in line with a deeper understanding of who we are and what we want—our spirit. Volume III discusses the challenges and decisions of life within the context of these essential human thoughts. The rigid life path that we follow so blindly is in need of scrutiny and repair. The question is whether this life structure is meaningful or logical? Every intelligent person must be able to answer this question for him/herself.

The discussions in this trilogy are mainly based on common sense and personal experiences of the author. Providing scientific proofs and research methodologies for all the conclusions is impractical and unnecessary for the type of 'mostly philosophical' remarks offered in this trilogy. Yet, most of the conclusions are in line with the studies of prevalent scholars, statistics, and social facts. Fortunately, the discussions and suggestions are generic and more of a general nature than definite solutions and conclusions requiring finite scientific proofs. Even if one undertook elaborate scientific research to test the theories of this book, people who benefit from the existing socioeconomic chaos always find ways to refute them just for keeping the public in their shells.

Many of us believe that too many things in our world are happening so irrationally, while another group counter-argues from a different perspective to justify them. For example, we destroy old forests for lumber and creating jobs, ruin marine life and pollute environment through industrial production and exploration of oil sands, by humans' reckless over-consumption and waste, etc. Many of us believe that these atrocities are all symptoms of our surrender to capitalism, wicked value systems for more consumption, and for keeping the economies of the world alive as long as possible. We all know that this extravagance cannot go on forever and it would never serve the majority. Yet, we still keep electing arrogant politicians who ignore these obvious facts with a smirk.

The quotes from various scholars used in this trilogy are merely for reflecting other viewpoints on related topics without prejudice. They are plausible opinions expressed liberally in public domains on such philosophical topics and have thus become relevant for general review purposes. Although the author does not necessarily agree or disagree with them, he believes they are interesting points that readers might be interested to check in those books for further detail and reflection.

PART I
Thoughts and Feelings

CHAPTER ONE
Humans' Fundamental Thoughts

We are made of similar cells and DNA, but our thoughts and feelings make us who we are—so unique. Scientists believe that we make 40,000 decisions every day, which in return shows the enormity of thoughts and feelings that support or stir all those decisions day after day. Accordingly, even our simple thoughts and feelings constantly interact and clash deeply and thus expand into an enormous (and often unmanageable and stressful) pool of thoughts, emotions, and decisions at every moment.

Our thoughts can be divided into three categories. First, *fundamental* thoughts about our existence, ideals, philosophy of life, etc. They help our self-awareness, spirituality, and growth. Second, *tactical* thoughts that relate to our general learning requirements, performing our jobs, making financial plans, finding our companions, etc. These kinds of thoughts usually cause the highest level of stress and disappointment. Third, *mechanical* thoughts about our mundane affairs such as where to go, what to eat, what to buy, and similar simple thoughts that lead to the majority of our daily decisions.

The structure of our lives, as discussed in Volume III, sets the overall path of life that majority of people follow rather robotically. This social structure is developed (and supported) mostly through our *tactical* thoughts and decisions. The quality of these thoughts and decisions, however, depends highly on the strength of our *fundamental* thoughts. Therefore, Volume I is devoted to exploration and analysis of fundamental thoughts in terms of their role for our growth and health, and for making wiser tactical decisions. If we are interested in finding a more meaningful path of life, we must examine our fundamental thoughts and their effects on our tactical decisions and thoughts, while we try to cope with social demands.

Normally, we do not remember even a few dozens of our thoughts in a day, if that. Yet, certain fundamental thoughts subliminally occupy the minds of intelligent humans almost constantly throughout their lives, every single day. They delineate some aspect of our lives, but also make us feel good or depressed about our surroundings and ourselves. Therefore, studying our fundamental thoughts is necessary for understanding the meaning of life and making sense of our actions and decisions. More importantly, however, we must somehow come to terms with these deep-rooted thoughts that boggle every intelligent person's mind, because that is the only way to grasp life, justify our existence, and feel good about ourselves. In fact, building a personal life philosophy by gauging our fundamental thoughts is a sacred mission we must undertake honestly and earnestly. Some of these existential thoughts are listed in Table 1.1.

Table 1.1: Humans' Fundamental Thoughts

1. Our reasons for living.
2. How to build a happy life.
3. How to define a complete life, in which our deeds, feelings, and thoughts have value and purpose.
4. The best way to enjoy life at its fullest.
5. What is the inner 'self' and 'who we are' as a person.
6. What is the essence of humanness and whether it can be enhanced.

7. How to effect change and improve social order.
8. What a wisdom path is and how to track it.
9. What freedom is and whether it is an achievable goal.
10. How to live practically but not submissively.
11. How to nurture our positive doubts while defeating the perils of indecisiveness.
12. How to fight depression but not fear it.
13. How to make major life decisions and survive.
14. How to find a reliable companion.
15. How to optimize our physical and mental health.

The above list covers humans' main life dilemmas among many others. These integrated thoughts, and our efforts to resolve them, preoccupy any intelligent person's mind for establishing his/her general life philosophy and defining a meaningful path of life for him/herself. In fact, none of the above dilemmas (thoughts) can be truly analysed and resolved without pondering and choosing a ground for the others. Accordingly, our thoughts become too complex, fuzzy, and confusing most often—because we must find a comprehensive answer for all these life dilemmas collectively, as an exercise in self-awareness, for making our existence more authentic and meaningful. In the end, of course, 'finding the means of a happy and purposeful life' is the ultimate objective of all the fundamental thoughts in the list. All these thoughts and dilemmas are instinctive urges for finding happiness—which is a myth by the way, anyway, as will be discussed later in this volume.

This Chapter reviews the above fifteen fundamental thoughts briefly. Everybody can benefit from a well-defined personal life philosophy eventually to address all these dilemmas collectively and arrive at a comprehensive guideline for making the best use of his/her life and thoughts.

1. Reasons for Living

As we reach some level of maturity, maybe even in childhood for some geniuses, we begin to wonder about our existence. We soon want to justify it, too, as though we did not deserve to live without establishing a rationale for it. Our doubts about the purpose of our existence, along with other fundamental thoughts noted in Table 1.1, always roll in everybody's subconscious or unconscious minds, although most of us with lower mental activity or curiosity do not ponder them actively. Looking for a reason to live, especially, feels like an instinctual (and perhaps spiritual) urge ingrained in our genes. We cannot avoid it, and some people may commit suicide if they are oversensitive or tired of seeking that elusive justification to live. The more intelligent a person, the more s/he feels compelled to justify his/her existence, which delineates the high price we must pay for being an intelligent species. Unfortunately, it is getting harder every year to find good reasons for living within the chaotic environment and lifestyles we have created for ourselves. It is becoming more difficult to promise a bright future to our children when socioeconomic conditions are fundamentally threatened and family problems are getting out of hand. Fortunately, however, the majority of us do not give up easily and quickly, as we pursue some passive crusades to find legitimate reasons for our existence. All along, we dwell on all kinds of doubts and adopt lousy motives to continue living without ever feeling quite satisfied with our reasons. Mainly our hopes and optimism make us believe that we would eventually find a better rationale for living. Yet, relying on some shaky purposes for living is still better than not inventing any reason at all. A lack of life purpose only heightens our frustration and depression. In a philosophical sense, people find fewer reasons for living every year, but fortunately some other instinctual urges, e.g., lust, still keep us hopeful and optimistic.

Of course, the other side of the coin is that any rational person needs even more reasons for not living. More people struggle nowadays with the thoughts and feelings of loneliness and desperation, which often appear like good reasons for not living. Still, most of us are stubborn and resilient enough to keep living anyway, as if programmed to tolerate suffering and rejections naturally. Even our doubt about the existence of some ultimate reasons for living is a positive urge to keep us going. Our doubts help us live longer, but also make us explore life, persevere, and wonder.

Nonetheless, our lifelong urge to justify our existence is an added pressure of living by itself while it also complicates our thoughts and feelings constantly. In fact, living is too difficult, because we feel obliged to justify both an eager existence and early exit, while no rationale seems to exist for either. Oddly, not having a good reason for living or dying does not automatically justify, and lead to, the other option. This deep inner conflict creates the most fundamental doubt in our lives—the biggest dilemma we struggle with forever. That is the question Shakespeare imposed, "To be or not to be?" The conflict Hamlet faces is because he needs reasons for both, although the emphasis appears to be on finding a justification for living. Our struggle to find a valid reason for either option never ends. Period. Meanwhile, we just plough on through life, suffer, think, enjoy, until we die.

As we get older, we realize the futility of our hopes and dreams, or even our lasting struggles to find a reason for living. We learn to merely amuse ourselves somehow until the end arrives. We grasp the futility of all those worries, thoughts, and solemn feelings that have crippled us for no tangible outcome. We eventually admit that life has no purpose when we are old and tired, if not sooner. This is a sad conclusion that poses another fundamental question for youth—about living an inherently purposeless life, if going by the testimony of wise elderly. Well, that is why they prefer to ignore the elderly advice!

The irony is that, at the end, we face a substantially more fundamental thought as soon as we realize two basic facts that: 1) No philosophical reasons exist for living, and 2) no rational reasons exist for not living either. Back to square one! Then, our new and urgent fundamental thought (and dilemma) would be: Can we learn to build a useful life for ourselves based on the above two simple facts without letting these existential thoughts and feelings torture us? This is a major conflict and intellectual challenge for many people and it can be resolved somewhat only after we learn to build at least a personal life philosophy.

2. *Means of a Happy Life*

Obviously, all our thoughts and actions are for one ultimate purpose: To lead a happy, healthy life in a meaningful manner. Well, if life has no particular purpose, can we at least find a means of being happy? Our innate optimism and hope make us believe in the possibility of finding happiness and tranquility. Our pride also goads us to believe that not finding happiness is a direct reflection of our unworthiness and failure. Occasionally, we get a taste of this elusive happiness, which raises our hopes about the possibility of making it permanent. Thus, we look for the wisdom of doing so by seeking all kinds of advice from gurus and experts. Part III of this volume is devoted to a detailed discussion of 'self' and happiness. It attempts to identify the characteristics of happiness, but mainly suggests that a special personality and outlook are needed to maintain happiness rather permanently. In line with building that proper (but rather unconventional) personality, our ultimate happiness depends on how well we come to terms with all the thoughts listed in Table 1.1 above. We need the right personality and convictions to resolve these dilemmas and a variety of doubts, feelings, and thoughts that overwhelm us.

An authentic 'personal life philosophy' must also augment a 'proper personality' to manage our doubts and decisions in life, balance the cycles of happiness and depression, and find tranquility. This combination would help us choose the right values and a simple lifestyle, and develop the right mindset and priorities. A proper personality nurtures a solid personal philosophy intuitively or through self-awareness. Accordingly, the person learns to adhere to his/her convictions and beliefs regardless of all the external forces that try to influence his/her thoughts and feelings.

The main challenge in life, of course, is to understand the characteristics of a proper personality and build authentic personal convictions in our materialistic societies. Even more difficult, however, is to admit the necessity of developing our beliefs and convictions. Unless a person is somehow blessed with at least some inherent goodness and curiosity for gauging his/her life options, s/he hardly sees the need for a personal overhaul or life philosophy. Thus, the question is, 'How a person with no inherent goodness or wisdom would ever care to consider his/her life options objectively and strive to build a personal life philosophy?' What other incentives may motivate him/her to change his/her lifestyle, and find happiness? How people with formed personalities and crooked philosophies can find happiness without first reassessing themselves and their ideologies? How can we find happiness before making a major overhaul in our mentality? How can we free ourselves from the luring rewards of materialism to build self-reliance and some sense of spirituality?

Answering these questions is difficult, but some guidelines to achieve this horrendous task are suggested throughout this trilogy. Three points are clear though: (1) Finding happiness requires a proper mindset and personality, (2) pursuing an authentic life philosophy for finding happiness would eventually lead to development of an ideal personality, and conversely, (3) an ideal personality would have no difficulty in choosing a personal philosophy that leads to some notion of happiness.

3. Making Our Lives Complete

We often feel a sense of emptiness and doubt the quality of our lives. Of course, external factors and luck always affect our moods, but mostly our boredom causes self-doubts and depression. Our dreams about a 'complete' life feel either unachievable or meaningless again after a while. We usually imagine a complete life in sitting at the beach with a cold drink, a handsome companion keeping us amused, and lots of money to do whatever we wish. Alas, not even all these rewards can give us a complete life.

If we get a little more philosophical, we helplessly question the value of our routine activities and resent wasting our precious lives so mindlessly. We like to know what else is out there that could make our lives a little more meaningful, and possibly complete. We blame ourselves for the void and not finding a more sensible path. During our struggles for a meagre subsistence, or while accumulating enormous wealth, after doing the same things over and over again, with every failure or accomplishment, we still doubt the purpose of spending our lives on those routines and dread the lingering shallowness of our existence. All along, in fact, we also feel the inherent vanity of life altogether.

We usually force ourselves out of these depressing moods by engaging even deeper in our routine lives and struggles, or seek more pleasures. Yet, a subtle sense of incompleteness resides in our subconscious throughout our lives and makes all our goals and struggles feel like a bottomless abyss. One day, this feeling becomes too deep and fundamental no matter how often and hard we fight the moods of 'incompleteness.' Therefore, one purpose of our personal life philosophy is to find a simple definition of life, instead of worrying about its completeness and means of enhancing the quality of our superficial lives. The prevalent lifestyles can never offer a complete life, nor can give our existence an essence.

The feeling of emptiness often surges from boredom, but not necessarily from the lack of activities and excitement. We may attempt to relieve our tensions by getting involved with more activities, pampering our sexuality, taking on new challenges, travelling all over the world, and looking for exciting ventures. But these distractions would not resolve our sense of void and vanity in the long run. Only when our adventures and experiences find authentic values or offer a new learning dimension, we grasp that mystical sense of spiritual completeness. Other activities only add to our feelings of boredom and void despite their potential for inducing temporary relief. We usually try to keep busy somehow or socialize non-stop to suffocate the lingering feeling of emptiness, which is often on top of our normal sense of loneliness, even when we are in a relationship. For spiritual completeness, as an alternative way of living, we must prepare for a long inner journey to overhaul our mentality, however.

Contrary to common perception, a complete life is not structured around 'things.' Rather, it depends on how effectively we use those special life 'resources' we inherently own, such as our potentialities, passion, compassion, and spirituality. Struggling for more of everything simply wastes our most precious resources of life, i.e., time, energy, and intelligence. However, people normally perceive 'completeness' in owning more of every *thing* that is out there. The mentality of our modern societies revolves around greed and egotism instead of needlessness and selflessness.

Our struggle to get more of everything we already have only raises the bar endlessly toward that imaginary completeness. Aiming for a balance of things, not more of everything, and an effective use of life resources are naturally the secrets of a complete life. The less time and mental energy is spent on things, the more resources can be devoted to fundamental thoughts and authentic needs in life, which provide a much higher value for 'completing' our lives, in terms of both the number of years (quantity) we live and what we do (quality.) A 'complete life' requires a full range of worthy thoughts, feelings, actions, and principles (life values) to fulfil a large amount of social and personal responsibilities. During this process, we seek the means of true happiness (peace of mind), bring 'self' in control of our actions and decisions, find a path of wisdom according to our life philosophy, etc. Our limited energy and intuition should guide us explore new, soulful experiences and attain self-actualization, which is the shortest path for normal people to get a sense of completeness and divinity.

A complete life contains a variety of simple events and ventures that produce purposeful learning and growth experiences, and at the same time, create childlike excitements and sense of achievements. Contrary to the common perception, 'complete' does not imply a stationary state in which everything reaches its perfection. Rather, a complete life is always dynamic and requires a high degree of change and risks. Two levels of challenges recur in a complete life. **First,** the challenges and plans necessary for maintaining our basic needs and health effectively—to build up a stable state of mind and body. **Second,** the challenges and plans that goads the process of personal growth—the dynamism of a complete life. This growth is achieved by new learning experiences and purposeful efforts throughout our normal lives. Growth is a natural process that contains schooling, learning, working, building a path of wisdom, making a family and raising children perhaps, plus all other routine decisions, actions, struggles, pleasures, and doubts. We must push and measure this natural growth, more harmonically and thoughtfully, for defining our existence and building our life philosophy. All these small experiences also provide the texture and beauty that add to the 'completeness' of our lives.

We can strive forever to explain some aspects of a complete life and choose certain fundamentals to achieve it. But, beyond all these experimentations, we can conclude that life by itself has no special properties to make it complete. We may assume that our universe is perfect as it is, but even that would be only another subjective judgment. The perfection or completeness of life is created in the mind of each person based on the soundness of his/her life philosophy and personal experiences. Therefore, in a philosophical sense, 'A complete life is the one that we know how to create for ourselves.'

4. Enjoying Life at Its Fullest

To most of us, enjoying life means having as much pleasure and extravagance as we can possibly muster. We rely mostly on our drives for sexuality, love, possession, and power to maximize our chances for enjoying life. For achieving these appealing goals, we adopt superficial values, waste time and energy to build a phony personality, and maintain a busy but boring lifestyle. This demented mentality has grown fast in modern societies and still people wonder why they are not enjoying their lives as much as they think they should or deserve. All those seeming pleasures actually make them feel lonelier and emptier every day. Despite our strenuous struggles to enjoy life and find the means of happiness, we still feel the incompleteness and emptiness of our lives. The rising rate of social stress and family breakdowns are the main symptoms of our present shoddy mentality. No matter how much pleasure, possessions, and power we enjoy, at the end we still face the same dilemma: How to make our lives a bit more peaceful or somewhat meaningful.

Therefore, it seems that maximizing our life enjoyment is merely a matter of reaching certain level of maturity and contentment. This happens only when we grow a mentality to perceive our life *complete* (meaningful and enriching) as is for a selfless self-fulfilling person. 'Enjoying life in its fullest' and 'making our lives complete' are the two sides of the same coin. Thus, for enjoying life we must again emphasize on making our lives meaningful and complete. But how must we go about doing this?

Ironically, we must first accept that no inherent 'complete' life exists to maximize our life enjoyments. Only we, personally, can define and make our lives relatively enjoyable and meaningful by adopting a simple life philosophy. In return, our simple life philosophy must contain the basic principles about humans' natural needs. Ultimately, the 'completeness' of life comes from inside us in the form of mental energy to use our unique potentialities and opportunities for reaching contentment and self-reliance. We cannot define one unique purpose, e.g., happiness, for life. We cannot devise a formula of completeness based on a combination of certain life purposes either. In fact, the irony is that the simpler the lifestyle we adopt, the more complete and enjoyable life becomes. If these conclusions are valid, they reflect why life cannot be complete (or meaningful) in itself beyond our personal mentality and inner strength.

Yet, we exhaust ourselves with our idle attempts to find the meaning of life, make it complete, and enjoy it as much as possible. Accordingly, we follow a lifestyle that feels incomplete and causes only more depression. A sign of incomplete life is the amount and intensity of our never-ending regrets for the opportunities lost and decisions not made, or made hastily or foolishly. Regrets could also be a sign of growing wisdom. However, if we cannot reverse or ignore the repercussions of our earlier mistakes, we can hardly hope for a meaningful and peaceful life. We can always try to make the best of our existing circumstances, but for reaching a permanent inner peace, we must make certain efforts and decisions at the right time. To have a complete life, we must plan for it—mostly in terms of life philosophy and path. We cannot 'live in the now' and expect to have a complete life too. Rather, planning is crucial for minimizing the unnecessary struggles of life and for avoiding irreversible mistakes that could cause lasting grief and regrets. Planning is for making our critical life decisions in a timely manner, while we also depend on our instincts and doubts to help us with those decisions. Foresight and planning are for not getting trapped in inescapable and regretful situations.

Another big irony is that, while life has no real purpose, we must set many personal purposes for our lives and thus make it 'meaningful' *merely* for our needs according to our objective mind and for helping us maintain our health. *The completeness of our lives depends on how consciously we try to define one for ourselves according to proper values.* The ideas offered throughout this trilogy can help on this regard, especially about the fact that life's 'completeness' depends on our ability to use our potentialities and time wisely. A big emphasis is placed in this trilogy (especially Volume III) on one's timing and diligence regarding major life decisions for making one's life complete.

While writing this section of the book, a sad story in papers many years ago shocked me deeply as a parent. On April 11, 1996, Jessica Dubroff who was trying to establish the record of the youngest pilot to fly across the United Stated had crashed soon after taking off at Cheyenne, Wyoming killing herself, her father and the flying instructor. Many of us may agree that Jessica who was only seven years old did not get a chance to live a life, let alone a 'complete' one. In a press conference, Jessica's mother felt that it had been Jessica's choice to be a pilot and that submitting to her wishes had been necessary. As reported by The Province, a daily newspaper in Vancouver, British Columbia, Jessica's mother commented:

"I beg people to let children fly if they want to fly." "... clearly I would want all my children to die in a state of joy." "... I would prefer it was not at age seven but, God, she went with her joy and her passion, and her life was in her hands."

It is hard for many of us to understand this kind of life philosophy and advice, although the point is not to make judgments here. But let us ponder a scenario in which our six-year-old kid asks us to let her/him drive a car because s/he enjoys it. When we say no and explain its dangers and illegality, s/he would say, "Okay, how about letting me fly then?" S/he would then try to convince us that s/he has suddenly developed this passion to pilot a plane and that if she did not fly across the United States within one year her/his life would be ruined.

We probably would not be serving any purpose, other than our Egos perhaps, to let our kids drive or fly even for the sake of passion. Is this passion something that cannot be dealt with in a timelier manner, perhaps in a few years? Would it really cause a deprivation of our children's souls and psyches to postpone the passion of flying, or similar adventures, a few years? Could not any other experience give our kids a similar joy and passion, until the time is more appropriate for flying, banjo jumping, skydiving and any other adventure that an independent youngster can decide to undertake for him/herself? Are not we, as parents, forgetting the role we must play in teaching our children self-discipline and patience, especially when we face their excessive emotions and passion? It is also hard to believe that a seven-year-old child chooses, or is even capable of judging and deciding, to fly in a bad weather for setting a record, which does not mean anything anyways.

The purposes behind the decision to become a seven-year-old pilot and all the subsequent decisions, may seem unclear, if not absurd, to many of us. This is not an isolated instance in our society by a long shot. Every day we set strange purposes and standards for ourselves and our children. We teach our children from the very young age that competition and winning is the most valuable purposes of life. We are turning our young girls into sex objects and confusing our boys about the kind of companions they need or should choose. With these kinds of attitude and beliefs, we set and impose a ridiculous perception of an ideal life for ourselves and our children, in which we are always winning, having fun, and surpassing others at any cost. We waste our mental energies and time on activities, competitions, spite, and struggles that have no purpose but feeding our Egos and causing more depression for the whole society along the way.

This story is only one of million simple examples of how we, as parents, and society in general, brainwash and spoil our children. We push them develop their crooked value systems and fanciful ambitions, which have no meaningful purpose and instead mislead them altogether when the time comes for making their major life decisions. Accordingly, we abolish their chances to be good parents or spouses in their own relationships.

One traditional principle always makes sense: There is a 'right time' for every decision and every doubt. We can leisurely follow our dreams and enjoy righteous experiences throughout our lives, achieve our goals, love, etc. But there is a 'right time' in our lives for certain things. There are only certain years that we can enjoy childish thoughts and plays. There are right times for building a career and a family. There is a right time for making a decision about marrying a particular person. There are *right times* for making all critical decisions of life. If we stand by and let the opportunity slip away, or make hasty or bad decisions, we face many disappointments in life. There is also an 'optimal time' for less critical life decisions, which are still important, e.g., for completing a college education if one intends to have one, for driving a car or piloting a plane, etc.

It seems hard for most of us to accept that only simpler life purposes fulfil the inner needs of 'self' and provide experiences beyond egotistical or materialistic values. Every piece of music can be rediscovered over and over. Every plant and flower has a different property, delicacy, or fragrance that we can feel for the first time every day. Our thoughts can stir the boundless energy that leads to unique creations and valuable experiences of tranquility. We can enjoy the feeling of achievement by doing small things like gardening, writing a short story, painting, meditation, or physical exercise.

Enjoying life is obviously more than having an occasional feeling of ecstasy, or even getting the sense of 'completeness' resulting from personal achievement and self-actualizing experiences. To enjoy life, the cycles of happiness experiences must be continuous and self-feeding, while we manage the pressures of depression cycles effectively too. We do not necessarily need major achievements and self-actualizing experiences to attain the highest sense of completeness and joy. Rather, we need many simple experiences that challenge and utilize our various potentialities. We need 'self' driven experiences, since only they release the huge amount of energy and joy that flow naturally within us. We need more of the experiences that are not based on winning and hostility, but rather on giving and forgiving. We do not need more pleasures and sexuality to enjoy life at its fullest, but only compassion.

5. Exploring the Inner 'Self'

We have an intrinsic urge to know 'who we are' as a person. We often question our truthfulness, identity, and personality. We like to self-analyse ourselves and perhaps overcome the causes of our phoniness and sufferings. We like to build a strong character and maintain our integrity. These fundamental goals and questions always boggle our minds, at least subconsciously. 'Knowing about ourselves' and understanding 'self' are major topics in this trilogy and are covered in various chapters, in particular in Chapter Two of Volume II.

We learn a lot about ourselves when we consciously attempt to do so, usually for developing a personal life philosophy. Our search revives and refines our inner 'self,' while we analyse our inner needs and feelings, get more in touch with our souls, and eventually learn to master our thoughts and decisions more effectively. Through this conscious process of building our beliefs and convictions, we strive to grasp the motives behind some of our superficial personal needs, reset our expectations from life and society more realistically, and then attempt to turn our thoughts into certain ideologies, philosophies, and lifestyles. Accordingly, our life philosophy turns into 'self'-driven guidelines, beliefs, and ethics. This primary wisdom and self-awareness becomes the platform for building the foundation of our thoughts and finding a relative sense of contentment and peace.

We use philosophy for grasping 'self,' and 'self' is our guide for building a sound philosophy. We ponder the urges driven by the less desirable aspects of our personality (i.e., Ego and Model) for developing our life philosophy, too, but only for grasping the difficulties of maintaining a 'self' controlled personality. (Detail discussions about the three aspects of personality, i.e., Self, Ego, and Model, are presented in Chapter Five.) Nevertheless, our personal life philosophy shows our self-image as well as our preference for the mental and physical atmosphere we like to live in, including the society, family, and friends.

Exploring the inner self and building our life philosophy is not a one-time exercise to decide on certain personal preferences and objectives. Rather, it is an ongoing process of learning and evolving, and then formulating our thoughts. This is often a natural process, though, in line with our efforts to understand our inner needs as we mature and think deeper and longer about our experiences and existence. As such, a personal life philosophy goes beyond the purpose of merely defining and formulating our thoughts, ideals, wishes, and morals. Instead, it must be viewed as the vehicle that carries us through the journey of 'self' realization, while we learn more about our dilemmas and doubts, and about the deeper side of us we have not known before. At the end, we reach the wisdom path that we have been seeking inherently. Afterward, a 'self'-controlled philosophy of life would guide us as we proceed on the path of wisdom with our souls free at last.

6. Defining the Essence of Humanness

Grasping our 'self' and becoming a 'self'-driven person also delineate our connection to a larger sphere and a collective humanity. We entertain the high likelihood of the 'self' being an integral part of the universe, which we believe governs the whole spectrum of existence. We imagine being a part of a whole picture, although our limited perceptions do not allow us to see this vague image of totality anyway. Sometimes we remember that we are only an insignificant part of the universe, but are often too self-centered and portentous around one another, as if we were gods in our own rights. Our thoughts about 'who we are' are quite inconsistent because we do not have a grasp of 'self' and the essence of humanness. Therefore, understanding the scope of our interconnectivity within the universe is another purpose of life philosophy.

We relate with the universe in the way we are part of the total energy, in the way we imagine our souls link us to eternity, and in the way we complement the other aspects of the universe including Nature and animal kingdom. We are related within this universe as humans with relatively equal intelligence and similar needs. The purpose of a personal life philosophy is to assess and develop ideologies for establishing and honouring these relationships. Feeling this natural connection can help us become purer human beings too.

A rather universal definition and perception of *humanity* can be drawn according to our current intelligence and world cultures. This perception, however, would be quite incomplete, complex, and too vast to grasp. Furthermore, people have a somewhat, and sometimes drastically, different views of 'being a human.' Being a human implies togetherness and care, but our social teaching has mostly replaced humanness with individuality (egotism). That is, we give our personal interests and needs a much higher priority over any public and humanistic interests.

And this is why our perception of humanness has become crooked and ambiguous.

The main theme (and purpose) of humanness is the prevalence of their common needs and interests as the conscience of individual and society. This idea has, however, been contravened by the domination of individuals' and special group's interests controlling the value and mental structures of the society. Thus, another purpose of a personal life philosophy is to nurture a more authentic meaning and perception of humanness in our minds. We have to fight internally with so many ideas and priorities that have misguided us, all along, as the criteria of being an individual but not necessarily a human. We have to switch from individual to human in a major way. We must give up the biases, brutalities, and prejudices that dominate our judgments when we measure and value things and people. We need compassion, love, forgiveness, and integrity to rule our deeds and relations with others and with the universe as a whole.

An authentic personal life philosophy should help us find ourselves anew in the context of pure humanness and humanity. We should transcend from the stance of isolated individualism to the realm of integral beings. Nevertheless, we may not discard our doubts about the purity of human nature, because in fact we are not pure beings. Like many other animals, we have instincts that often prevent us from becoming a pure human being. Yet we may at least rise above animals to appreciate the vanity of all the sufferings and killings in the world, usually for no reason but stupidity and greed. Even animals' instincts stop them from killing their own kind for such trivia. How is it possible that humans' instincts and egoism have demoted us below even that basic standard, while we boast about our supreme intelligence too?

All these thoughts and doubts about humanity occupy our minds regularly, but we usually do not know how to deal with them and change our mentality. A personal life philosophy can enhance our understanding of humanness, to become fairer, unbiased, impartial, and compassionate. This minimal morality might then also goad us to play a role in spreading some values of humanness and promoting the ultimate goals of humanity and harmony of life.

Sometimes, we feel outright ashamed when we notice—maybe, eventually, by some magic—that not even an ounce of human essence is in all the weight we carry. And sometimes, we feel so sad when we witness how the people we love—our parents, children, friends, and spouses—are so empty of human essence.

7. Effecting Change and Improving Social Order

While we pursue happiness, peace, and a 'self'-driven life, we sometimes think about devoting some of our energy and time to the welfare of others directly or indirectly. We like to play a role in strengthening social infrastructure and mending its broken pieces. We feel obliged to do our share in the construction of facilities, ideas, and systems that can support and protect life and the health of our planet. A personal life philosophy demands active participation in the affairs of societies, organizations, countries, and governments. Our pure intention for charity emerges in our careers and through personal initiatives without any expectation for monitory rewards.

We mull over our responsibilities despite our disagreements with many social parameters and the people influencing them negatively. Our varied responsibilities extend toward our family, socioeconomic needs around the globe, the welfare of humanity, and the health of Nature. Each type of responsibility, e.g., family, imposes certain facts and demands. 'Becoming a purer human,' as discussed in the previous section, is also a *personal responsibility*, not only a whim or ideal. Thus, understanding our varied responsibilities and means of fulfilling them are other purposes for developing our fundamental thoughts and life philosophy.

We have learned to view 'relationships' as a mechanical and automatic process of dealing with other individuals. But this is not a realistic picture. Every worthwhile relationship carries a great deal of responsibility for pinpointing its parameters and means of nurturing it. Especially with the rising chaos in family relationships nowadays, learning about the role we must play effectively in this regard alone is becoming more obscure and overwhelming, but also more urgent. We spend a lot of energy, feelings, and thoughts on relationships and still face more doubts, disappointments, and cynicism about human nature every day. At the same time, we burden our relationships with our unrealistic and fanciful expectations instead of understanding the nature of companionship and the purpose of teamwork.

We are quick in acknowledging our social and family responsibilities, but we cannot create some solutions for discharging them more compassionately. Our scepticism and pride cripple us to act upon our responsibilities in a full-heartedly and sincere manner. Therefore, while we need to learn about all facets of our responsibilities philosophically, we also need to find better ways of honouring our social and family commitments. We must get creative about the means of discharging our responsibilities. Merely showing a lot of sympathy and concern is not enough. Rather, a plan of action is required with a clear definition of the role that everybody can realistically expect of him/herself to play, instead of becoming more demanding. We need a better social order to facilitate and encourage a sense of global responsibility.

8. Choosing a Path of Wisdom

We believe we know a lot about life and people because we are smart, have gone to school long enough, got many years of experience, made lots of money, built a huge Ego, and similar reasons. We trust our knowledge and ability to analyse and understand facts, situations, and people perfectly, so we do not hesitate to make hasty judgments and premature decisions, and take precarious actions. Yet, behind all that haughty confidence, we always have some lingering thoughts and doubts about our egoistical perception of the world. We might eventually sense the need to follow a path of self-awareness and curb our lifetime desire for self-importance. During this journey, we notice the possibility of a different reality behind our rigid perceptions and haughty interpretations. Maybe a more sensible reality actually corresponds with our nature more *realistically*. Only then, we may realize the naivety of our beliefs and the limitations of our knowledge about ourselves, people, and things. We sense that our conventional beliefs and knowledge are only illusions built around an imaginary world. We see how our misperceptions and misjudgments distort our viewpoints, desires, decisions, and doubts. We remain doubtful chronically when we should decide, and we decide hastily when we ought to doubt.

When we reach such a critical point in our lives, we see the need to develop a personal life philosophy and a more reliable path of life. We like to understand and remove our prejudices that contaminate our judgments, decisions, and actions. We like to find a means of overcoming our nativity, conviction of superiority, or any other misperception resulting from living within the boundaries of a 'perceived world.' Some lucky individuals achieve this milestone and follow a path of wisdom eventually after years of feeling lonely and empty while pondering and doubting their ways of living.

Following a path of wisdom starts with a personal conviction, or perhaps a deep inkling (doubt), that there is a 'real world' that supersedes the laws and values of the 'perceived world' we are accustomed to. We believe that, by attempting to understand some aspects of the real world, we get a chance to open our minds, souls, and hearts to a new vision of existence. With this basic commitment, we may step on a path of wisdom that would ultimately change our vision of the 'reality' we have known. We start to doubt the value and importance of all the 'facts' we have embraced so unthinkingly. As we progress on this path, we find more about life essentialities and realize how we have been wasting our time and energy on unnecessary struggles and worries. Gradually, wisdom replaces our perceptions and assumptions. We commit ourselves to a self-awareness routine in search of the truth and real reality; to soar to the highest level of 'self' recognition and wisdom—the summit.

Following a path of wisdom is not a mythical concept the way it usually sounds to us. Yet, we cannot overcome our doubts about the existence of a more authentic approach toward life than the one we are used to follow. Dr. Wayne Dyer's book, *You see it when you believe it* delves into this concept in a particular manner. He suggests that when we believe in the things that have all along appeared unrealistic and mythical, such as God, they would become a reality and we can readily *see* them. Many of us may find this method as another way of inventing and perceiving things according to our imaginations. Dr. Dyer's suggestion is plausible though in the sense that we should break away from our existing perceptions, so that we can build simple, meaningful beliefs and convictions. However, we should not replace one type of perceptions with another kind through self-hypnosis. The philosophy we can realistically adopt is that, by following a path of wisdom, we do not need to believe in so many things in order to see them. We should not force ourselves to believe in something that is not evident to us. That would be just another manner of mental conditioning to accept (force) the authenticity of a notion. We do not need to commit ourselves to too many new beliefs at the outset, anyway. Rather, we can start with a simple belief that 'we have most likely misled ourselves in life with some perceptions that we or others have imposed on us.' Thus, by following a path of wisdom and self-awareness, we attempt to get rid of those misperceptions for achieving a more natural contact with life and our 'self.' Once we step on this path, new meanings start to evolve gradually along with our sincere desire to become self-aware and selfless. The new knowledge and concepts would actually evolve naturally from within us. The only challenge is to stay focused in the process and trust one's 'self' to follow this path patiently with courage and confidence.

The 'things' we see are only the reflections of our minds' and hearts' reaction to events, situations, people, and material things. We see concepts, ideas, people, people's intentions, situations, and the whole universe differently in a new context once we set out to question our minds' and hearts' way of seeing and interpreting things. We would suddenly have more doubts about so many things that we were sure about before. These are positive doubts and precious. At the same time, we would have less difficulty making decisions that had appeared so hard before. Personal problems would seem less significant and often unimportant and irrelevant completely. This new perspective of life makes our decisions much easier and clearer.

The new path of wisdom gives us the perspective of a life that is enjoyable merely by the reality of our existence, which is easier to tolerate too. It would show us the options of living that are not obvious from within the perceived world. Following a path of wisdom helps us distinguish the essential facts and decisions of life from amongst the mountain of supposedly important dilemmas and situations piled up in our head about the 'perceived reality' world. It would give us the power to know when to doubt and what to doubt. At the same time, it would give us the insight, eventually, to see those things that are authentic and thus less doubtful.

9. Gaining Our Freedom

Freedom is not free by a long shot. In fact, we must pay a big price for even a small dose of it, let alone absolute freedom that is a myth anyway. Our endless craving for freedom and the feelings of entrapment at work, in family, in relationships, and society as a whole, torture our minds consciously and subconsciously to no avail. Instead, we get more frustrated every day, because gaining even a relative freedom is getting more difficult, as we feel trapped by our financial and emotional needs and dependencies. It is impossible to sense real freedom if we like to live in society and have a family, not to mention the compliance we must show to our government and our employers.

In all, we must develop a kind of life philosophy that can free us from the influences and impositions of social systems and people to some extent. We must find an optimal but practical position for us, where we can have enough independence and some feeling of peace without isolating ourselves from society. Most importantly, however, we must somehow learn about the degree of freedom we can muster before our lifestyle makes us feel so helpless, isolated, or depressed. We must decide eventually about the level of independence and freedom we can bear and/or need to lead a practical life, and then learn to adapt ourselves to that kind of lifestyle.

Feeling free is a relative state of mind depending on a person's interpretation of life, which is itself a function of his/her intelligence and general perceptions. When we accept the conditions and impositions of society as a reality of life, we do not feel our freedom jeopardized too much. And when we do not feel deprived of freedom, we do not appreciate what it is, although everybody feels, and suffers from, the stress of living in this imposing environment. Occasionally, as we face and sense life's unfairness and impositions, we suddenly crave our precious freedom. Still, despite all the stress of living and our relentless thinking about at least some relative freedom, we remain absorbed in the rules and conditions of society. We go on living the way our parents have lived, the way we have grown up to be part of the transitory life and absorbed by it. Our inner urges for a companion, pleasure, compassion, approval, and other incentives keep us quite needy to others. Our neediness has grown so immensely we willing give up our freedom and maybe even our soul and integrity.

Fortunately, more people are starting to see societies and economic systems as hindrances to their natural freedom—which is merely not a matter of having a right to vote. Our democratic processes have in fact become quite infected and thus defy the sense of natural freedom that, for example, gypsies have had without any need for democratic pretences. We may be awakened by a cold slap on the face to feel the value and meaning of freedom, which is vastly different from the perceived freedom we are conditioned to imagine. Despite the stress and anxiety of social living, we seem to have no choice but to accept our illusion of freedom as a 'reality.' But some of us at least appreciate that our stress and anxiety are the symptoms of a larger problem. It relates to our inability to lead a 'self'-driven life without being labelled as rebels and terrorists. We wish that exercising our freedom did not come at the cost of losing the trust, contact, and respect that we expect to receive from people and society.

As long as we are absorbed by our existing lifestyles, we would not understand, feel, or care about our freedom. And if we do not understand or feel a lack freedom, our lives go on erratically and mechanically. The stress and anxieties would, however, continue to mount without us really knowing their cause(s). Eventually we face two scenarios. We either continue to live with stress and anxiety to the point of a nervous breakdown, or find the strength to look beyond the symptoms of stress and anxiety to explore how our loss of freedom has created our life drama. There may not be easy solutions before we delve into a lengthy exploration of 'self' and finds a path of wisdom. However, we may at least learn about the sources of our problem and stress.

Even when we see socioeconomic orders as constraints to freedom and 'self'-control, our natural reaction (and social teaching) is to adapt ourselves and live with them somehow. We do not know what else to do and are not ready for the risks of unknown or untested options. We like to think and act practical. Most of us cannot survive without the fringe benefits of social living. This is one of the real dilemmas of living. We have grown up within these socioeconomic systems and adaptation feels like a natural and practical choice. But then one day suddenly we feel the need to be detached from some of these social values. Like our numerous other irreconcilable dilemmas, it is hard to balance these two opposing needs. On the one hand, we want to be attached to the systems that seem to feed our needs and Ego so nicely. On the other hand, we want to become detached when we suffer from all the stress and anxiety of social living, or when we feel our integrity is crushed beyond our tolerance.

Many complex dilemmas, including the situations related to our financial and love needs, keep us deeply dependent upon one another and social systems. However, numerous simpler habits, which we embrace so casually, also make our task of gaining our freedom impossible. A simple example is the extreme use of all sorts of financial credits to buy houses, cars, furniture, computers, vacations, shoes, and on and on. These facilities encourage us to consume more, often beyond our means. With the outrageous interest charged on most of these credit facilities, we end up spending most of our income on repaying our debts. In all, the existing excessive use of credit has caused tremendous disorder in both overall economy and financial life of people, especially when it encourages people to spend beyond their means. For gaining our freedom, thus, a basic remedy is to resist the temptation of a credit-based life. While using credit facilities prudently and rarely, we should detach ourselves from this popular habit in our societies and thus feel freer with less stressful jobs to do too.

Another simple example is the influence of movies and television that are forming our cultures and lifestyles. To make these programs and movies appealing to the naïve audience, a higher level of extravagance and excitement are built into them every day. They continuously increase the amount of violence, grotesque ideas, and sexuality in movies and television programs (including commercials) to keep us attached. Accordingly, we adopt the crooked values and phony personalities promoted in these programs to shape our lifestyles. As our minds get confused and lose the ability to distinguish reality from perception, we get absorbed deeper in this world of illusions and imitate these violent behaviours and phony lifestyles. Some people have lost their minds and touch with reality so drastically they have turned into criminals with no sense or motive. Random killings and family murder/suicides are signs of frustration due to the lack of a clear perception of reality and one's value of life. Personal expectations of life have drastically tarnished and everybody looks for more excitement, money, sex, and power. When these fantasies and unreal expectations do not materialize—or often even after they are satisfied—people feel only more hollowness and confusion.

We are becoming dependent on some individuals, groups, professional sports, and movies to make our lives complete or miserable (e.g., when our favourite sport team wins or loses). Although the feelings of depression and anger may last a few hours or days, often the effect on our nerves and mind is permanent and substantial. Some people even gamble their monies on these games, which makes the impact on them even more severe and longer lasting. We get addicted to invalid social symbols and values that give us both joy and depression, often in large doses. We depend on movie stars and athletes to give us joy and excitement, but also to reaffirm our identity. They have become our idols and heroes; and their failures make us equally angry, hostile, and depressed. Some sports are pure inhumane and violent, just because excitement increases with the amount of violence and generate more revenues too. But, even those less violent sports can influence our psyche and affect our moods, attitudes, and reaction to others and things significantly. We try not to take the winning and losing personal and not to take the outcome so seriously and just enjoy the game. But it is difficult. The question is whether it is worth our time, energy, and nerves to be subjected to this much torture as a price for a short excitement and joy, e.g., from watching sport events. Not an easy question to answer for the majority of people.

How can we be proud of societies that promote such horrendous amount of phony perceptions of life through movies, television, magazines, and other means of propaganda to control the freedom of people? How can we learn to live in such perplexing environment without losing our identity and integrity completely? How can we maintain some level of freedom without being totally rejected and isolated from society? These are main dilemmas that we have a tough time sorting out when we crave some level of freedom.

Of course, our social endeavours and competitions add texture to our culture and our personal lives. However, they drag us further away from the realities of life. We get too distracted to explore a more authentic path of life and gain our freedom. The attachment or detachment from each type of social system, being credit facilities, professional sports, or others, is a part of an individual's life philosophy. We cannot and do not want to isolate ourselves from the excitements and privileges of living within socioeconomic systems. Yet, at the same time, we must be wary of these attachments' effect on us and our children for maintaining a relative 'self'-driven and tranquil life.

A personal life philosophy intends to assess the balance of our attachments and detachments in society in order to minimize our stress and anxiety-inducing dependencies. Some attachments, like a family life, cannot be easily avoided despite their high stress potentials. We must somehow learn to honour and deal with these natural attachments in an effective manner. However, some attachments are questionable and can be avoided if our personal philosophy helps us see it that way, such as attachment to work beyond a reasonable limit. It would be a personal decision as to how much credit one should use to consume more things and services and how much TV and professional sports one would like to get attached to. A personal life philosophy determines the extent of our attachments and sets the limits of our sacrifice needed for gaining a relative sense of freedom.

Our decisions and doubts about our attachments and detachments are personal, but a general rule may apply to many of us: When no philosophical ground exists for attachment, we need strong reasons for remaining attached and dependent. Otherwise, we should seriously think about our addictions to such thoughts and activities. We must know and admit why we are hooked, and then take action to detach ourselves from them as quickly as possible. All these thoughts and feelings might eventually help us increase the relative degree of our freedom.

10. Living Practically but Not Submissively

So, we set out to impose a balance between our attachments and detachments in order to maintain our independence and integrity. We adopt a life philosophy that sounds practical for dealing with others and social systems with the least amount of frictions. We strive for certain personal ideals, while practising popular ideas in society to survive. Meanwhile, we like to push new and revolutionary ideas to spread our humanistic ideals. We plan to be flexible and open-minded with regard to our new thoughts. We strive to build a practical personal philosophy, although it may appear odd and absurd within the recognized social boundaries. Moreover, practicality requires extensive efforts to understand other people's needs, habits, and expectations. By flexibility and practicality, we like to maintain a quiet life and bearable relationships with others despite our differences in needs, habits, and objectives in life. We cannot simply expect others to think like us or grasp our needs or life objectives even if we explained it to them for many hours, or even a lifetime. People's points of reference in life differ drastically. Obviously, we cannot understand others either, because we do not have the patience, mindset, and incentive to do so. Even a psychologist never understands a person thoroughly, as his study usually has a targeted professional purpose. He works only within a limited timeframe, circumstances, and environments, which never contains a person's full routines and thoughts.

We could try to understand the needs of at least those who are close to us and try to respond to their needs favourably as long as our beliefs and convictions are not highly threatened. A majority of us, however, has difficulty grasping or caring about the seemingly imposing needs and expectations of others. Yet, we must try harder every day to find ways of living in harmony with everybody without arguing, challenging our differences, or trying to impose our needs and wishes on one another.

We get frustrated quite often when we cannot get along with people, because i) they do not understand us, our logic, or our viewpoints, ii) our attempts to change people, to see and do things our way, fail, and iii) we remain doubtful about the possibility of people ever learning anything. Deep down we believe they can learn and change somehow if they stopped being so stubborn. We believe they are only resisting to become who we wish them to be. We feel helpless and frustrated, because we perceive the value and depth of our relationships and friendships based on the amount of agreements and similarities in thoughts and actions. The danger is that when we develop personal philosophies, we become even more dogmatic in assessing other people's behaviours, thoughts, and lifestyles.

The irony is that we must prepare ourselves for even vaster personal differences, as societies continue to promote individuality more than humanity and harmony. As societies become more complex and violent, people are forced to look for better means of defending themselves and surviving. Furthermore, we encourage people to be assertive, positive thinkers, and fighters, looking for opportunities and success in a highly competitive world. All these expectations (aspirations) contribute to self-centredness and ego-driven personalities who build their own crooked perceptions of the world and give their personal needs ten folds more importance than the common needs of groups—being a family unit, an organization, a community, etc.

These facts show the need for refining our life philosophies to allow for more flexibility every year, in order to accept and live with other people despite our rising differences in thoughts and lifestyles. We should expect situations or thoughts that contradict our philosophies, but nonetheless be able to live with the situation or person. This happens a lot in families, where the nucleus of most important relationships and communications are developed. When personality differences block the possibility of communication, only refined personal philosophies can prevent disasters and breakdowns of otherwise acceptable relationships. Volume III of this trilogy discusses some of these ideas in detail.

In all, we should prepare ourselves for tolerating less bearable relationships and situations. We must gain that extra patience and tolerance through our refined life philosophies, and then lower our expectations from life and people accordingly too. We should admit that we (as a society) are inherently incapable of reducing individual differences even if it were a desirable thing to do. We should admit that hardly ever another person can really understand or care about our viewpoints and needs. Even if they did, they would never sympathize with our seemingly different or radical ideas, because their own views would always remain dominant and valid in their minds. Only when two people have the same basic needs, at least on the surface, they might understand each other better tentatively until their higher needs begin to interfere again and create new conflicts. Generally, we must admit that people's varied backgrounds and visions make them different and dogmatic. We should also admit that we cannot change people as much as we wish and try, and as much as they may appear, or promise, to change.

We must learn to live and let live. The purpose of a personal life philosophy is to prepare us for this kind of mentality and expectation. People have different needs and priorities, and they have an absolute right to live anyway they wish. We should beware of our Egos that insist we can change people. We must remember that although we may influence or manipulate others temporarily, we cannot control them permanently and fully. The silliest expectation we all entertain regularly is the notion that, 'Why he or she is not as perfect as we would like him/her to be,' while we imagine that our standards of perfection and correctness are valid. We have only ourselves to blame when we refuse to understand and accept these simple facts, and while we cannot learn to be quite flexible. Our life philosophy and new mentality must eliminate these self-imposed sources of frustrations and agonies.

On the one hand, we need life philosophies that strengthen our divine self and help us *relate* to others rather passively but effectively, instead of struggling to change them to fit our needs. Only through patience, tolerance, and compassion by using the 'self' aspect of our personality, we might live a peaceful life alongside the people and symbols of our modern societies. Otherwise, we cannot survive in our families, work environments, and society as a whole. This mental adjustment would present a big challenge and dilemma for us to resolve, because adapting ourselves to social values would threaten our principles, thoughts, and beliefs all the time.

On the other hand, adaptation and tolerance do not mean compliance. We intend to respect others and live with their quirks that often conflict our philosophy of life. However, we do not want to let them influence or weaken our convictions about life. We intend to make our lives practical in the light of personal life philosophies and knowledge of individual differences. Yet, it does not mean we should submit to the desires of others and even society if they contradict our fundamental beliefs and personal commitment to a path of wisdom. We should not allow the purpose of practicality becomes the cause of our submission to the mainstream life. Of course, we can change personally, too, if we find it useful, but only based on our life philosophy and newer convictions, and not because of someone else's demand.

11. Nurturing Our Positive Doubts

Another flawed teaching of our societies, which is reinforced by positive thinking schools too, is that our 'doubts' slow us down and prevent us from taking risks and moving forward decisively. This notion applies only in special circumstances, but not as a strategy for decisiveness and social appeal. Our prudence (doubts) in pursuit of new ventures and adventures is an instinctual defence mechanism. However, it is also becoming an essential tool for fighting deliberate schemes and misinformation in our corrupt societies. 'Doubting' goads us to take a break and think deeper and longer about issues instead of making hasty decisions. In particular, *doubting* the teachings of our societies is extremely enlightening, as they make us *ponder* our life options more thoroughly.

Most decisions require serious doubts and thoughts in order to, (a) subdue our emotional tendencies or egotistical assumptions about our knowledge of facts, and, (b) withstand other people's pressure on us to make a decision. Raw certitude ruins our ability to look for more options patiently. Saying that decisions require thinking and analysis is not enough. Rather, the nature of our prior doubts determines the scope and extent of the factors scrutinized. Without deep doubts, we do not take advantage of an inner voice and intuition that emerge beyond any logical thinking process. As an example, nowadays we have learned that the phrase 'I love you' may be more mechanical, or perhaps even cynical, instead of authentic and useful. Sometimes, we may doubt the sincerity of a person without any logical reason or proof of insincerity. Without our innate doubt, we may accept and use the information s/he gives us readily.

Having positive doubts is different from being suspicious of everything and everybody as a habit. Chronic suspicion reflects our inability to doubt objectively and instinctually. Doubts are necessary for making a sound decision, but also for making us less judgmental and opinionated. Often we turn into a suspicious person because of bad experiences with people often due to our gullibility, naïve trust, or not knowing how to nurture our doubts. Thus, we become cynical because of our negative perceptions and psychological reactions to our experiences. For example, we become suspicious and jealous of our friends because their odd behaviours hurt our Ego. These negative doubts are symptoms of psychological shortfalls, although instincts still play a role too. Suspicion and jealousy derive from personal insecurity and erratic thoughts that raise our tension. They only waste our energy and intelligence. This is in contrast to 'doubting' objectively, based on a whole set of factors, for a specific purpose, e.g., gauging the depth of our friendship. These positive doubts are 'self' (not 'ego') driven.

Analysing our doubts is a kind of meditation that requires a tranquil surrounding and a relaxed mind. Pondering our doubts is a major part of self-awareness as we proceed on the path of wisdom. Meditating on our doubts leads to answers accessible only in our unconscious mind. Our doubts usually induce some tentative tension, but they eventually exert an immense source of inner energy in the form of intuition and compassion, which then relieve the original tension too. Positive doubts exude energy and intelligent decisions—not lethargy and cynicism.

Our 'doubts' are often a *positive* attribute for relating to people and environment effectively and peacefully—most often for the purpose of giving them the benefit of our doubts and seeing them more positively. Conversely, our 'doubts' stop us from trusting people naively and automatically. Intuitively, our thoughts concentrate on positive possibilities and give people the benefit of a doubt when we are not sure about their intentions completely. And we see things with an open mind in positive light and purpose when negativity is not interfering. This is contrary to cases when suspicion and jealousy direct all our energy immediately toward negative thoughts and possibilities. The *true* sense of 'doubts' makes us flexible and tolerant of others and gives us the chance to view and deal with life in a practical manner. With positive 'doubts' we remain less critical of other people's positions and lifestyles.

Even when 'doubts' manifest as *negative* attributes in our judgment, such as the time we doubt someone's sincerity, we can use them mostly as an alarm mechanism. We can use this opportunity to meditate and evaluate the consequences of a major decision that is necessary to prevent irreversible mistakes or harms.

Entertaining our doubts during the decision-making process increases the quality of our decisions. On the other hand, this needed pause should not stop or delay the whole process of decision-making. In particular, if we delay the timing of crucial decisions of life, repercussions may be grave. Without a habit to use both our positive and negative 'doubts' effectively, our judgments and decisions become prejudiced. Negative doubts (prejudice) lead to cynicism and withdrawal. Conversely, positive doubts (rationality drive)—without proper justification and application—cause indecisiveness. Sometimes, they lead to gullibility, too, when we keep giving people or events a benefit of our doubts instead of making a bigger effort to study people and incidents more carefully.

Maslow refers to a similar phenomenon when he attributes the indecisiveness of his self-actualizing subjects (as) a major weakness. He states:

"The main danger of B-cognition is of making action impossible or at least indecisive. B-cognition is without judgment, comparison, condemnation or evaluation. Also it is without decision, because decision is readiness to act, and B-cognition is passive contemplation, appreciation, and non-interfering, i.e., "let-be." So long as one contemplates the cancer or the bacteria, awe-struck, admiring, wondering, passively drinking in the delight of rich understanding, then one does nothing." Toward a Psychology of Being, Abraham Maslow, Von Nostrand Reinhold, 1968, p. 116.

"The main danger, then, is that B-cognition is at the moment incompatible with action. But since we, most of the time, live in-the-world, action is necessary (defensive or offensive action, or selfishly centered action in the terms of the beholders rather than of the behold)." Ibid., p. 117.

(The phrase 'B-cognition' referred to in the above quotes means the 'Cognition of Being,' which is a humanness state of mind—love, caring, etc.—that self-actualizers are characterized by.)

Through a personal life philosophy, we strive to use our instinctual and objective 'doubts' to our advantage. We learn to distinguish positive doubts from suspicion, jealousy, and cynicism, which are destructive and contrary to the purpose of doubtfulness. Instead, positive doubts are viewed as a source of raising intelligent thoughts and accessing our unconscious. Therefore, any positive doubt should coincide with *active* contemplation. The ultimate purpose of positive doubts is to help us develop our solid convictions and make the right decisions in life with a sensible frame of mind within a logical timeframe. Part VI in Volume II discusses the nature and role of human doubts in detail.

12. Fighting but Not Fearing Depression

We must deal more proactively with the rising sources and level of depression as our societies become more complex and less friendly. Our modern lifestyles make us more alienated from one another and from the humanistic principles that must supposedly form the foundation of a society and our togetherness. Despite the prevalent positive thinking slogans, deep down we all feel lonely and betrayed. We feel the vanity of life and doubt the viability of our lifestyles. Our eagerness to show off our resilience and optimism actually demonstrates our disappointments and deep insecurities. All this hoopla reveals our rising need for such defence mechanisms to keep our hopes high. Often our struggles for positive thinking seem more like a gimmick or a refuge to hide our frustration, desolation, and depression. After all, life is hardly proving to be a joyous or meaningful journey. Without our innate hope keeping us going, many of us would have committed suicide already to get out of our laborious, boring lives. No wonder the level of violence, depression, and suicide is rising so fast.

All the evidences hint that the level of depression would increase as the merits of social living decline. Instead, we encounter pervasive social disorders, including the loss of compassion and patience, unemployment, tax burdens, unreliable social services, loss of privacy and freedom, higher cost of living and basic needs, reduction of real income, lack of any form of job security, severe labour competition in international markets, and fast deterioration of political systems, social values, and morality. In these types of societies, people's interactions and relationships become increasingly more antagonistic and a major source of depression.

Unfortunately, in today's overactive societies, everybody is inadvertently dragged and trapped into shoddy lifestyles that cause plenty of confusion and depression. Youths, in particular, would face more overwhelming doubts and decisions, which they must handle in a timelier and speedier manner too. Our communication barriers are increasing fast and we find it impossible to understand and respect one another's needs and opinions. Personal doubts, stress, and anxieties keep piling up, and, under these pressures, we also destroy our chances for building meaningful relationships with others. At the same time, we transmit our frustration throughout the society and add to the public's overall level of stress and anxiety.

Sadly, the future of humanity is doomed. We are already trapped in an accelerating process of no-return deterioration. The environment, economies, social values, etc. are all under severe pressures. Simply, the situation is hopeless. With the risk of being labelled a chronic pessimist, many of us seriously doubt that this deterioration process can be stopped or reversed. Too many strong and opposing poles already overwhelm the social structure; they can neither be replaced nor brought into control and balance. For example, we witness governments' difficulty to bring national budgets and debts under control, simply because the means of achieving this goal requires higher taxes or cutback in services, neither of which the public like. A government cannot be popular and elected if its socioeconomic platform does not respond to the immediate needs of individuals, especially the rich running the world. This is like having a sick child decide whether to take his medicine or not based on its taste. Governments are influenced and run by elite groups and conglomerates and thus have lost their objectivity and effectiveness to make proper socioeconomic decisions for the welfare of its citizens. The gullible poor are selling their freedom and democratic rights so cheaply, too, when they are lured by measly incentives or promises. The needs of business enterprises and labour forces can never be reconciled. When business should become more ruthless to survive in the highly competitive international markets, workers lose more jobs and psychological security, so they fight back. There are numerous examples of imbalances similar to this business-labour dichotomy, such as the needs of industry and conservationists, the needs of wealthy versus poor countries, the needs of the exploiting and exploited nations, the needs of individuals versus various interest groups, the needs of two individuals in a relationship, etc.

Besides the external pressures, we also contribute to our own frustrations and depression by setting untenable objectives and expectations for our lives instead of attending to our real needs. Furthermore, we do not know how to deal with our occasional depressions that are natural, especially the mild ones erupting after a happiness cycle.

For all the above depressing facts, however, we must deal more effectively with three sources of depression: i) the external (including socioeconomic and relationship) pressures, ii) personally induced stress caused by our fanciful objectives and expectations, and iii) the natural depression cycles emerging at the end of some (if not all) the happiness periods.

The purpose of a personal life philosophy is to keep us aware of the sources of our depression. Understanding and rationalizing the causes of our depression is important. We aggravate our depression unknowingly and unnecessarily when we do not study its sources carefully, or when we try too hard to fight those unchangeable features of social structure. The enormity and nature of these major sources of depression are discussed in detail in Volume III of this trilogy. Furthermore, we often allow one type of depression cause other types. Thus, we must learn to treat each type of depression according to its source, study its causes in detail, and then develop practical methods of curbing it somewhat. We must accept depression as a real feeling that need not be feared, but only managed. Like all other human emotions, depression need not, and should not, be suppressed or controlled artificially. Rather, it should be grasped to our advantage and expressed creatively. We should learn not to feel guilty or lose control of our minds and thoughts when caught in a depression mood. Nor should we blame ourselves or even others for it, but only determine whether any of our mistakes or misperceptions is causing our depression. A depression experience can in fact help us learn (from) our mistakes and reassess our perceptions about life and society. Only we must stay objective without allowing self-pity, anxiety, or laziness taint the process of studying our depression.

Instead of fearing depression as a negative experience, we could learn to emphasize on the opportunity it provides to learn more about ourselves and our life philosophy, etc. We must work on its real roots actively, instead of letting it pile up in our subconscious and turning into a melancholic and nagging habit. Getting trapped within a depressed personality is neither an appealing social stance nor a useful attitude for building a personal life philosophy. Instead, evaluating and learning about the sources of our depressions can make us strong. While the presence of depression is normal and acceptable, we must stop it from dominating our lives or becoming a habit. By regular analyses of our mild depressions, we must disallow them to root.

Ironically, we can often learn more about our 'self' and unconscious mind during a state of *alarming* depression than when we are lost in our *numbing* happiness moods and pleasures. As a major human emotion, depression can provide access to deeper layers of our being and initiate a natural process of meditation and evaluation. It is strange that our intuition and unconscious may be easier accessed and moved by negative emotions, such as depression or sense of loneliness. Many philosophers, scientists, artists, yogis, and Sufis have reached their height of wisdom through isolation and some form of depression. In fact, real wisdom emerges only through solitude. Of course, this does not suggest that we can or should awaken our 'self' merely through solitude or seek depression for any purpose. However, the world we can find and touch during our depression moods is unachievable in happiness periods. Each aspect of a happiness-depression cycle has a unique benefit and lesson for analysing and grasping 'self.'

The depression-induced urge to seek privacy and do 'self' evaluation is mysterious, as if Nature were trying to give us a chance to heal our wounds during a period of inner privacy and reflection. In that sense, depression can be seen as an instinctual mechanism for 'self' preservation through reflection. A major cause of depression nowadays is that we are afraid of loneliness and we are not trained to benefit from this natural need of humans. Instead, we insist on socializing to fight off the depression of not knowing how to be alone and independent.

Ignoring our depression or facing it with artificial means, such as drugs, deprives us from the opportunity of learning through instinctual healing. We often avoid dealing with depression or unbearable thoughts on the ground that we are too busy to do so, or on the assumption that it would go away better by ignoring it or dampening it by more socializing. Accordingly, we not only pile up depression to a point of explosion, but also miss a chance to really feel and express our deep emotions, which are often creative and heartfelt. This deprivation could eventually suppress our ingenuity and damage our psyche. In today's busy world, we may not find time to even appreciate and deal with our depression until its effects cripple us—almost the way we weaken our bodies from sleep deprivation and maybe even excessive pleasure. At that level, we simply lose control of our lives. Depression, at a normal level, is a sign of body and mind requiring a rest and reconnecting. Ignoring this vital sign would not remove the problem. Attending to it would release the boiling tensions within us before it explodes; and if used properly, it might even lead to creativity and finding the path of wisdom.

13. Making Major Life Decisions

We ponder our life options regularly and build our beliefs routinely as we mature. Especially during adolescence and early adulthood, we hope to develop some kind of guidelines (life philosophy) for handling our niggling doubts and decisions. We look for rigid standards and criteria to arrive at right conclusions and avoid costly mistakes. We try to stay logical and insightful for making effective decisions, some of which we believe are crucial for our long-term welfare. We also like to learn self-discipline and patience, to tackle a large variety of life dilemmas with proper scrutiny. The main purpose of all this torturous contemplation, of course, is to maximize our chances of enjoying life's grand opportunities, while minimizing the risks of social living and facing dire disappointments. In all, we realize that most of our decisions and actions benefit from a methodical justification and a profound life philosophy.

Accordingly, personal life philosophy reflects our deep convictions and standards. We attempt to apply it uniformly in our relationships and social activities with our earned self-discipline and patience. And we depend on it for assessing our options within a hectic social structure imposed upon us so casually and callously. We hope to find life's essentialities and a path that can help us materialize our true potentialities and feel actualized, instead of sinking deeper in the illusory world that our naïve perceptions have created.

Understanding the complexity and risks of a dozen or so decisions in life is particularly important. Therefore, Volume III of this trilogy is devoted mainly to discussions of the most important life decisions. The natures and purposes of our doubts and decisions, especially regarding major life decisions, are explained in Part VI in Volume II.

14. Finding a Reliable Companion

Having a companion is a basic, instinctual need and extremely helpful for maintaining our mental and physical health. However, unfortunately, this affair has become the main source of frustration and stress in society in the new era. We are highly doubtful about the nature and purpose of relationships nowadays and the level of reliance and trust we can have in another person in such a chaotic relationship environment. The situation is getting out of control fast, while we spend so much of our lives wondering how to find a reliable companion, how to relate, and how to avoid the rising hassles of being in relationships. We ponder this topic a lot, almost as much as we think about eating. Overall, relationship dilemmas pose some of the most critical decisions of life nowadays for everybody. This subject is in fact so critical in the author's opinion that he attended to writing a book about it first while delaying the completion of this trilogy. *The Nature of Love and Relationships* tackles the major issues and obstacles of relationships in the new era. Part III in Volume III of this trilogy discusses this matter in some detail too.

15. Optimizing Our Physical and Mental Health

All our thoughts, doubts, feelings, and actions should lead to one ultimate, but basic, objective our entire lives, i.e., maintaining our mental and physical health. The focal point and reference for building a life philosophy and all the *fundamental* thoughts behind it, as explained in this chapter, as well as our *tactical* and *mechanical* thoughts, are just for serving our body and mind the best we can. Mental and physical health is indeed the main criterion for the correctness and worthiness of all major life decisions. All other objectives and thoughts, including our search for happiness or a reliable companion, are valid and useful only if they can serve the main purpose—our mental and physical health. Thus, any thought, feeling, action, or relationship that does not fulfil this ultimate objective is wrong and worthless. Now just imagine the absurdity of all those thoughts, feelings, actions, and relationships that damage our mental and physical health. It is hard to imagine anybody having any trouble relating and adhering to this very basic philosophy of life permanently. That kind of ignorance would only reflect the impact of current superficial lifestyles on our mentality, e.g., when we let our health and professions get ruined because of love, greed, work, power struggles, etc.

Maintaining our physical and mental health is an obvious fact, though many of us forget this basic principle for living effectively. Yet the overall health is merely the first step, because we have the ability to expand our minds significantly for optimizing our health and happiness. We can seek the higher intelligence and wisdom that most humans can potentially acquire for not only living healthier, but also reaching a soulful enlightenment. All we need is the willpower and maturity to fight off the influence and demands of our perceived world. We need a divine 'self' power to bypass the temptations of the superficial needs and values that society propagates. We need new visions and thoughts to overcome the effect of our tainted misperceptions, especially about the purpose of life and our futile search for the elusive happiness within a tainted framework. We need a strong 'self' to reveal our gullibility and childish whims to us, and then perhaps take us to those territories of boundless intelligence and energy, which only a healthy mind and body can reach.

Our brain has a vaster capacity and potentiality than we normally recognize and utilize. We use only 3-5 percent of this capacity on the average, if that. Even the most intelligent scientists and geniuses have not used their brains beyond this low level. Thus, there is plenty of potential and intelligence in humans that have not yet been tapped because of the way we have restricted our minds to confined thoughts and habits—mostly due to religions and charlatans exploiting our minds and existence. We certainly have some doubts about the enormity of human's potential and intelligence, as it sounds more like a hedonistic, abstract notion, especially when witnessing all the human naivety and ignorance around us. However, the possibility of humans' higher wisdom could materialize if we eventually distinguish life essentialities, become an integral part of the universe, and emerge as a selfless enlightened person.

Obviously, with a weakened physical and mental capacity, we cannot utilize even the bare minimum potentialities that might be considered normal for humans nowadays. To go beyond this minimum level, though, we need a divine physical and mental capacity. We need an absolute, unconditioned, and untarnished psyche and physics that a man could naturally own and control. We should always maintain reasonable doubts regarding the high impact of upbringing, genetic defects, and social conditioning on our mental and physical health, which are mostly irreversible. Yet, with our primary intelligence, most of us can assess our physical and mental health as a first step toward a minimum self-awareness. If we succeed, we quickly realize that we are not as clean and clever as we naturally could be or believed to be. Subsequently, we could attempt to resolve some of our weaknesses through a rigid self-awareness regiment and self-therapy, or by referring to a specialist. By acknowledging both our deficiencies and inherent human potentiality in general, we may be able to refurbish our troubled psyche and weakened spirit. We could diagnose and admit to our idiosyncrasies, and then treat them with care and passion. This is a part of self-cleansing (awareness) process that can prepare us to enter a path of wisdom.

Occasionally we feel too vulnerable and face some moments of weakness and chronic doubts. In such times, we must draw on our primary wisdom and patience to maintain our convictions and beliefs, and then raise our self-awareness by studying the sources of our depression and desperation. We could also remember that we are at such a state of vulnerability and learn how to resist the temptations and scapegoats that entice us during such periods. For example, when we are lonely, we feel particularly deficient and depressed. Knowing this fact, we also recognize that in such situations or moments we could get into habits or activities that are psychologically and physically harmful, or make irreversible, erroneous decisions. Despite this awareness, it is still difficult for most of us to subdue our vulnerability; so, we get into those harmful activities, addictions, or lifestyles, anyway, just to overcome our loneliness and void. We prefer self-destruction to self-awareness, perhaps because it is easier and because we have a hard time justifying our existence anyway. We lose our reasons (and even our plausible doubts) about living. Thus, we give up and let go of our mental and physical health. Self-destruction feels more natural than self-awareness to ordinary men, but we can choose not to remain an ordinary man.

We need a high level of awareness about these inevitable moments of weakness in our lives, and a strong conviction to avoid making irreversible mistakes during those periods. There are also those inevitable cycles of depression, but a healthy mind realizes that some moodiness of personality is natural. With this awareness and free spirit, we can handle and perhaps even take advantage of a depression mood. These moodiness states are the natural symptoms of a happiness-depression cycle, hormonal changes, or a moderate case of personality swing that are normal and manageable at these levels. Our chronic doubts about the purpose of our existence cannot be avoided and they always cause depression. A healthy psyche knows how to deal with a mood change or a mild depression, instead of being threatened by them.

Physical weakness not only allows diseases take over our body fast and easy, but also sabotages our spirit and ability to think straight. By letting body lose its vitality beyond the reasonable aging process, and not following an informed health regiment, we only increase our chances of failure and sufferings in both physical and psychological fronts. Conversely, without the proper nurturing of our mind, the physical aspect of our existence is drastically threatened too. Body-mind connectivity (including their linked welfares) is a fact we must always remember and honour. Without defining a plausible direction for our lives and making firm commitments to achieve certain worthy goals, we would leave ourselves at the mercy of the Devil. We would kill our spirit and existence if we do not take control of our lives. Forget about 'living in the now' in any moment when your life direction is not fully planned and pursued proactively.

Our actions and decisions should always have plausible purposes for enriching our mind and body, while we minimize those random living aspects of our life that have no tangible benefit or purpose. Referring to the simple example noted briefly before, one of our major pastimes is to watch professional sports and cheer for a few teams. The higher the consequence of the games, i.e., play-offs or finals, the more the outcome of a game affects us emotionally and psychologically. This is a prevalent habit and a major phenomenon in the world today, in the way athletes and celebrities have such great impact on the quality of our mental and physical health. We feel sad for no justifiable reason at all. Why we strain our brains by our obsessions is inexplicable. Is it because our lives are too empty and soulless? If yes, why cannot we come up with healthier pastime to overcome the burdens of our mundane living and avoid all these extra pressures on body and mind?

Humans' *fundamental* thoughts briefly discussed in this chapter, as well as our *tactical* and *mechanical* thoughts, consume a great deal of our energy, and induce depression and destructive urges quite often too. They stir a large variety of lingering doubts in our heads throughout our lives and they demand major life-changing decisions. All these thoughts, doubts, and decisions also provide the opportunity for learning about ourselves and finding a path of wisdom, though they occasionally turn into main sources of depression and stress during the process, as discussed in Chapter Seven.

CHAPTER TWO
Perceived and Real Worlds

The world and all its luring features, events, and interactions appear so natural to us and thus we take them as our 'life realities.' Yet those 'realities' are mostly the reflections of our imaginations, desires, and interpretations. These subjective impressions and judgments are tainted by not only humans' sensual limitations, but also people's dynamic tastes and preferences in various circumstances. Therefore, humans' 'reality' is merely a distorted view of the truth and the universe. Actually, our misperceptions impair our view of even simple facts, such as humans' extreme vulnerability despite their rising haughtiness. We have even come to believe that God has a special interest in us and perhaps even has created this whole universe for our sake. What a weird, conceited notion!

Meanwhile, many of us also sense a real, absolute world that exists out there independent from human impressions and interpretations. We do not know what it exactly is, but have enough knowledge and logic to acknowledge its existence and purpose outside our naïve impression of it. Thus, we have two worlds: The *imaginary* world created in our heads by our perceptions—let us call it the 'perceived world.' And then this *absolute* world that exists beyond humans' thoughts and imaginations—let us call it the 'real world.' To get a better grasp of these two worlds, their main characteristics are briefly noted below.

Characteristics of the 'Real World'

1. This is a world beyond human imaginations, which holds the *absolute* truth about the universe—a minuscule part of which includes humans' existence too.
2. It sets the attributes of all facets of existence, including the nature of man.
3. Deviations from the nature of things cause chaos and conflict, which in humans' case leads to their ongoing confusion and suffering. That is, as long as we humans try to create absurd imaginations, rules, and thoughts beyond reality and our natural needs and capacities, we make our lives more whimsical and unmanageable.
4. The natural connection between humans and the universe emerge instinctually in the form of their inherent drives and spirituality needs.
5. No religion or human intelligence (or any other kind of imagination) can reveal the true nature of the 'real world.' However, our limited intelligence might eventually help us map a path of wisdom that enhances our sense of connection with the universe. That seems to be the only way for humans to find peace of mind and live more in harmony within the essence of the 'real world.'

A fuller picture of the real world is provided on page 82.

Characteristics of the 'Perceived World'

1. This is the world created merely by human impressions, rules, ethics, ideals, and desires.

2. We have learned to fully accept this world (our own perceptions) as the real truth, instead of doubting its authenticity.
3. We make our judgments and decisions based on values and criteria that have evolved in this illusive world also based on humans' subjective standards. Accordingly, our logic and judgments are not aligned with any truth beyond human inventions, which are made for their convenience and according to their limited intelligence.
4. Because of the above conditions, and due to our greed and ambitions, we have created more superficial needs for ourselves gradually through history and raised our expectations from life and one another, to a point where our lives have become too complex, unattainable, whimsical, and stressful.
5. We have developed wrong self-images and phony identities that have little relation to humans' natural capabilities and needs. We seem to need these superficialities to assert ourselves and adapt within our competitive societies.
6. Our socioeconomic structure and values have also evolved in line with humans' unrealistic impressions and demands and thus they cause not only more confusion and hardship for people, but also reinforce the cycle of human misperceptions about life and themselves.
7. With our vast illusions and self-deceit about the purpose of life and our position in society, the 'perceived world' is gaining an unprecedented momentum and becoming more superficial and misleading every year. The gap between the two worlds of 'real' and 'perceived' realities is widening very fast, which means less possibility for peace and practicality of human life.
8. People, including world leaders, are in total denial about the deteriorating path that humans have taken and still focus on immediate needs of businesses and governments instead of the welfare of humanity in the long run. After many millenniums of trial and error with our wars, science, philosophies, and political systems, we still do not have a basic democ-

racy even in most advanced nations (despite all their propagandas), and we still put our greed and power above all humanity. We humans are still as infant as our Stone Age ancestors about the welfare of humans, or maybe even worse when we consider all the killings and carelessness in the recent eras.

9. People and governments are too optimistic about the present state of the affairs and the viability of the existing socioeconomic systems despite all the evidence indicating our humongous failure.
10. Living in this 'perceived world' has impaired our judgment and willpower to find a solution for human survival and humanity. Many people, but especially our egotistical leaders, have simply chosen to ignore this important mission for human race—to look for peace and salvation.
11. The 'perceived world' has many lasting repercussions on our personal lives too. For example, it has made us raise our expectations, e.g., about work environments, while in reality the majority of us must face our bosses' egotistical demands and bullying. Or how naively we have come to believe in love and happiness.
12. We also like to believe that human nature is pure and life is a place to enjoy ourselves—just two other gross misperceptions.

A major book should delineate the characteristics and perils of the 'perceived world.' But only a few evidences are offered in the coming pages to make the above observations more clear. They show how we have hypnotized ourselves with some imaginary ideals and shallow ideas and then hurt one another in this phony world of perceived realities. The book *Empire of Illusion*, by Chris Hedges, Alfred A. Knopf, Canada, 2009, illustrates the depth and the sad effects of people living in this illusory world and suffering the consequences of their choices and habits.

Some of our most crooked perceptions in society are discussed in the following pages.

Perceptions about Our Identity

As elaborated in many parts of this trilogy, we would never understand who we are. Sometimes we sense our struggle with our personality and inner conflicts regarding who we can be and the image we are trying to portray to others. In general, however, we are too absorbed in our phony personalities to worry about our real identity. It is actually getting harder nowadays to establish our identity in such a hypocritical society. We do not even care to understand at least the plausible essence of humanness and our authentic needs as the building blocks of our identity. Our pleasure seeking attitude, ambitions, sexuality, and greed prevent us from finding who we really are. We simply imitate others and cherish crooked values and lifestyles that have evolved in our societies and serve only our Egos. We build a shoddy mentality hypnotically and we create a fake identity to guide us for defining life and setting our plans. We become phony and arrogant in order to portray our fake confidence and individualism. And we try to manipulate one another with our exaggerated show of love and sincerity. We know how phony and flimsy our communications and promises are. The overall trust in society is at its lowest ever, and still we continue to behave arrogantly and deceivingly, while bragging about our integrity and trustworthiness. People not only can see the phoniness and shallowness of one another, but also notice the vanity of their own identity when they self-analyse themselves occasionally and use their conscience to get a glimpse of who they have become. We have developed false identities to adapt ourselves to social settings, hoping to get more things and compassion in society. Our shaky identities are a direct symptom of living so enthusiastically in our perceived world. Accordingly, we have become distraught about the purpose of living in such a chaotic environment. We have also lost our chance to explore the true meanings of individualism and 'self.'

Perceptions about Dependence and Independence

In line with our shallow identity, we have become extremely confused about the level of independence and individualism we wish to attain, compared with the amount of dependence we need and wish to maintain with others, especially our spouses. As humans, we need both dependence and independence, but we have not yet been able to find the right balance between these two conflicting needs of ours. Actually, the effect of living in the perceived world has made the task of finding the right balance of dependence and independence extremely difficult. With our eagerness to place so much emphasis on individualism and independence, we have become more arrogant and demanding, but also both oversensitive and insensitive. This condition has impaired people's capacity to find, or even know, the amount of dependency they need or can realistically expect to maintain. Deep down, however, they feel the deficiency and do not know how to remedy the situation either. A detail discussion of this phenomenon is provided in *The Nature of Love and Relationships*. The main point is that people have deep, irreconcilable misperceptions about their conflicting needs for independence and dependence and assume that a workable balance would automatically emerge despite their rising Egos. Even worse, they assume they can have both as they switch from one position to the other and expect people around them to adjust themselves according to their erratic preferences for independence (freedom) and dependence (compassion). This wishful thinking and naivety is itself a direct outcome of living in this perceived world and making all sorts of far-fetched assumptions.

Perceptions about Love

Another evidence of our perplexing mentality in the 'perceived world' is the way people have become too romantic and believe that everybody can and should find an everlasting love. They not only have wrong inclinations about the nature of love, but also assume everybody can find it or nurture it. The irony is that they have become too arrogant, oversensitive, and antagonistic while insisting on getting more compassion and affection. They are personally incapable of understanding and giving love to others, but demand it obsessively. They have also made love the main factor for the success of relationships. Thus, anytime they feel a bit less love than their imaginations demand, they get offended and depressed, which often leads to the collapse of their relationships too.

Perceptions about Religions

Religions stand out probably as the most significant evidence of humans' persistence to live in this perceived world all across the globe. It is amazing how we humans ignore the simple logic that the existence of so many conflicting religions eradicates the validity of all of them, especially considering the amount of wars and controversy among these religions. The matter is even more horrific considering the extreme hostility among various sects within every religion for small disputes, which realistically should not have any effect on the actual words of the prophets per se. Not even the purpose of religions is clear anymore. Has it really supposed to be a means of God's contact with humans? If yes, for what end? To make humans more civil and ethical? What has He or us achieved after all this time?

The basic tenor of the main religions is that there is One God, Who demands peace and morality from His creatures. So ultimately, all religions must worship the same creator as a first test of authenticity of any of those religions—and all for the simple purpose of propagating compassion and forgiveness and not animosity and egotism. Even humans' basic logic dictates that there must be no multiple Gods and no acrimony among religions, but only simple uniform messages from Creator. This God would supposedly send His messages through prophets to warn humans about His existence and the repercussions of not following His rules. Actually, we should assume that the only reason He would send multiple prophets had been the lack of proper communication systems at the time, or else one prophet would have been enough! Anyhow, you would expect this God convey the same messages through all His prophets and ensure not only those rules are consistent, but also given to people without any side interpretations by the prophets. He had definitely trusted them, too, to stay faithful to His instructions and words. So why would He send different (and often conflicting) messages through His prophets? Has He tried to confuse humans and then punish them at the end too? Should not He have also known that a variety of interpretations could erupt and cause such a chaos?

Islam professes that God has sent 124,000 prophets so far, although only five of them have been GREAT! You wonder how persistent and optimistic God has been all along—never giving up, at least not until Prophet Mohammed, the last Great one, was appointed to this seemingly irresolvable intention of God. Maybe He has finally given up on sending more prophets after Prophet Mohammed, either assuming that he would fulfil His intentions once and for all, or believing that sending prophets would be useless for the kind of humans He has created. Well, the point is that after 124,000 prophets, we are still in this big mess!

On the other hand, you would imagine that a just, proactive God would not allow such havoc and gullibility continue under his name, if he had anything to do with this whole shenanigans. He would have made sure by now that his name and reputation were not abused so much, forever, through all these misrepresentations in various religions. He would have stopped all these mistakes and ended all the fighting that continues among so many religions, which He has Himself supposedly created every few centuries. In the final analysis, He is responsible for all this religious mayhem destroying the world then. How could He remain the cause of so much pain on Earth, all because of His righteous decisions to enlighten humans and make things better for them? Would not have He by now tried to reverse His past mistake of trusting His prophets and their successors? Has God failed so miserably?

With our limited logic and no direct interests or reputation at steak, any one of us can imagine how He would have acted differently to avoid all these confusions and chaos—if we could respectfully be in God's shoes for a second and had all His power. Let us say, He sends Moses with the Ten Commandments and the Torah to enlighten people. Then, fourteen centuries later, still not happy with the outcome, He sends His beloved son to correct the situation. He says, "Jesus, go tell people that Moses was my prophet and they better listen to what he brought to them under my name. Tell them that those instructions are authentic and necessary for them to follow. You may also correct all the misinterpretations and add a few clauses to tighten the guidelines in the Torah. That's all! Go my son and be careful."

But then Jesus starts a new religion and writes a whole new book. God, would tell him, "My son, why did not you just do what I asked you to do, to only make sure people understand my earlier instructions. I have not changed my mind and there was no need for a new religion and a whole set of new guidelines. Why did you write another book to confuse these daft humans, and get yourself killed too? Maybe I should not have resurrected you as a punishment for your disobedience!?"

Then still unhappy with the way humans are behaving six centuries later, He sends Muhammad now, again with the exact instructions and intention, to affirm what He has been trying to do for people and to ensure His instructions are followed. "Just listen, Muhammad. All you must do is to confirm that Moses and

Jesus are saying the same things and that they both were my GREAT messengers, as you are. Tell them that Jesus was (in fact is) my son, now safe and sound, and will return soon as promised. Just confirm my consistent wisdom and stress on what I have been saying in the last two millenniums. Only make it clear for them that those books are my words. Just make it easier for them to understand my existing instructions. For God's sake (My Sake), please do not write another book. Are you with me?"

This would have been a logical way for a God with enormous foresight to handle all the rising controversy and affirm everything He has been trying so hard to do for His people for two long millenniums, *at least*. But then again Muhammad comes down the mountain proudly and writes still another book that causes a lot more controversy and wars. It is hard to believe that any powerful and insightful God would allow this much travesty under his name. "Did not I specifically tell you not to write another book and only affirm what I have been trying to tell my people already? Why nobody listens to me? What kind of humans have I created? Such stubbornness! Why everybody likes to be an author these days more than a holy messenger? Why nobody likes to only affirm my previous messengers and messages? I have to keep thinking again for a better way of communicating with my people. Everybody knows that I really want to communicate with my people, but somehow I do not know how anymore! Unless I use the internet now that this service is finally available and everybody is so addicted to it as well! I feel so helpless because of these humans. It feels weird, especially after creating this humongous orderly universe! Is this Satan's fault too?

(I am absolutely sure that God will send me directly to heaven for defending Him so adamantly in this chapter.)

Despite the impossibility of a rational God playing any role in the creation of religions, prophets have tried to raise morality and intelligence of people in the best ways they could, but then things have gotten out of control. All prophets have had their honourable intentions and did their best regardless of their connections and family ties with God. However, it is reasonable to believe that one intelligent God would have never allowed so many contradictory religions disrepute Him. All religions are still respectable and worthy, but they have clearly failed to represent a wise God. There is no point to pick on a particular religion, either, like the way some scholars, including Salmon Rushdie, have inadvertently or intentionally done with Islam. All religions have their own merits and demerits, but none of them could have been the creation of a proactive God. Reviewing the petty differences among many factions of each religion makes all religious claims more questionable and disheartening. Only a cynical creator might have liked to cause so much mayhem for a simple objective—unless for having some fun perhaps! This is just too hard to believe, of course, though we still must not dismiss the possibility! *Just in case He has a big sense of humour!* Therefore, the most reasonable conclusion is that He has had nothing to do with these books and messages, despite all the good stuff in them. Hell, heaven, and afterlife are all merely our illusions in the perceived world. Period.

Aside from the way these religions were initially created, we still want to play even more silly games with God by trying to re-interpret some of His words according to our newer needs, e.g., about the gays, abortion, etc. We people are demanding flexibility from religions in order to match our perceived world's values or else we do not like that religion. We are asking God to be flexible with our needs because we have created our 'perceived world' and are happy living in this illusion with no sense of ethics. We just want to do things our ways or no religion. We want to build our Gods according to our needs, again. As far as God is concerned, we are telling Him that it is either our way or highway! We want our God to change His mind regularly as we see fit. In the older times, we made our gods in the shape of wooden idols and now we want to build them around the erratic values of our perceived world.

At the same time, it is amazing how we wicked, ungrateful humans (mainly clergies) claim so much nonsense about God and His instructions so fearlessly and arrogantly. How can we be so foolish and selfish, especially disregarding the possibility that a real God might actually exist and be witnessing our ignorance, hypocrisy, and fraud? We are so arrogant, not willing to even respect and appreciate all the great things He has done for us, starting with our mere existence. Not even atheists would dare be so stupid and say all these lies and contradictions (and made-up stories) without the fear of retribution. Only gullibility and arrogance can make us so confused about God and religions. What other evidence do we need for our wickedness and full absorption in our crooked 'perceived world'?

Various religions and their sects believe that only they are right while the rest are wrong, evil, and perhaps even charlatans. Therefore, one day we must finally choose between the two obvious options: That we are either worshiping different Gods, or only making up so many (if not all) of those religious claims. In either case, the bottom line shows humans' amazing tenacity to ignore that these religions and guidelines do not work. Instead, our attitude toward religions reveal the depth of social naivety—a phenomenon that humans may never be able to overcome. We are simply incapable of admitting that so much confusion and bloodshed only show how badly we have failed to build a culture for human coexistence regardless of God's existence. We just love our ignorance. We prefer to deny that an able, logical, and consistent God would send only one set of rules, which are by the way fixed and final. Nobody likes or accepts an inconsistent God. Our deliberate refusal to ponder these simple facts demonstrates the debilitating influence of the perceived world. Even our humanly substandard logic can detect the depth of our flawed reasoning, let alone the supreme logic that must exist for explaining the rules of the universe and the wisdom of an extremely artful creator. We are so entrenched in our ignorance and perceptions, however, we insist on closing our minds and eyes to even the simplest humanly facts and logic.

Of course, some of the messages are consistent across the main religions, which offer interesting conclusions by themselves. For example, they refer to 'Judgment Day,' which implies that, first of all, humanity would (and should) come to an end. Second, we would not know about the outcome of our deeds and sins until all humans have died—and not right after each person's demise. (Let us hope we do not have to wait for all other intelligent creatures in other planets to die as well, as a requirement of reaching the Judgment Day all at the same time, because they are the creatures of the same God, too, after all.) Anyhow, this predicament reveals God's absolute pessimism from the beginning about humans' ability to acquire enough intelligence, create a harmonious world for themselves, and avoid their extinction. Or that God knew from the very beginning that the level of sins would get so unbearable, He must end the whole damn thing and put people out of their miseries. He already knew from day one about the imperfections of His creations. Then what? Why send prophets then? Who is responsible for all humans' defects that He had already anticipated from the beginning? And is it now fair that humans be punished for someone else's design flaws, especially since they had been obvious to Him from the very start?

We can offer thousands of evidences about our naivety, especially regarding our views of religions. We can write hundreds of books, and argue among ourselves until hell freezes over, but we are not going to give up our naïve logic, perceptions, and love affair with the fantasy world we prefer to live in. We are not going to admit that, unless we look at all the religions together and make some sense of them (or not) collectively, nobody would grasp the properties of a credible God, at least for communicating amongst ourselves a little more civilly. At this point, however, all these religious imaginations in people's minds only reveal the dominance of the 'perceived world' in our lives, not only in terms of our historical illusions, but also for demanding new interpretations and upgrades according to our new needs, e.g., sexual liberty or gays' status in a religion. Our stubbornness and resistance show how deeply humans have become an integral part of the perceived world they have invented for themselves. We just keep expanding this world every day with more energy, persistence, and imaginations, perhaps as fast as the universe is expanding. We will never find courage, intelligence, and willpower to think more fundamentally to grasp our identities and 'self.' We have always assumed that humans are at the centre of the universe and the most important feature of God's smartest creation. But then we have proven to be the wildest of all creatures in His kingdom and the most foolish one too.

Perceived and Real Worlds

We normally do not get a clear sense of either 'perceived' or 'real' realities to choose a more fruitful path of life. These two worlds cannot be thoroughly mapped because: First, the 'perceived' reality has evolved over centuries around fluid social values and rules permeated through people's minds and imaginations with little foundation or logic—so it is merely a mishmash of flimsy, unstable perceptions. Second, as each one of us sees these values and rules differently, we relate or refer to them based on our unique personalities and needs. Things and ideas are valuable to people because they perceive them as valuable, e.g., for soothing their unique insecurities. And they also perceive, assume, and accept facts and rules, because they are conditioned to do so, as part of their attempts to cope with, and belong to, a social group, religion, community, or organization.

It is even harder to have an understanding and definition for the 'real world,' because, at best, it is real for the 'self' only, i.e., a selfless, needless, and conscious person, which is hardly an attainable state. Few reach this height of enlightenment and, even so, their ability to explain it and our ability to grasp it are too restricted. That is, until we reach a high measure of consciousness required to personally feel and understand the meaning of 'real' at certain level, we would never grasp its nature, let alone gain an ability to explain it to others. Even if somebody could explain it to us, its dimensions and absoluteness remain enigmatic due to our subjective personal interpretations and our inability to digest such visions. (Maybe this is a good excuse for prophets' inability to convey God's messages uniformly—though God could have potentially prevented this bottleneck!)

The point is that the interpretation of every reality still suffers from human limitations. Any kind of *presumed* reality feels real only to any person according to his unique level of consciousness at an exact moment. No two individuals' comprehension could coincide, since they never have the same level of consciousness or become one in any form or shape, at least while they are alive. Neither people nor science can really understand, define, or explain spiritual experiences, although they try to do so through psychology and philosophy at least. The best thing we can do at this time is to speculate and speak *only* about the implications and consequences of the real world for a person, a group of people, or society.

Nevertheless, an overall picture of these two parallel realities, as general concepts, can help us contemplate and make decisions about our existence and a viable path of life. We need tentative definitions for perceived and real worlds, as the two extreme boundaries of human consciousness and their desire for piety and spirituality.

A general definition of the 'perceived' reality may be built based on the prevalent perceptions of the public, as reflected in social culture and commoners' personalities. On the other hand, 'real world' is much harder to define, as it contains the ultimate and inherent secrets of the universe, while our interpretations of this 'absolute and immense' phenomenon remain forever subject to humans' tainted logic and low personal awareness. One way to make rudimentary definitions of, and compare, these two worlds is to use the notions of 'summit' and 'submit.' This general picture (and contrast) is the best we humans can ever envision for developing our mindsets about these two worlds. Then, we could speculate about the *potential consequences* of living within the real and perceived realities respectively, which merely satisfies our thirst for philosophical debates regarding our life paths and personal choices.

At the *base level* of the 'perceived reality', a person *submits* to common values and rules totally, out of ignorance and weakness. S/he is fully dependent on people and things outside him to receive material and mental satisfaction. S/he never challenges ideas and concepts, does not have a positive self-image or self-confidence, has no personal integrity, cannot or does not know how to think and for what end, and is incapable of seeing the inner self that exists within him even when some signs appear to him. A small group belongs to this utter level of ignorance.

Conversely, at the 'real reality' level, an individual reaches the *summit* of the truth, inner realization, full consciousness, and wisdom, which stands beyond the world of appearances, pretences, and phony feelings. This experience has not been fully explained or understood, despite the horrendous attempts by philosophers, theologians, psychologists, sages and saints, and those who believe (or claim) to have felt this ultimate state of enlightenment. Socrates, the Buddha, Rumi, and many other scholars pursued this path to their ends and left us with some clues and teachings. For most of us, however, we may only imagine its splendour through contemplation from one of the finer life paths that we might eventually explore. We might achieve this privilege by reflecting upon our personal experiences, logic, and feelings up to this point in our search for the truth, even though we are only travelling on a path far away from the summit.

Numerous levels of awakening and corresponding paths exist for people. Diagram 2.1 shows peoples' maximum and minimum levels of needs and their dependencies on the perceived world.

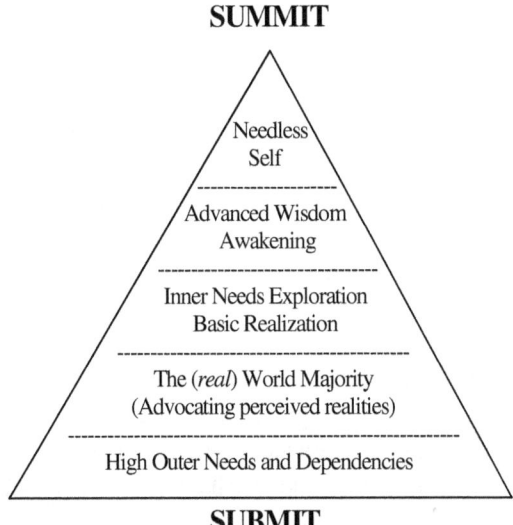

Diagram 2.1: The Paths of Awakening—Eros Dimension

The phrase 'real world,' which everybody uses regularly, is in fact people's common definition of, and reference to, the 'perceived world.' This perceived reality (which we take as our real world) is where the large majority of us adopt on the Eros dimension (in terms of the level of neediness versus self-awareness). This path is slightly higher than the SUBMIT, but much below even a basic self-awareness level. At this level, we need a stimulus, influence, or incentive to start looking for the higher paths. Close to the half way on the Eros dimension, some people reach the level of morality and wisdom required to rid themselves of their needs for phony lifestyles and appearances. They begin to explore their real inner needs instead. They become relatively selfless and self-driven, and thus achieve spiritual joy and energy that guides them through life. The Advanced Wisdom level is the same concept with higher intensity. At the imaginary SUMMIT level, perhaps no definition of needs, either outer or inner, exists. At this level, human needs do not have a sensual merit, as one's being theoretically coincides or combines with the reality of the Supreme Being, the God, the nature, the universe, consciousness, the energy, or whatever exits beyond the limits of human logic and mind.

The above two extremes are the opposite realms of the same continuum—the dimension of Eros, wisdom and awakening. Based on our level of awakening, however, we have different needs and outlooks on life. Therefore, in the hierarchy of Eros, the lowest level is full dependence on outer needs. At mid-range a person breaks away from outer needs and delves into inner needs. And at the Summit—a theoretical concept—s/he becomes needless, since the finite need to connect with the Supreme Being has been achieved. This height of human achievement is probably more theoretical than practical for normal people. The possibility of even saints and prophets having reached that level of immense blessing is doubtful too.

However, regardless of the path we choose and the height of the truth that we find in ourselves, the experience is 'personal' and unexplainable. Once someone experiences his/her 'self' and feels its permeating joy and energy, his understanding becomes his mental definition and guide for further exploration. However, the option for a novice, who needs some evidence to be convinced and motivated, is to choose a basic self-exploration path to experiment. S/he may begin his search by studying books or other individuals' experiences, including members of his/her family and community. Another good source for exploration is people who have been transformed spiritually. Something has happened to them, such as having a NDE (near death experience). We can read about them, listen to them, or ask them about the extraordinary inner energy they have suddenly gained. Then perhaps we can draw our conclusions, just for the purposes of starting our own thinking and search.

Exploring the Real World

There are many evidences and ways of confirming our inner self and attachment to a real world beyond the perceived world. For one thing, we often feel that our routine perceptions of our identities feel too shallow and unnatural. Our conscience also hints the existence of a hidden wiser 'self.' Other people, despite their biased perceptions, can also give us some clues about our character and how we come across as an individual.

An individual's level of consciousness also provides clues for differentiating 'real' and 'perceived' realities. For example, as a child, when we become aware of the reality of death for the first time, we send this information to the lowest level of our consciousness after the impact of this shocking news devastates us for a few days or weeks. Afterward, death remains in our minds only as a 'perceived reality.' That is, we know that death is a fact and, sure enough, we see and hear about it almost every day. However, we prefer to keep it in our lowest subconscious and we do not totally believe or feel that death is our destiny as well. All perceived realities are like this: A superficial image, feeling, or understanding of some things or values; they remain superficial as they reside merely in the deepest level of subconscious. The real reality, on the contrary, begins to manifest only at a state of full (or at least high) consciousness and awareness. We can imagine that our experiences at full consciousness bring us closer to our self and the real world. Then, 'Is death possibly the ultimate venue for abandoning our perceptions, reaching full consciousness, and entering the real world?' This is an odd, improbable concept even if we wish to believe in our immortality. Reaching full consciousness during our normal existence also seems impossible, despite all the speculations about our inherent connection to the universal consciousness!

Nevertheless, our real reality (possible consciousness), as an individual, is something that we can explore personally only through extensive and sincere self-analysis and 'self' development, and by challenging our perceptions. But can we ever bypass our perceptions? How much consciousness can any normal person, who is raised within such domineering perceived reality, ever achieve?

In his book, *A Second Way of Knowing, The Riddle of Human Perception*, Prentice Hall, 1991, Edmund Blair Bolles discusses the limitation of our perceptions and how our lives are affected by them. Some excerpts from his book are printed here as another point of view about the concepts of perceived and real reality and humans' capacity for consciousness. He says:

"Deciding who sees reality becomes harder when the objective truth is not so easily defined. At this point one's own prejudices enter the sense too powerfully to be called science. How shall we judge an old study of shape constancy? Using the technique described in Chapter 7 (of his book), students from England and India looked at inclined disk and then matched their perceptions against a chart showing possible shapes. The Indian students showed stronger shape constancy than the English students did. The British, not surprisingly, took the finding as evidence of their superiority over Indian perceptual backwardness. Indian perception was said to "regress to the real object." Anybody familiar with the role racism has played in psychological and physiological studies will suspect that the opposite result too would have served as proof of British superiority. The Indians could have been said to show a regrettable tendency to miss the real object." Ibid., pages 107-108.

As noted in the above passage, we not only perceive things differently and superficially, but also interject our personal interpretations and prejudices in the way we like to see and use things. In the same book, Bolles refers to the biography of Georgia O'Keeffe to reflect how perceptions are interpreted personally and how they build an individual's understanding of the world. He quotes:

"Georgia was suddenly struck by the realization that her feelings governed the way she saw the scene. It was a moment of transformation: the entire visual world, she realized, was dependent on the emotional world. That day she learned the artist's secret. What you perceive depends on who you are. Analytical thinkers have generally assumed that we perceive reality as it is; they then use a process of abstract reasoning to interpret that perception. O'Keeffe realized that the perception is the interpretation. It rests on an internal reality that governs the meaning we find in our sensations. To be an artist she needed techniques for drawing accurately what was out there and she needed to develop a grammar for expressing what those things looked like to her. With the realization that perception depends on an internal reality, O'Keeffe was on her way to becoming an important artist." Ibid., pages 121-122.

The way we perceive things is naturally also dependent upon our intelligence and social conditioning. Bolles says:

"We know not only what our senses detect but what those things are worth to us. These qualities, though entirely private, are absolutes of our psychological reality. They form the ground on which the rest of our world grows.

These absolutes are not the same things as emotions. Emotion is where memory enters an experience. It is powerful, but different." Ibid., page 129.

We each have our own absolute psychological realities that make us (mis)perceive the world in our own way. Our senses create, and at the same time limit, our understanding of a real world in its absolute form away from our personal judgments. In all, we have difficulty perceiving the real world at normal conscious level that we apply to our everyday living. Even facts are only our interpretations of some perceptions. They are not necessarily *real facts* in an absolute term in the world of real realities. Bolles states:

> *"Calculating that a tree is a tree has turned out to be more difficult than expected. The tree really is out there, but the fact of its being a tree is not. Facts are not just floating about freely in the physical world."* Ibid., page 136.

The last sentence (above), i.e., *Fact are not floating about freely...*, should however be rephrased or complemented with a qualifying sentence such as, 'Humans' prevalent facts are indeed floating about too freely in the physical world, rather recklessly, which merely reveals their shallowness and invalidity. They are developed and tested only by humans' perceptions, intelligence, and crooked logic.

Most of us can understand and feel physical evidences rather readily, but we have great difficulty with abstract ideas, such as the ones suggested in the last few pages. Yet, the best physical evidence of the real world can be found only in the subtle and mystical energy that many of us have felt on some special occasions. Sometimes, those sensations have even turned into some form of awakening and deep beliefs. Only those kinds of personal experiences can provide the needed clues about a more fundamental reality beyond the perceived world we are accustomed to. The energy that suddenly emanates from a spiritual experience flows through our minds and bodies, elevates our spirits, increases our physical and mental abilities many folds, and results in undeniably superhuman creations and thoughts. We may eventually learn to count on this energy to experience the feelings of even higher significance.

However, for us to remain honest and objective, we cannot talk about the sacred paths at the higher levels of Eros. We may talk about any personal experience only in a discussion of a lower path. The limited definition of SUMMIT provided here is what a philosopher may give, or it might have been generated from our projections of *summit* sensations based on our primary personal experiences at the lower paths.

In fact, both 'submit' and 'summit' extremes are philosophical and theoretical. Most of us follow a path somewhere between these two extremes, though much closer to the Submit. Yet, even these two extremes and all the paths between them are all possible human realities. It is only up to us what kind of life we wish to lead and for what end. Some of us may get the power and wisdom to project the sensation of summit based on our experiences at a lower path. Or we may change our paths several times in our lifetime as we mature and hope to eventually reach a satisfactory level of Eros and enlightenment. Since we are moving on the same dimension, it is possible to do various experimentations without so much difficulty. In fact, a long, uninterrupted process of self-exploration and meditation elevates the person to the higher paths automatically depending upon the level of his focus, , sincerity, sacrifice, and stamina.

Sometimes we lose our focus, when pursuing a finer, divine life path, or get influenced by some external factors. We are often forced to deal with our immediate needs and life pressures, so we let go of our spiritual aspirations for a while. Yet, our gained wisdom and new perception of life still help us cope better with the crude realities of the perceived world with more patience and compassion. Many people have joined a convent, followed a path of certain spiritual nature for several years, then given it up and returned to a regular everyday life that they felt more comfortable with, maybe even marrying a nagging, wicked spouse to avoid loneliness. Yet, they carry and apply their new wisdom in whatever environment they choose to live. All life paths revolve around humans' perceptions, after all, as another option on Eros dimension. Life paths only differ in terms of our level of consciousness about the realities of the perceived world. This single Eros dimension contains all human perceptions and encompasses all the ways of living in the universe, society, and family with their specific demands on us. After all, humans are by nature from the same origin and dimension, regardless of the odd reality they build for themselves due to their naivety. We are all helpless but also inquisitive about our existence. Biology has already proven our basic origin, yet we often like to show off our superiority with such pathetic arrogance and self-importance, as if we had created our own body and mind. Of course, we have our preferences for choosing the path we can master according to our potentialities, personalities, and perceptions. At the same time, everybody has an inherent inner power to free himself from the path of a passive being and evolve to the higher paths of wisdom, freedom, and inner peace. The higher paths are approachable and achievable by everybody just as soon as we prepare our thoughts to go there and become a bit more conscious.

A Picture of the Real World

What is a reasonable meaning or description of the real world then? Actually, two conflicting definitions of the real world emerge for our practical purposes. First, we perceive and define the real world as an absolute, inherent entity in the sense that physical life and perceptions of humans cannot change its nature and characteristics an iota. The physical life of humans is merely an offshoot of it without affecting its absolute totality, like dinosaurs' extinction not hindering the reality of the universe even a bit. The real world is the universe separate from our perceptions, observations, interpretations, and existence. It continues as is, even after humans go the way of dodo. Therefore, the first aspect of the definition intentionally excludes human beings from playing any role in the real world, let alone being at the centre of it— as we always like to put ourselves.

In the second definition, we do exactly the opposite. That is, we attempts to place human beings at the centre of attention, because it is our lives and reality that we are interested in grasping and trusting for creating a practical means of living. In this context, we imagine our existence is so important that only a direct connectivity to the universe could be meaningful for studying the nature of the real world.

Thus, a big dilemma for humans is to somehow reconcile these two opposing definitions of the real world mentally. While in the first aspect of the definition we stress the sheer absoluteness of the real world, in the second definition we focus on the significant connection of human life to it. This special attachment to the universe feels of absolute essence, even though we usually realize the ambiguity and the fluid nature of this connectivity. Most likely, we are connected but irrelevant! In our minds, of course, we cannot stop feeling as the most relevant aspect of the whole existence. This significance is not only for our sake per se, but also as a required element of Creation. We conceive ourselves at the centre of the universe and believe that everything revolves around us. That is why the universe was created! (This way of thinking, of course, has a great significance for establishing human beings' identity in their own minds.) However, in spite of our conviction of importance, identity, and close relation to the whole universe in a fundamental way, we also suffer for not knowing about the nature of this connectivity. That is why we look for a supreme wisdom to solve this puzzle. The urge to understand our true 'self' is a struggle to find our identity in the scope of the wholeness, and not even merely as a spiritual individual. We need such a sacred identity, not merely as particles, matter, consciousness, or souls, either, but rather in terms of the full physical existence and characters that we must carry around day after day. We like to establish our *relevance*. Instinctually, we are driven to find some kind of connectivity and that is why so many of us are lured by religions—simply because we do not know how else we could find this connectivity (and our purpose of living) independently through thinking and experiencing on our own.

Some scientists have tried to explain the connectivity of humans and the universe through quantum mechanics theories and full consciousness, but there is no certainty about their assertions or the nature and mechanism of this connectivity. Is it contained in the physical dimension of humans, or does it reside at some other dimension where we are not readily aware of or can access directly? Gary Zukov states that:

> *"At the subatomic level, we cannot observe something without changing it. There is no such thing as the independent observer who can stand on the sidelines watching nature run its course without influencing it.*
>
> *In one sense, this is not such a surprising statement. A good way to make a stranger turn and look at you is to stare intently at his back. All of us know this, but we often discredit what we know when it contradicts what we have been taught is possible."* The Dancing Wu Li Masters, Morrow, 1979, New York, pages 112-113.

Although the real world is an absolute, inherent entity, it is impossible to explain, touch, and imagine it even remotely the way we grasp the perceived world so naturally. While we (including scientists and spiritualists) are making judgments from within the perceived world about the real world, which is somewhere outside our present wisdom and reach, the whole concept of REAL remains abstract and the PERCEIVED notions feel real. We can never get out of this loop. Therefore, the definition of reality becomes cumbersome and appears abstract, arbitrary, and imaginary. Everything we can say about the real world comes also from our perceptions about an absolute world that we hope and desire to exist as an alternative to the perceived reality that is forcing many erroneous facts about life on us. Because we can see the problems and chaos in social order and human life, and as we fear mortality, we become philosophical and look for eternity and meaningful facts. Some clues also make us wonder about the possibility of a softer and purer nature in human beings than what we see nowadays in the existing cultures. So, we become interested in cultivating some morality and sense into all the chaos, ignorance, and wickedness that we are forced to live with and participate in in the perceived world.

The real world reflects the truth behind all the illusions of the perceived world. We hope that searching for that truth and grasping even some of it would provide an antidote for all the chaos, ignorance and immoralities that we wish to believe are not the real nature of human beings. In fact, we may even feel victimized by all these mayhem that we have inherited from previous generations without a fault of our own.

How all these corruptions and ignorance have emerged is a different issue. Yet, we take them as facts of our societies and cultures and wish to find other alternatives. One quick interpretation of the reason for development of chaotic and corrupt cultures may relate to a lack of adequate wisdom when human race first started to establish social life. Those early cultures were goaded by trade (evoking greed), and subsequently, tyrants and ruling powers emerged (evoking superego). Although prophets and spiritual figures tried to force morality on people, the fact that people did not understand or believe in the need for it, the whole idea of religion and spirituality was presented and adopted in a wrong way, mostly forcefully and through blind faith. The right way to grasp spirituality, when a person intuitively understands the real purposes of morality and humanity, was never given a chance. That kind of knowledge would have been the only possibility for an authentic transformation, and for moving to a wisdom path that could possibly give people a proper identity and sense of spirituality. Instead, some religious ideologies have only misled people beyond their existing confusion about the nature of reality (both the perceived and real ones). Well, older generations might have had good excuses for their ignorance. What are our excuses now? Must we still be so greedy and egotistical?

Our inherent identity, which we may refer to as real 'self,' is an abstract presentation of an individual who believes in, and starts to recognize, the possible purity of his nature. Although humans are most likely not pure by nature, they could possibly approach it only through the proper means of enlightenment and the use of their brains. Maybe that is the challenge that God has designed for us. Maybe He is waiting to see whether we can eventually use our brains to become better human beings despite our crooked nature. It is a big challenge, but maybe someday a group of people can eventually take it on. Maybe a sound logic can annul the effects of our bad nature.

It is possible that someday a new human identity emerge as they enter the higher paths of wisdom by a stroke of 'self'-awareness. This new wisdom would reveal the voids of immoralities and give them the energy to disengage themselves from the entrapments of perceived values and norms, including greed and egoism. Eventually, the absolute 'self' reveals humans' inherent essence for connecting to the universe. His new wisdom helps him explore the purpose of his being in this body and mind form for a limited time. Whether he finds the full wisdom to grasp even a sense of the real world is uncertain. An ultimate wisdom is needed to answer many fundamental questions, including whether 'self' would definitely live (in whatever context it may be) beyond this worldly life or not. It is amazing how the majority of us, including many intellectuals, believe in life after death when there is absolutely no reason to believe in such a bizarre notion.

On the scientific front, we have been told by prominent scholars, including Albert Einstein, that time is nonexistent in the form we conceive and use it. Time, as a measurement tool, however, fits very nicely in the framework of the perceived world. We have applied it consciously in every single moment for our convenience despite our limited knowledge of science and our shallow observations of the things that happen around us. It is very difficult for a person of average, and perhaps even high, intelligence to understand the meaning and implications of time-space as one inseparable continuum. In the same way, the mathematics we use, like the concept of infinity, are abstract rules that are useful in explaining the variables in the perceived world, but are most likely meaningless in the real world.

Thus, on the one hand, we have created the science that explains some aspects of the universe and related phenomena, and, on the other hand, we declare that the main component of all these concepts and mathematics, i.e., time nonexistent (or meaningless) in the real world. This seeming contradiction shows the limitation of our knowledge, especially about the real world, which remains an abstract reality in our minds. Since time is nonexistent, we believe that everything is happening at the same time. There is no past, no future and none of the words that we use for our communication makes any sense in the real world. So what is making our days and nights look transient to us, for example?

Gary Zukov states the following about the abstract reality of time professed by Minkowski, Einstein's mathematics teacher who was inspired by Einstein's theory of relativity:

"Minkowski's mathematical exploration of space and time were both revolutionary and fascinating. Out of them came a simple diagram of space-time showing the mathematical relationships of the past, present, and the future. Of the wealth of information contained in this diagram, the most striking is that all of the past and all of the future, for each individual, meet and forever meet, at a single point, now. Furthermore, the now of each individual is specifically located, and will never be found in any other place, than here (wherever the observer is at)." Ibid., page 154.

A timeless sphere fits the philosophy that all events are predestined and are for specific and definite purposes. Yet we know that in the perceived world we spend many hours of labour to make a living and our pains are real and lengthy. We feel, perceive, endure, and count every minute of our labour and agony day after day. We enjoy every moment of a pleasant experience, and thus we conclude that time is real! But it is not, we are told. We also strive to plan and make decisions because relying on fate alone does not make sense—actually feels stupid!

We may speculate about the meaning of the real world forever, but what can we hope to achieve that could possibly guide us in our daily lives and soothe our suffering? Therefore, the only purpose of drawing a tentative picture of the real world is to serve merely as a general notion for all the upcoming discussions in the future chapters. Many of us would never get enough of philosophical speculations about our world and our universe. It is fascinating and it is about us—the real us within the realm of the real world—though presently trapped within the complex realities of the perceived world.

PART II
Facts and Myths

CHAPTER THREE
The Essence of Facts

"It's just a simple fact!" we tell one another as if reiterating the absolute truth formulated by God. We rely on facts for being rational, making good decisions, and building the foundation of our thoughts. But what is the meaning and value of facts in a world of perceived realities where we live in the midst of our deep illusions and phony personalities? We grow up with naïve fantasies and shallow ideals, and we define life according to shoddy social values and lifestyles. So how can any of our judgments about 'facts' be useful for understanding our 'self' and for guiding our lives on a peaceful path?

Our history, cultures, and religions have drawn a crooked picture of reality for humans over time in many ways. First, decades of human imaginations and desires, driven by unique personal urges and idiosyncrasies, have created our basic perceptions of the world, life, and destiny. Second, the vast influence of social trends, advertising, and propagandas in recent decades, has further contorted the historical perceptions of reality and 'facts' of life. Social values and conditioning encourage our whimsical vision of the world and our boosted Ego and greed further disorient us about the facts of life. Third, our rising needs and aspirations along with our obsession to prove our identity and individualism have made our perceptions of 'facts' even shakier nowadays beyond the illusive picture of reality that society imposes upon everybody. We believe we deserve everything in the world, like movie stars, because positive thinking experts force us to think so, or else we might as well pack it up and consider ourselves total failures. In all, everybody's reality has nowadays become too complex, unique, and incompatible with the truth that should logically exist outside our perceptions and presumed facts. That is why people's worlds and realities are so flimsy and unreliable for personal guidance. And that is why people cannot relate to one another and thus their relationships fail so quickly. The bottom line is that we can neither trust the perceived reality ruling us, nor define the truth eluding us.

The process of building our perceptions about the presumed facts of life is mechanical and straightforward. Initially, we encounter only simple things, ideas, and events as we grow up in our dysfunctional families. We also absorb the cultural teachings, which are mostly permeated through nonsensical television programs and movies. These basic experiences build the primary elements of our thoughts and minds. However, quickly enough, we begin to interpret and define each of these experiences in a personal and peculiar way, and then try to associate them to one another, hoping to find some profound perceptions and universally acceptable meanings for them. We like to draw some conclusions regarding life and its purpose. Hence, our compound perceptions evolve merely in response to our conscious and unconscious needs and intellectual ability to interpret and associate basic experiences and thoughts.

In time, our needs, emotions, insecurities, and intelligence converge, instil special meanings for our experiences, and erupt unique perceptions, which would eventually become a rigid foundation for our beliefs—our reality and facts. We can expand this principle in several ways. For example, we can say that our beliefs and facts stem from our misguided needs and insecurities. Or, they are the result of our experiences. Or, they are a reflection of our complex perceptions. Nevertheless, it is obvious that the perceived world is simply a reference to this unique set of personal perceptions and beliefs that we compile and depend on for making decisions, taking actions, and building relationships. In this sense, we each invent our own world, despite societies' keen intention to create and depend on uniform values, a valid culture, and universally understood criteria for judgments. This mishmash of personal and social perceptions is another reason why our culture is disintegrating.

This book would not pursue these thoughts and many directions that they can take us, because each would be a complex and lengthy discussion by itself. The purpose here is only to reflect upon the simple conclusion that we are at the mercy of some absurdly developed perceptions and beliefs to run our lives and make judgments and decisions. Accordingly, we use the words 'facts' and 'myths' to express our beliefs about the factuality (or fictionality) of things and concepts. Yet, since we are making this assessment from within a personally defined perceived world, our interpretations of things, ideas, and concepts cannot be independent from our personal needs and beliefs—not to mention the illusions permeated in our crippled culture. Every fact or myth has a different meaning and implication not only for each person, but also according to his/her needs, perceptions, and beliefs, which fluctuate regularly as his/her brain grows too.

When we want to pass a judgment about an issue or idea, we try intuitively to establish its truthfulness; we want to know how factual it sounds, which means we are interpreting its validity based on some preset criteria and personal beliefs. However, even our criteria and beliefs are based on our perceptions, and thus our analyses and criteria cannot be of great help or value either. Therefore, the question is, 'What do we really know about facts and myths to base our thought processes and judgments upon?' In order to answer this question, we should find out more about our perceptions and the way facts and myths evolve from them.

The Complexity Levels of Our Perceptions

People's ability to communicate and relate is deteriorating fast due to the rising incongruity of their perceptions of one another's intentions and honesty, social issues, and common concepts. People's perceptions have many levels of complexity, but overall, they are getting more convoluted every year in line with higher social immorality and corruption. At simpler levels, people normally have a more uniform understanding of a concept. However, at higher levels, not only perceiving and understanding become more difficult, but also the variations in interpretations and meanings increase drastically among individuals. For example, 'chair' is a simple object and demands a simple perception, but we still make many interpretations about it. When we hear the word 'chair,' we each perceive a special kind of chair from the image that comes to our minds. Furthermore, we quickly associate some properties to it, which become an intrinsic part of our perceptions of a chair. We think of some adjectives like nice, big, comfortable, etc.; and then we also think of its purposes. We each interpret the purpose of a chair differently and assign a set of meanings to it in this respect. In some cultures 'chair' is viewed differently from what people in the western world are accustomed to; sitting on a chair has special inclination in their perceptions, e.g., a sign of pomposity or importance. Even when we look at the same chair, it still appears and means differently to each one of us, although we all see the same image. When even a simple object such as a chair finds different meanings and perceptions for each one of us, just imagine how vastly different people's perceptions of more complex issues and communications gets.

Studying a more complex (non-physical) perception like 'love' easily reveals that people's interpretations and meanings become more cumbersome and irreconcilable. Studying a compound concept like 'relationships' shows how differently we interpret each other's needs, actions, and reactions, and perceive various aspects of our relationships according to our own mindsets. For this category of perceptions, we are mostly quite aware and comfortable about everything we are doing and saying, and then stubbornly presume that we are right about all of them. Unfortunately, we are not willing, and in fact not equipped psychologically, to doubt the possibility of being wrong in the way we interpret the same ideas, treat one another, or communicate. Despite our persistence about our understanding and accuracy in perceiving various aspects of our relationships, we usually make all sorts of erroneous perceptions and assumptions about our dealings with others. Relationship problems mostly relate to the incongruity of partners' perceptions leading to atypical personal viewpoints, priorities, judgments, etc.

In the next higher level of complexity, we may think of complex ideas and concepts, such as biological construct of animals and humans, or the structure and laws of the universe that goes beyond our humanistic ability to perceive. Although we do not quite understand most of these scientific concepts, we still create our perceptions and opinions about them anyhow. For example, we personally do not know exactly how vitamins help our health, but based on experts' suggestions (which are often conflicting too), we build our shallow perceptions and opinions and decide whether to take some vitamins daily or not in hopes of benefiting from their properties. We know we do not understand these phenomena, but still maintain some kind of image and significance for them at any point. We find some personal rationale to make a decision about their meanings.

At the highest level of complexity, we deal with such concepts as Creation, God, human spirit, etc. For these concepts, we do not even have any scientific proof. We do not even have consistent methods or uniform means of explaining them. These concepts are not about tangible objects or ideas, but rather consist mainly of some form of speculation and myth. We have the highest difficulty understanding these concepts, but actually deal with them so intimately every day through our beliefs and religions. Our perceptions are vague and confusing, yet we create silly images in our minds, because we are intrinsically programmed to have beliefs in some supernatural phenomenon. We can see ourselves walking right into the heaven, for example. There are enough questions and clues out there to make us wonder and create our personal perceptions about the nature of these mysterious phenomena.

In all, there is a big range of perceptions that we build our thoughts and lives around. Simpler perceptions are what we usually refer to as 'facts,' and most complex ones are what we call 'myths.' Of course, we do not stop to distinguish and analyse the level of complexity and factuality of our perceptions consciously anytime we think about something. Rather, we have combined all these perceptions in a vast compound perception of the world, life routines, and realities. Even more bizarre is the fact that many people take some mythical notions, e.g., God, as ultimate truths. They put their whole existence on line for their absolute faith in certain notions that they have adopted as solid facts. Obviously, these people have the highest difficulty to examine their identities and grasp the true nature of facts and reality.

The Meaning and Implications of Our Perceptions

Someone may ask very rationally, 'How our perceptions matter anyway, especially since we can hardly change them?' or, 'Why should we care about individuals' huge perceptual differences?' The short answer is that even our basic awareness about the impact of our perceptions—both positively and negatively—on various aspects of our lives can help us in many ways. As noted before, our difficulty in communication and relationships mainly relate to the rising incongruity of basic perceptions among us. Our perceptions also cause our personal deficiencies and biases that prevent us from dealing with social and work issues effectively. Our crooked perceptions develop and drive our mindsets, values, attitudes, personalities, judgments, cynicism, and decisions. They make us dogmatic and useless. Naturally, our perceptions stir our emotions as well, while our erratic emotions and thoughts influence our perceptions of things and people and our reactions toward them, too. Emotional people usually have a more complex perception of the world, and sometimes their oversensitivity causes major misperceptions and relationship conflicts. Nevertheless, we all filter the messages and ideas through our perceptions, some of us with higher intensity and some with less consciousness.

Obviously, the strength of external stimuli affects our perceptions too. While our perceptions trigger our emotions drastically, our personal emotions enhance our receptivity to sensitive external stimuli as well. Some people perceive the meanings of art more profoundly because of their perceptive cognition and means of grasping and interpreting it. But then, perceiving art and music masterpieces induces special emotions as a unique (positive) experience in that instance. Even a highly sensitive person needs an external stimulus, maybe even a simple thought, to activate his emotions. And all these *activating* happen through our unique perceptions of things, e.g., art and music. Nevertheless, our perceptions seem to be crippling our understanding of at least the nature of facts and myths, which we have adopted for making our judgments and nurturing our habits. We are depriving ourselves from the opportunity of using our thoughts and wisdom to drive at least a good portion of our decisions and actions. We cannot make good decisions and see our options properly because we do not challenge our debilitating perceptions.

Of course, our perceptions are not always dysfunctional forces, but in fact they can be the source of valuable intuition and inspirations. While artists have a more perceptive cognition, the rest of us are less emotionally perceptive (or vulnerable). Because of their unique perceptions of realities, artists create special art and music that even we can enjoy, in spite of the fact that we do not extend any emotion of our own in creating them. As we appreciate other people's perceptions, e.g., an artist's or writer's, some higher instances of communication become possible and life feels valuable, while a higher sense of consciousness also enriches some moments of our lives.

Artists' perceptions give them ecstasy and actualization and perhaps some feelings of desperation, loneliness, or even suffering. On the other hand, some individuals become completely ruthless because of their perceptions of the world and life. In general, some of us perceive things with more attention and compassion, while another group turns into cold-blooded criminals who can kill and torture others with no sense of remorse, guilt, or shame. And then there is the majority of us who are uncertain about our emotions and our needs, and thus cannot grasp a proper or meaningful perception of the world.

We are standing on the borderline, sometimes becoming cruel in our relationships with others and even our families, and sometimes we become emotionally moved by simple incidents such as the suffering of an animal. With the increasing rate of violence and apathy in relationships, there seems to be something drastically wrong happening around us in our societies and cultures from which we draw our perceptions. It seems that, with our shallow perceptions of things, ideas, and events, we are drifting away more and more from our natural tendencies for living in harmony and peace with one another. Instead, we are destroying and hurting one another with our unleashed Egos and ideologies, which have evolved out of our false perceptions. Our erroneous perceptions are also the sources of our personal suffering, futile struggles, and unsatisfying lifestyles. All along, these crooked perceptions weaken our spirits to the point of neglecting life values that can enrich our existence. Overall, learning about the limitations and the misleading nature of our perceptions can help us understand our deficiencies better and opt for self-therapy.

We can never solve the mystery of the truth behind all our crooked perceptions. Only some of us can gradually see some aspects of the realities beyond the perceived world. Yet, we all should face the realities of living regardless of our perceptual or factual nature. We can never stop doubting the meaning and purpose of things, and still we must interpret these meanings and purposes within the context of a hypothetical framework of facts and myths.

We are inherently driven to distinguish between facts and myths that constitute our points of reference in life in all respects, including the main question of, 'Who we are.' However, a more challenging task for us is to reconcile our perceptions of facts and myths in some manner, in order to prepare the foundation of our thoughts and beliefs as profoundly as possible. That is, we must find ways of trusting our intuition about the truthfulness of some myths that do not succumb to our humanly logic. However, at the same time, we must convince ourselves to doubt the validity of some things, ideas, and events that we so readily believe are true and factual. We must realize that facts are not necessarily factual realities, and myths are not necessarily untrue because we do not perceive their truth. This does not mean that we want to become more doubtful and confused or religious. Rather, by reconciling our perceptions of facts and myths, we intend to expand our tolerance for seeing and accepting alternative definitions and meanings of facts and myths. We want to become aware, and accept the limitation of our beliefs and convictions resulting from our erroneous perceptions of the world.

Facts, Myths, and Challenges

We consider facts as concepts that reflect absolute truths beyond any doubts and imaginations—like day and night. However, even facts are still the figments of our observations and raw logic, and therefore some type of perceptions. We have adopted these facts merely because we have learned, over the centuries, that they are more reliable (and stable) concepts than our other perceptions. They have evolved as solid and inherent assumptions to build our lives around, and we accept them with total certainty (rather naively) concerning their truthfulness and consequences. They have become simple, proven *perceptions* that build the basic elements of our logic, intelligence, and thoughts.

On the other hand, myths refer to those concepts that we consider imaginary or even hard to conceive or achieve—like heaven or happiness. They appear fictional and we do not have any logic or approach to understand or sustain them as part of our routines and living aspirations. They are complex perceptions that cannot be associated with any physical or tangible phenomenon. Yet, despite our scepticism about their viability, we do not want to (or cannot) deny the possibility of their existence. We prefer to give a benefit of a doubt to their viability, though our clues are often only what others have told us, rather than a firsthand personal experience. Therefore, we have a hard time deciding whether to let those myths play a role in our thought processes and judgments or reject them totally.

Our lives consist of major 'challenges' to deal with facts and myths—for example, for finding a *reliable* companion or *lasting* happiness. These challenges force us to develop our ideas, decisions, and actions. They also reflect our outlooks, values, and attitudes, which cause our pleasures and sufferings. We like to believe that these challenges are necessary and achievable with reasonable efforts. We believe they are comprehendible and justified within the existing framework of human knowledge and logic.

Facts, myths, and challenges often materialize in a package of thoughts that demand decisions and actions. Therefore, while we might look at facts, myths, and challenges in separate domains with varied significance, they collectively build our cognition of things, ideas, and events. For example, when we express an opinion, it would be based on our cognition of all the related facts, myths, and challenges that we have personally experienced about that subject.

Several important reasons exist for analysing facts, myths, and challenges in this and next chapters. First, it would help us detect our motives behind our actions and habits, and thus learn more about ourselves. Second, we would realize our dogmatism to live within certain shallow boundaries we have accepted as facts of life, mostly because of our conditioned mentality. Third, we would appreciate the undeniable impact of myths in our lives and beliefs, even though we try to remain logical about their authenticity as much as possible. Fourth, we would understand the underlying structure of our value system, and gauge our readiness and motivation to choose a more spiritual and humanistic path, compared with a path dictated merely by misleading facts. Fifth, distinguishing facts, myths and challenges (as shown in the next chapter) would show the roots of social problems. It would reveal the difficulties of communicating and trusting the alternative modes of thinking and living.

In all, studying the nature of facts, myths, and challenges (in the next chapter) would provide a clearer understanding of our perceptions, their sources, and their effects. Facts and myths are mostly raw information stored in various levels of our consciousness according to our intelligence and experiences. Naturally, while our unconscious mind remains untapped, our understanding of the world and life, as well as the capacity of our perceptions, remains too elementary at best. Thus, some personal efforts to distinguish facts and myths fully at a conscious level, and pinpointing our special challenges for interpreting and reconciling them, broadens our perspective of the world, realities, and facts. Mastering such a transformation would bring us new insight, creativity, and courage to set out the course of our lives and beliefs more effectively and proceed to establish a meaningful philosophy of life.

A philosophical interpretation of life and the obstacles for achieving a higher wisdom (or at least less gullibility) has been the greatest, and the least accomplished, challenge in human history. While the possibility of a less formidable and more tolerable form of living cannot be promised to anybody, we may still have the opportunity to enlighten ourselves as individuals by first learning about the hurdles of living more independently, and then trying to overcome or mitigate them. The best way to study the obstacles for such mental growth is to establish one's position and reaction to facts, myths, and challenges as interrelated principles affecting one's existence. We should reconcile all our facts, myths and challenges in order to strengthen our decision-making power according to our positive doubts while minimizing the negative effects of our doubtfulness.

Establishing a Framework

We can prepare a tentative list of commonly perceived facts, myths, and challenges for our discussions. The list is not intended to be comprehensive, but rather a tentative framework only. Initially, I decided to think of ten items for each of the 'facts', 'myths', and 'challenges' categories without consideration to the order or relationships amongst them. Later, while attempting to find a logical order for presenting them, it appeared that I had subconsciously selected items that have some inherent relationships across the three categories. It was possible to order them rather logically while establishing the relationships among those facts, myths, and challenges quite nicely. Nevertheless, Table 3.1 in the next page appears to provide a good approximation of most people's mindset. It also constitutes humans' main mental reconciliations needed for attaining a simple notion of the truth.

Table 3.1 also provides a platform for studying some of the main concepts that occupy our minds and thus strengthen the a foundation of our thoughts. If some new logic or other kind of evidence, including extra-sensory notions of spirituality, could convince us to revise our facts and myths table, we may accordingly test the suitability of our discussions and conclusions at that point—maybe in the future editions of this book!

However, if we decide to revise or recreate the structure of facts, myths, and challenges in a different form from the one in Table 3.1, we may have to continue those discussions in a different domain altogether after it is defined properly. (Actually, we might even end up creating a domain where these facts are not accepted as facts and these myths are no longer myths.) Some aspects of our discussions in Chapter Two, regarding the perceived and real world realities, constitute the 9th fact and myth on the list.

Table 3.1: A Suggested List of Facts, Myths, and Challenges

FACTS	MYTHS	CHALLENGES
1. Physical (outer) self	1. Spiritual (inner) 'self'	1. Humanness & humanity
2. Life (living)	2. Freedom	2. Valuing our doubts
3. Nature	3. Love	3. Relationships
4. Physical growth	4. Truth	4. Psychological growth
5. Social living	5. Everlasting happiness	5. Coping and adaptation
6. Economic constraints	6. Chance/luck/fairness	6. Contentment
7. Personal limitations	7. Enlightenment	7. Life decisions
8. Personal needs	8. Purity/piety	8. Needs gratification
9. Perceived Reality	9. Real Reality	9. Psych. & physical health
10. Death	10. Creation/creator	10. Spirituality, self-actualization

A brief discussion of the above topics is presented in the next chapter.

CHAPTER FOUR
Main Mental Reconciliations

Grasping the interconnections and relationships among the facts and myths listed in Table 3.1 (at the end of the previous chapter) requires a large variety of mental challenges and reconciliations. These facts, myths, and challenges constitute humans' main dilemmas and thus discussed briefly in this chapter. The task (objective) of reconciling them mentally is, by itself, a major life challenge that everybody pursues consciously or subconsciously according to his/her lifestyle and intelligence.

1. Physical Self, Spiritual 'Self', Humanness

Birth gives us a physical (outer) self—a very special privilege that we often forget or even abuse. It provides a horrendous opportunity for living and contacting the environment, humans, and animals, etc. The *fact* of our existence is evident only in this physical form (self). At least according to the norms of the perceived world, *being* per se is the most significant and relevant 'fact' for a person—the simplest fact that cannot be denied, especially as our sufferings constantly remind us of our pathetic lives. What lies beyond this basic existence is only speculation and a myth.

Naturally, we cause our own suffering when we undermine the health of the body, for example by drugs and alcohol. Our crooked lifestyles and values induce high stress and confusion, too, which we would then try to hide or overcome by more pleasure, sexuality, and egotism, all leading to the demise of our psyche and further suffering. In effect, our misguided brain is killing the rest of the body because of social pressures and our weak personalities. Thus, we are the biggest threat to our existence—both as a person and collectively as human beings. Our brain is merely an abused organ of our physical self, too, after all.

On the other hand, our brains (senses) let us reach within and without ourselves, think, and *feel* emotional impulses. These emotions and psychological reactions, along with other brain functions, e.g., analytical ability, bring us to the threshold of dreams, imaginations, and divine creations. At this stage, we enter the domain of the spiritual 'self,' which is a myth. Within this realm, we become capable of expanding our existence beyond its apparent limits, where our sufferings may subside too.

We know from what we have learned, or possibly experienced personally, that we have an extra-sensory ability to achieve a higher level of consciousness beyond the boundaries we apply to our normal life situations. This high consciousness brings us in contact with beauties, energies, feelings, and inner happiness that are inaccessible in normal life; they are experiences of the supernatural and spiritual nature. This higher consciousness is a myth as we have no concrete evidence regarding its existence, and not even a uniform and tangible definition of its nature. Many people who have claimed achieving such levels of high consciousness have expressed their experiences and their sources differently and incompletely. We are not talking about religious beliefs or practices, although some may find religions a source of reaching high consciousness. Rather, high consciousness is more a matter of individual's state of readiness for transcendence that leads to a search for, and an experience of, selfdom and spirituality. It is also plausible that some form of spirituality is achieved through self-actualization experiences, which has been a dominant field of study in psychology. Still, in spite of scientific findings, most of us do not understand or know how the process and objectives of self-actualization (and the spirituality induced from it) can be pursued and achieved. Therefore, while such experiences of spiritual 'self' or 'self'-fulfilment are beyond a person's normal consciousness, it all depends on his/her state of readiness and inner search to evoke the spirituality power within him/her. The problem is that our conditioned mindsets make us see and sense reality from a rigid frame of mind—through perceptions. Thus, most of us have difficulty penetrating our inner dimensions and higher consciousness to release our divine potentiality and spirituality. We do not find this human dimension realistic and feasible within the context of our perceived world.

As much as our physical self is taken as an irrefutable 'fact,' we have been conditioned to accept the norms and values of the perceived world as facts, too, for defining and nurturing our physical self. We have become defenceless against the conditioning forces of our perceptions—which we have learned to accept as facts of life and necessary for understanding our existence. In this context, fact-driven realities in this world refer to our perceptions of physical needs, actions, emotions, and relationships. For example, we need food to satisfy our physical self and thus everything we do to satisfy this need, including education, working, cooking, etc. all become routine facts and reality. We do all these things because they are fact-driven realities, and we seem unable to avoid or deny them. We do all these activities without questioning their ultimate purpose as if they were inherently programmed in our DNA. Thus, at the end, we have no chance of avoiding the conditioning forces that our perceptions of facts impose upon us.

Another deficiency of our fact-driven reality is that, most of us, only accept tangible and sensible things as reality. In this respect, we make our judgments solely according to the sensitivity level of our five senses, and thus limit our understanding of the world to the level of perceptions that we are personally capable of developing through our five senses. This is, of course, a natural and humanly logical way of seeing the facts of life according to our physical senses. This implies that to a deaf-born person the concept of music is absurd, let alone the judgments of enjoyment from some particular music and headache from some others. Thus, we are bound by the sensitivity of our senses in our understanding of life and the universe, and also in our definitions of facts according only to their sensible physical identity. Yet, there are most likely many other realities out there that do not fit our humanistic senses or our expectations of tangibility and sensibility. As a whole, we are conditioned to accept certain things as reality not only due to the influences of rearing, teachings, and personal sense of presumably fact-driven realities, but also due to our limited sensitivity and knowledge of other sensations beyond our five physical senses.

Our physiological existence and reality is a tangible fact and easy to notice, while our psychological reality is not so clear and measurable. In spite of our superficial impressions of, and limited ability to understand, our psyches, we have learned a great deal about our psychological dimension in recent decades, to a point where psyche has now been recognized as a factual reality. We are learning more every day from our personal experiences, and also from scientific information, that our psychological health should be given as much and perhaps a higher priority than our physical health and needs. This urgent need is becoming a serious matter of 'fact' too.

With this initial acknowledgement, we must accordingly place more emphasis on learning about our psyche in a more proactive and conscious manner. Almost all the problems we encounter in our lives, including physical illnesses and short life, have been found to originate from the weaknesses and sicknesses of our psyches. Yet, in spite of this knowledge, we appear unable to do anything about it. We are facing more stress and suffering, as we seem helpless at the presence of our rising psychological needs. The 'fact' is that our psyches are in control of us, whereas ideally we should be in control of them for the sake of maintaining our sanity. We need to come to terms with our souls, which becomes possible solely by controlling and strengthening our psyches. Accordingly, for controlling and strengthening our psyches, we must control our shallow needs and aspirations.

The eastern philosophy of karma is based on a belief that human souls are given repeated physical lives in order to heal the burdens of their actions and experiences in past physical forms. And that we are reincarnated numerous times until we complete the healing process. This regimen is deemed necessary for gauging our worldly failures and sufferings until we learn how to control our psyches and how to redefine our physical desires and needs in line with the kind of piety and clarity that a free soul requires. While the idea of Karma and reincarnation are myths of the highest level, the idea of reconciling between our physical existence and soul sounds quite plausible.

We must go beyond our physiological needs to look for happiness and psychological growth, which is required for reaching a higher level of humanness and understanding of humanity. Our salvation begins as the spiritual 'self,' which is inherently within us, is grasped and revived. Attaining a certain level of humanness is our main 'challenge' for reconciling between the 'fact' of our painful physical self and the 'myth' of redemption through spiritual 'self.' But, we do not know how to get there, and we do not even believe that such a thing (which we call 'self') exists.

An inner 'self' that is strong and full of energy and wisdom seems so obscure and unbelievable, it is a myth! On this ground, someone may present a strong argument—which, by the way, shows his inner struggle with his conscience: He may argue that, "We know the 'fact' that our body has a limited life and every second of it is precious, and thus why not use it only on factual things, including the pleasures of the perceived world? And let us forget about the 'myth' that happiness comes from inward awareness and actualizing the spiritual 'self'; it feels like a waste of time and energy to search for something that may bring us some sensations we do not understand or can anticipate its nature?" Using a counter-argument against this personal position would be useless. Only personal motivation and inner conflicts may lead to awakening, a higher conscience and consciousness, and then clarity about the purpose and possibility of inward reflection and self-awareness.

In all, although myths remain as mysteries for the foreseeable future, we cannot ignore their impact on our lives. Myths are the causes of our positive 'doubts' in a substantial way. Even for those who pretend not to believe in myths such as a spiritual 'self,' there is always a major DOUBT about this possibility in their subconscious. They may feel that some efforts and sacrifice might bring them a high level of consciousness, which would supposedly eliminate or reduce their stress and hardships of living. This is a real dilemma for a great majority of us, and too serious (important) a 'doubt' to ignore.

More and more people are becoming anxious and stressed with their works, family lives, loneliness, social injustice, etc. The psychological impacts of this social chaos are quite grave. Everywhere we go, we find people in search of salvation and remedies for their stress and confusion. The outcome of various methods of positive thinking and psychotherapy has proven futile and now many of us are in doubt whether a search for the spiritual 'self' and inward awareness can be our ultimate recourse for liberation and alleviating life's sufferings. Somehow, we should deal with this doubt and make a decision. This is, in fact, a serious decision about the role and impact of myths in our lives and thoughts.

Whether it is due to our doubts or because of an insight, we may decide to do something about the weaknesses of our physical self, most likely by discovering our spiritual 'self.' At this stage, our 'challenges' start. At this point, we have realized the ambiguity of our 'facts,' encountered our 'doubts' about the possibilities of 'myths,' and have intelligently decided to face the necessary 'challenges' that may reconcile our facts and myths. In all, our 'challenge' is to reconcile between facts and myths by accepting their connectivity; or conversely, their irrelevance. For example, it may be reconciled that bodily pleasures have no relevance to (or impact on) inner happiness that can be found only at the spiritual 'self' level; or show a possible connection between a healthy body and a healthy mind, which would then lead to understanding of the spiritual 'self.'

Our challenges at this level, through ongoing exercises of deeper consciousness, reveal our higher qualities, to become a more compassionate human, to understand the meaning and implications of humanness, and walk into the domain of 'self.' The first challenge is to admit and accept that life is a place for suffering and disappointments (especially as our lifestyles and economies get more complex and unreliable every day). Therefore, we must adjust our mentality to face these challenges head on the best way we can. Also, our challenge is to find the elusive happiness in the depth of the mythical 'self.' We all recognize those cyclic moods of happiness that are temporary and mostly superficial. Obviously, they cannot overcome our permanent, deep suffering. However, we also have some vague notion of, and a strong desire for, a happiness that is complete and permanent; a real happiness that would subside all thoughts and feelings of suffering and instead brings us a deep sensation and satisfaction of *being alive*, and *being* per se.

As physical self is a 'fact' of existence, living has always been a source of suffering and confusion. It is possible that our sufferings are partly due to our misperceptions about the true nature of facts—for example, the purpose of life. Of course, our sufferings are also due to our misperceptions about many ideas that we take so seriously as 'facts' of life, when indeed these presumed 'facts' have no real factuality and we are only being fooled by them. We are simply drowning in the ocean of our perceptions (presumed facts). We just keep swallowing more water in hopes of satiating our thirst for happiness and survival, as we have assumed and accepted our perceptions as facts of living.

It is interesting to return to the list of facts, myths, and challenges in Table 3.1 and see how every single 'fact' in this list is a direct cause of our sufferings. Similarly, we can detect the soothing effect of myths and challenges on our lives. Accordingly, it seems plausible to make the following observations:

- Every essential 'fact' is always surrounded by one or more related 'myths,' and certain 'challenges' that we intuitively take on to reconcile between all these facts and myths.
- All facts (both real and perceived ones) are causes of human suffering, starting with the real fact of existence.
- Myths are the insights that may annul or question our perceptions of 'facts,' raise our positive doubts, and thus mitigate our sufferings through mental adjustment.
- Challenges are the healing processes that can help us relieve our pains and free our souls. Our main life 'challenge' is to explore our positive doubts and to reconcile the facts and myths engulfing, and often crippling, us.

2. Life, Freedom, Valuing Our Doubts

Life itself—the mandate to live—is the second 'fact,' as defined and measured in terms of both its length and quality. The 'quality of life' is finding a higher importance for us in recent decades, however, while life expectancy increases too. Remarks such as, 'He did not have a good life,' or 'She lived a great life,' reflect our emphasis on *how* a person lives more than *how long*. As a matter of *fact*, nowadays, we expect a special quality or outcome from life. Yet, even defining the meaning of life is difficult, let alone agreeing on what makes it great or how to achieve it. Instead, we are gradually learning that life's quality is only an abstract notion—another whimsical perception. We will soon be convinced again, like our ancestors, that life is merely a cycle of erratic experiences and reflections regardless of our health and wealth. Our impressions of life's quality depend also on our age, state of mind, and background. The simple activities that make life feel wonderful to a child in a developing country have no meaning for a spoiled teenager in North America and so and so forth.

Realistically, 'life' mostly denotes our journey through hardships, occasional joys, uncertainties, loneliness, and our lingering doubts about the purpose of it all. Despite our eagerness to grasp life's quality, it is easier nowadays to explain a bad or miserable life—due to its prevalence. As a matter of 'fact,' our incessant doubts about many facets of our lives, along with our erratic choices and decisions, make it impossible to sustain any kind of quality in our lives. All along, the only remedy is to keep ourselves amused with our duties and creativity as a possible healing process, which sometimes brings us some joy too. We must just learn to embrace various challenges in hopes of making sense of our lives eventually, perhaps through self-actualization and spirituality for some luckier people.

Our efforts to define the quality of 'life' bring us to the domain of myths. The most common symbol and criterion for 'life's quality' is individual's 'freedom.' It implies a relative sense of independence and salvation despite the unavoidable hassles of living, human ignorance, and social chaos. The word 'freedom' here is much broader than its common use, of course. This kind of freedom protects us from the evils of propaganda and social conditioning. The real freedom of mind enables us to function independently regardless of common judgments and social demands. It safeguards our spirit from the vast hypocrisy and corruptions engulfing us, even within family members and friends. And it is obvious again that we are talking about a myth, the myth of freedom, because living in society drastically restricts our chance for real freedom.

There is no real freedom in our present lifestyles when our options are so limited and imposed through propagandas, dispiriting economic systems, and addictive social values. These fake symbols of freedom are merely the means of exploiting our intelligence and spirit. The freedom in so-called democratic societies is merely another way of obstructing our chances for real freedom, while different methods of conditioning and advertising constantly reinforce our needs for more things and shallower lifestyles. No real freedom comes from greed, wasteful consumerism, spoiling our kids with more things, and giving high values to pomposity and sexuality. The freedom that one requires for a good life is exactly the opposite, i.e., the courage to resist all those temptations.

For real freedom, we must find our souls, which is still an even more obscure mythical phenomenon. It is an abstract ideal, a myth, for the practical purposes of our social and family lives, which we cannot easily give up. For freeing our souls, we must break away from all the hypocrisies and dependencies of the physical world, its values, and its institutions. This is an impossible task when we must think practically, even though finding our soul is an instinctual drive we have a hard time ignoring.

In the absence of true freedom, our challenge is to create at least some kind of a relative freedom. This requires our efforts to strengthen our minds, understand who we are, and prepare a simple life philosophy. That is the only way to fight the debilitating forces of social living that always strive to limit or undermine our freedom. We often doubt the authenticity of our lifestyles and values when our struggles to find peace do not lead to any tangible outcome. However, we usually do not value the clues hidden in these subconscious nagging voices that are trying to make us stop and ponder our life choices. Once we come to terms with our doubts, in the manner explained throughout this trilogy, especially in Volume II, we may set out to find a more enriching path of life with higher conviction and commitment. We would make decisions based on a thorough understanding of our real inner needs rather than pursuing the superficial needs implanted in our heads and dampening our spirits. We would understand our life objectives and avoid social traps that taint our integrity and independence. That is the only means of attaining a relative freedom and bringing some quality into our lives.

The 'fact of living' is most tangible by its nature—in the way it contains disappointments, natural disasters, and frustration. The main premise about the fact of existence is that it would be full of hardships contrary to our naive imaginations for happiness and a blissful journey. The sooner a person accepts this basic fact of life, the sooner s/he might get the right perspective and motivation to deal with it instead of blindly search for an illusive happiness through more pleasures or other superficial means. The main fact of life lies in its inherent demand for struggles and suffering. Our challenge is to make it bearable by valuing the hidden clues in our positive doubts about life and our purpose of living, and to eventually gain that mythical freedom, away from the seemingly factual social values.

Again, it is obvious that the fact of 'life' (the mere requirements of living) is associated with pain and tough choices. The myth of 'freedom' is the ideal target to relieve our stress. And our challenge—the healing process—in this case is mainly the task of 'valuing our doubts' and testing the validity of imposed social values. Our 'challenge' is to find at least a relative sense of freedom and peace by grasping our real purposes of living.

3. Nature, Love, Relationships

Nature and the universe seem like the most tangible and obvious facts surrounding us, even though they impose the greatest mysteries for us to tackle. Studying the intricacies of Nature and the complexity of its laws is always intriguing, but mostly overwhelming. The matter of Creation, why and how, is never going to be solved and yet we accept all its symbols, symptoms, and mysteries as undeniable facts. We simply take our illusion of Nature and Creation as facts. More importantly, we feel our deep connection to them when we step outside our routine dull lives to explore our identity. We believe that human life is an extension of Nature and an integral part of the universe—yet another set of facts we have adopted haphazardly. We take our connection to the universe as a 'fact,' although no scientific proof is available, nor can we say anything sensible about the nature or implications of this connection. Yet, anybody coming in closer contact with Nature understands more about his/her own vast *inner nature.* During those contacts, our deeper feelings and passion make us cognizant of our needs for freedom and humanness. Despite our deep cynicism about human nature and purity, we often feel an urge to find a purer sense of humanness in ourselves when we explore Nature and our inner need for spirituality is aroused. In all, Nature and our connection to it are considered 'facts' in our conscious awareness, although we seldom get a chance to appreciate their implications consciously too.

For one thing, we notice and believe that people's experiences with Nature often stir love and compassion, along with a sense of selflessness and resignation. Even the love between two humans is merely a symptom of internal reflections and outward expression of feelings between two members of Nature. We are each an element of Nature with basic interrelationships. Love, when not confused with desire, is a heavenly and spiritual connection between a person and Nature. This feeling pervades the whole universe and humanity as well as one's own inner nature, which itself is Nature. The expression that, 'They found their love in heaven' is a hint that love runs through Nature (heaven) as a media of exchange between two or more entities within Nature. The love of Nature itself is the purest of all loves, because it transpires unilaterally with no expectation for reflection or response.

The unconditional love of Nature, and sometimes another human being, is selfless and soothing. It creates compassion and transcends one beyond the realm of facts to soar into a fantasy world, which is filled with beauties and myths. The insidious and pompous love nowadays, and the mechanical engagement in sexual activities, suffer from the lack of Natural connection. They lack Nature's (natural) tenderness that connects a person with his/her inner and outer natures. The real love then remains a myth, especially in the materialistic surroundings that one lives in nowadays. Love remains a myth as one constantly feels the enormous inner need for it, and anticipates the possibility of reaching that state of super being. Yet, the harder s/he tries to find it, the less it takes the right form and meaning. Our love of Nature remains always plausible and educational, though—if we understand it and learn how to benefit from it. Once we experience the beauty of Nature and absorb the reflection of our love extended to, and through, it, the myth of love becomes more sensible and soothing.

In order to maintain and build constructive connections with Nature and others, obviously our challenge is to better define the purpose of our relationships and accept some practical guidelines for relating to one another, while respecting people's need for independence and individualism. Yet, it is getting more difficult every day for people to relate to one another and to Nature. We have lost our natural ways of building even simple relationships, let alone understanding the complex implication of love that we all hope to find in our relationships so obsessively. The level of social stress and personal pain keeps rising because our challenge to define the purpose of relationships has failed. Our challenge to connect to Nature has failed too. We are destroying Nature in general and have lost sight of our inner nature, the 'self', as well, while we submerge deeper in our phony lifestyles. For example, we try to find love amidst our insatiable drive for sexuality.

Since we are from Nature, which is the only source of collective love, we need to keep it as natural and unharmed as possible. Distracting Nature's order and reflections through pollution and misuse of natural resources threaten all facets of human life, including love and harmony for humanness. We are stubbornly obstructing the survival of the love source and sensation, which we all so deeply and psychologically need. For being a human, and for satisfying our own unselfish needs, we need to respond to our thirst for authentic love, the love that is only in the reflections of Nature.

Our challenges are obvious here. With the world's socioeconomic order in such shambles, creating a balance for industrial expansion and job creation, without ruining the Nature, looks impossible. It is hard to believe that humans would ever overcome their neediness and their rising greed for more things. Yet, no price is justified for the destruction of Nature and thus depriving humans from this unique source of love. Our challenge thus remains to protect Nature, our nature, and our environment, if there is still a chance to reverse the effect of the harms we have been inflicting all around ourselves. We must stop ozone holes from expanding and we must stop the destruction of forests and all other aspects of Nature. We need to establish a higher personal awareness of ecology as the vehicle to save our source of love. This is a major challenge. However, even a more difficult challenge is to define a simple purpose for our relationships and learn how to relate to one another effectively and perhaps even spread love a little more naturally. The challenge is to somehow maintain our natural urge for love, despite the misuse of this concept to satiate our love deficiency and other psychological flaws. Our challenge is to prevent our impression of love getting ruined forever due to the symptoms of love affairs in our so-called cultured societies and our depressing marriages.

Although Nature is the source of true love and humans' access to their essence, it causes a great deal of pain and distress, too, like all other facts of life. The beauty and love that we can potentially derive from Nature remain concealed from most of us and this deprivation makes us suffer deeply. The fact remains that Nature is also the cause of horrendous disasters, which brings grave sufferings for humans. The floods, earthquakes, tornadoes, storms, fires and many other kinds of disasters are caused by Nature. We cannot control them and when they occur, they result in massive devastations, deaths, and injuries. Therefore, the reality of Nature, as a hurtful 'fact,' remains indisputable in spite of our love for it. Love, as a myth that we can never truly conquer, is mainly a reflection of Nature and manifest only through our sincere integration with it. Therefore, we must resort to the loving aspect of Nature to compensate for the destructive force of it. Our challenge, the healing process, is to understand our relationships with both Nature and other humans. We must learn to relate more efficiently, personally, politically, and universally, in order to minimize human suffering. We must also take drastic ecological steps to save Nature. It may seem too late for all these wishful measures to save Nature and our neglected inner nature, yet we still have to face the challenges ahead. We can make at least a little impact by preventing the selfish and careless destruction of Nature, and by expressing love and affection to, and through, it somewhat more honestly and compassionately.

4. Physical Growth, Truth, Psychological Growth

The embryonic and hereditary aspects of physical growth are the 'facts' that affect one's body, health, and potentialities. It continues on a fixed path although we might influence some aspect of this growth, e.g., by more exercise and nutrition. Particularly, brain's growth is important in so many terms other than directing our thoughts and activities. It stores our psychological experiences and needs and it manages our thoughts and emotions. It must even grow its capacity vastly to distinguish and balance all the 'facts', 'myths' and 'challenges' we impose upon it. The growth of brain or mind is measured in terms of its capacity to make choices and decisions, and for establishing a value system or philosophy that could lead us through life via a healthy psyche. To do this job effectively, our brain requires standards and criteria to make sound judgments. Therefore, it keeps looking for the absolute 'truth' and a perception of an ideal world. The search for the 'truth' remains a lifetime struggle for our minds, because we never give up the idea of perfecting our grasp of the real world—an ideal world that really makes sense contrary to all the chaos we must deal with daily in the perceived world.

However, we humans still do not agree on any standards and criteria collectively that fit the laws of Nature too. After many centuries of thinking, experimenting, and suffering, humans have not yet been able to agree even on a remotely universal truth to guide them. Therefore, 'truth' remains a myth, while we cannot stop thinking that there must be an absolute truth somewhere outside the humanistic logic and dimension. The fact that we have not found it does not mean that it does not exist. This simple fact—that there must be an absolute truth—keeps our search and curiosity eternal. Our eagerness to find the truth at least about simple stuff, such as the purpose of living or the path of happiness, is an intrinsic and instinctive need in humans. We simply cannot stop chasing this myth and our own interpretations of it. We are delighted by our findings on some occasions, and grossly disappointed in other times, but search continues. We need to live both the life of facts and the life of myths in order to facilitate our maturity and psychological growth, even though we realize that we can never grasp the ultimate truth.

The challenge we chase from the date of birth to the minute of death is to facilitate our psychological growth. The curious eyes and hands of an infant inspecting a new toy shows how this process is taking place; and we can witness this thirst for the truth in all of our relationships, researches, meditations, contemplations and intuitions. The general psychological growth of the public seems to be happening, albeit slowly. However, our search of the truth, as a point of reference for humanistic standards, is derailed by our superficial needs and lifestyles. Thus, not much mental progress is possible, despite our eagerness and continuous personal search. We are simply too absorbed in a fake 'truth' that society wants us to believe in, rather than the 'truth' that is inside us and must be found through our instincts and spirituality.

The physical growth is a 'fact' that causes us pain and stress at both physiological and psychological levels. During the process of biological aging, we witness our body's deterioration and face our continual disappointments about our ignorance and inability to find the truth. Illnesses, worries about inescapable fatal deceases such as cancer, and the thought of death itself are sources of major agony. The only escape from these painful thoughts and suffering is to build a stronger psychological platform. Only our psychological growth can alleviate the sad fact of physical growth and our failure to find some kind of truth about life. As a myth, 'truth' is hard to grasp and hold on to, but even our imagination of such ideal is soothing. Our challenge is to turn all these sad facts and the soothing myths about the eluding 'truth' into a healing process. Searching and finding even bits and pieces of the truth offer a chance for psychological growth and relief, which would in turn bring us closer to the truth faster.

5. Social Living, Everlasting Happiness, Coping and Adaptation

It is a 'fact' that humans are social creatures and cannot survive in isolation on a long-term basis. We need love and belongingness, and our basic needs for food, shelter, health facilities, etc. can be satisfied best in social living. A large variety of social systems, including education, marriage, and even the simplest concepts of economy, somehow connect us to the social structure that we are defencelessly accepting as a 'fact' of living. But then, from our continuous suffering, and from what we see and read, social living is the cause of all our agonies and hardships. Social values and conditions, cruelties and injustice, crimes and drugs, etc. are all chewing away our mental connection to our 'self' and our humanness. We have lost our instincts because they do not safeguard us in the context of social structures anymore; some inconspicuous systems or ruling entities determine what we can or cannot do, what is good for us and what is bad. Thus, we resort to artificial means, e.g., more pleasure and power, to adapt and defend ourselves in this environment. Contrary to all other animals that can use solely their instincts to make quick and correct decisions, we have lost our instinctual abilities and we have become extremely incapable of making decisions while struggling with a variety of doubts. We cannot recognize the validity of our values and options.

Yet, we cannot run away from these facts of social living and values. We are attached to them and have become an integral element of their totality. On the other hand, as defenceless as we are, we also find the courage occasionally to look for an escape, for an alternative. We search for the elusive happiness that we believe we *deserve*. We have not found it within the realities of social living and we may have even looked beyond the world of perceived realities for a miracle that would give us this supposedly inner happiness. We hope to find the source of everlasting happiness, which supposedly elevates us to a rather stable state with certain static emotions and connections, e.g., a fulfilling job and a reliable companion. But our emotions and connections would never stay stable and reliable for a long time. The law of Nature demands that all things and thoughts be dynamic and transient. Therefore, any source of happiness outside a person is bound to change and necessarily impact individuals' emotions that induce a state of happiness.

Eventually, we realize that the ideas of an everlasting happiness and a path for reaching it are simply myths. We accept that happiness is a relative term, too, as it merely reflects our reaction to a new refreshing experience in relation to a sad state of mind or subsequent to boredom. Once the comparison with the past mood, and the freshness of the new happy experience, fades away, we lose our happiness state. Recurring boredom is one main reason we cannot maintain happiness on a long-term basis.

The main obstacle to achieving an everlasting happiness is the mere fact that we hope to reach this mythical level of 'self' fulfillment outside ourselves through self-gratification. We are seeking happiness by depending more on our chaotic social structure and values that demand more compliance and hypocrisy. Yet all the clues and teachings of spiritual leaders indicate that the only path to an everlasting happiness is the path of wisdom and inward search for contentment. While we look outside ourselves to find the truth and happiness, we are only increasing our addictions and dependencies on social order and its shallow teachings.

However, looking inwardly feels like an abstract concept, too, which requires a lot of meditation and time for self-awareness. Besides, it is hard to imagine how and what one would achieve from all these unorthodox efforts, anyway. Therefore, the idea of inward search becomes another myth. Not only the objective of everlasting happiness is obscure and a myth, but also the means of possibly attaining it is even more abstract and mythical.

Yet, it is within our nature, and a requirement for our survival, to continue our search of myths, including happiness, in a constructive way, perhaps on a trial and error basis, without necessarily committing our whole focus and energy to it until we see the changes that should come from within us like flickers of wisdom. Afterward, we may devote ourselves to the task, and simultaneous enjoyment, of 'self' realization and spiritual growth. Meanwhile, we admit that the concept of everlasting happiness is a myth, not as a cynical standpoint, but rather as a platform for adjusting our life outlook and expectations. While tolerating hardships and disappointments more patiently, we concentrate on other objectives, such as peace of mind, through actualizing our 'self.'

Our endless struggles for social living, and for finding that elusive happiness, are major challenges that we embrace in order to adapt to our surroundings and connect to people with minimal frictions. Our challenge is to cope with the rising crookedness of social living, which is misguiding us horribly about the sources of true happiness. The challenge is to somehow adapt ourselves to the routines of social living while pursuing our search for inner sources of happiness. This adaptation demands sacrifice and wisdom to reduce our dependency on social living without turning against everything and everybody. Is this possible and easy? Not unless we are really determined to find inner happiness and peace instead of only pursuing pleasures, wrestling with irreparable social conundrums, or losing our patience.

6. *Economic Constraints, Fortune/Fairness, Contentment*

Another main feature (fact) of social living is the economic means and opportunities that it is supposed to offer to its citizens. We are expected to make concerted and collective efforts for the benefit of everybody according to some economic model. This is an ideal perception of social living, with a proper structure of economic systems maintaining it. In reality, however, this has never happened. There have always been social classes and frictions because of the deficiencies in the economic order and governments. In our new societies, the situation is deteriorating faster than ever, and we continue to face more economic constraints than opportunities. We have become less secure mentally and financially by the way our economic systems are controlling our lives; and naively we sometimes even blame ourselves for missing those limited opportunities—e.g., to get rich. We have reached a point where we now have little confidence in the ability of the existing economic systems to provide a dependable means of honourable work and survival. Even for those luckier groups who have a job now, and live in affluent countries, there is a constant threat of unemployment and ongoing concern about their financial security. Even the rich and haughty upper class would not be safe in the upcoming economic failures. They would suffer the most, even though they believe they are immune against all the tyranny prevalent in the present socioeconomic environments.

A realistic (and humanistic) evaluation of our economic systems reveals that they are merely economic constraints while the related opportunities are becoming less tangible and generalizable, and while they subdue individuals' choices and independence. They cause more frustration and insecurity for people than offer a stable source of economic welfare. These economic constraints are established 'facts' that prevail in many fronts, including job opportunities, access to education, competition, tax systems, markets, technology, organization and labour discriminations, and many other social facets. These elements of economic systems are painful facts of life, while we naively depend on them for subsistence, and while the greedy, incompetent executives run corporations for their own financial and egotistical benefits. As discussed in Volume III of this trilogy, work and organization have become main concerns and sources of suffering for all of us. This is in spite of the ideal notion that work should be the source of security at least, and hopefully a means of self-fulfillment and inner satisfaction if it happens to be the right kind of work. As a whole, economic conditions in our societies not only limit individuals in satisfying their basic economic needs, but also deprive them from achieving their full potentials and self-respect.

In capitalistic economies, everybody is led to believe they have equal opportunities to make lots of money and build a fortune. However, this is untrue due to economic constraints for one thing, but also other uncontrollable factors such as luck and opportunity. 'Fortune and luck' are myths, but we know that destiny plays an essential role in everybody's life. If a person is born into a rich family, his/her chances are much higher to get the right education, have his/her business laid out and ready for him/her upon graduation, and s/he usually ends up marrying a wealthy person too. Compare this scenario with the situation of a person born in a less fortunate family with all kinds of social issues, mixed up with street gangs, etc. The point is not to stress on wealth as a means of happiness, but rather to highlight the shallowness of propagandas and our beliefs about the equality of opportunities.

Many people who end up making something of themselves admit that good luck and opportunity have helped them; or maybe even a divine force driven their fortune somehow. This may be luck, the universe, or God. Nobody knows the nature of this external intervention, though all kinds of people have experienced it—intellectuals, rich, poor, aristocrats and commoners. We might have felt the impact of luck, or that somebody is watching over us, somehow. These experiences occur frequently enough, in such a profound way, we cannot deny the existence of some external source of power in the universe that supports us, at least occasionally. Despite its irrationality and our passive mentality for exploring it, the myth of fortune resides in our subconscious as a real possibility, and we resort to it from time to time through prayer or meditation. That is what hope is based on and all about.

Another source of frustration lies in our persistent expectation for fairness from this world. We expect to be treated fairly and to receive the recognition that we think we deserve from the society, from the organization we work for, from our family and friends, etc. In reality, however, fairness is only a myth too. We can touch or exercise it from time to time, but, as a general rule, no such thing as fairness exists. Again, fairness is a relative term, too, and related to luck and fortune. It also depends on the state of mind of the person expecting it, and those who precipitate unfairness with absolute cruelty or stupidity. Unfairness is a torturous fact, but fairness remains a myth.

Despite all the unwarranted unfairness, while struggling within unmanageable economic constraints, social living still demands serious decision-making, intelligence, originality, perseverance and all other sorts of personal traits. We strive for the betterment of our economic/materialistic lives with all our might, and subconsciously hope that luck and opportunity aid us in achieving our fantasies as well, and we hope that the sources of achieving our fantasies as well, and we hope that the sources of unfairness, prejudices, and discriminations are eliminated.

Pressed by the inevitable economic constraints as a sad 'fact' of life, while pondering the myths of fortune and fairness, our challenge is to stay content (without losing our patience, identity, and individuality). Our goal is to avoid getting caught up completely in the machinery of the pervasive materialistic life, and precluding ourselves from the opportunity of evolving as humble humans out of this mess. We must somehow adapt to the unpleasant features of socioeconomic environments. We need all the luck and opportunity to cope with the socioeconomic problems of our world. But, more importantly, we must stay content and humble to bypass the temptations of the socioeconomic rewards, which are always contradictory to the values of divine humanness. We need strength and wisdom to bear unfairness and resist narrow-minded people who love to make life miserable for other fellow humans just for feeding their Egos—to prove their meagre existence.

As another 'fact' for survival, most of us usually attend to our economic and basic needs before pondering and pursuing our spirituality needs. Our challenge is to understand social constraints, find our limited opportunities, and bring luck on our side by believing in our 'self' and the potentialities within 'self.' We must maintain some level of faith, amongst all our doubts, that a divine force or fortune lives inside every one of us. This is not a religious belief or remark, but rather a psychological and medical assessment by prominent professionals that contentment frees our spirit, facilitates objective thinking, and releases the higher energies that we need to survive and succeed.

7. Personal Limitations, Enlightenment, Life Decisions

Personal limitations and potentialities are discussed in some detail in Volume II of this trilogy as they affect our life outlook and plans. Naturally, the genetics, rearing, and educational opportunities play major roles in the aptitude and psychological strength of a person. We usually have unique talents and needs, which often remain hidden due to our negligence or missed opportunities. Nonetheless, our potentialities and limitations make us different, even if we were to believe that all humans had the same basic essence. Not many people can develop the vision of Einstein about the universe, no matter how hard they tried. And there is no science or education to make many of us think and perceive things like him either. Thus, recognizing our potentialities and limitations is an essential 'fact' for setting our life objectives and plans wisely and realistically.

We know these 'facts' deep down, yet often get carried away by our ambitions, greed, or positive-thinking propagandas that claim we can achieve anything only by visioning or wishing it. Getting ambitious does not eliminate our limitations, nor does it affect the type and depth of our potentialities. Naturally, positive thinking can help us change our attitude and outlook on life, and thus explore those undeveloped special powers within us. But we should not confuse ourselves about our potentialities and limitations that can hardly be altered. A peculiar feature of our perceived world is that it deliberately ignores certain 'facts' about our limitations and pushes us to become dreamers. Instead of facing reality about our limitations, we just force ourselves to dream about so many far-fetched and often futile symbols of success. Of course, it is always wise to challenge ourselves, have ambitions, and set high goals for ourselves. How else could we ensure that our measures of our potentialities and limitations are valid? But the trick is to remain realistic too. This is a big dilemma that makes the 'fact' about our limitations and potentialities both confusing and pressing. Yet, the bottom line is that we must somehow resolve all these doubts quickly and choose a life path. That is why unravelling this 'fact'—about our inherent limitations—demands special efforts, in particular. As an important first step, we could at least avoid the obvious traps. For example, we can stop the common wasteful approach of trying to imitate or fake some peculiar personality or pursuing imaginary goals. Instead, we should remain simple and independent in gauging our potentialities, problems, and limitations. Hence, we give ourselves a chance to see the possibilities for improvement. By denying ourselves the opportunity to learn about ourselves, because we wish to imitate a special role model, or simply remain a dreamer in our world of illusions, we only increase our limitations while pushing our real potentialities to a deeper level of neglect.

We need to learn about our potentialities for making the right decisions for the rest of our lives, but more importantly prevent major setbacks, depression, and possibly even losing our sanity. And we need to learn about our limitations in order to know ourselves better and control our personality flaws in the way we do and say things, especially within our closer relationships with family and friends.

If the process of learning about ourselves (especially our limitations) goes deep enough, while we delve into self-awareness, we gain the insight and wisdom to choose a more realistic path of life. It is an amazing 'fact' that the more we understand and acknowledge our limitations, the more enlightened, selfless, and humble we become, but also feel more confident and free. We can make more effective and independent decisions about the course of our lives and the most rational lifestyle for us. This realization, at the intersection of the wisdom path, sounds mystical and a myth to many of us who have not experienced it personally. We have probably heard about mysticism, miracles, and the power of enlightenment. However, unless we have had personal experiences in these areas, we remain sceptical about the experiences in these areas, we remain sceptical about the reality of such power and its possible effect on our lives. We continue to face them passively with deep cynicism. We doubt our ability to grasp or experience these kinds of mythical phenomena. However, during some moments of weakness and need, we resort to the same kind of mystical power and plea for salvation. Many of us seem to have an inherent, though untested, belief in an energy source that mysteriously helps us in the moments of despair; and this is in spite of all our doubts about these mythical phenomena. Some truth may exist about all the energy sources that we consider mystical. And enough clues exist about the possibility of reaching personal enlightenment if we allow our hearts, minds, and beliefs grow in the right direction. Enlightenment is a conceivable reality, though it has various levels. Our view about luck and destiny might build our belief system, but enlightenment is a direct, active means of finding our connection to this mysterious force in the universe. Nevertheless, for most of us who are not following a wisdom path toward an ultimate 'enlightenment,' or are just beginning to search for it, our logic dictates that we deal with it as a 'myth.' We merely seek a kind of wisdom that could make our choices and decisions easier with less stress. Together, our real potentialities and limited enlightenment give us enough energy to deal with the real issues of our lives and avoid irreversible situations and repercussions.

Our psychological strengths help us grasp and pursue the mythical path of enlightenment. Then, together, our divine potentialities and the wisdom of enlightenment, would guide us through the most difficult task of our lives, i.e., the challenge of making major life decisions in a timely manner. Decision-making parameters are discussed in some detail in Volume II. Some decisions have long-lasting impacts on our lives and sometimes the lives of others. The challenge is to be prepared and make proper choices when we come across major life decisions and while we have the opportunity to plan a productive life for ourselves. But we must make all our decisions according to a proper criteria developed based on our level of 'self'-awareness and enlightenment. Making sloppy decisions, or postponing the making of decisions, is bypassing the life opportunities that are offered in particular orders and timeframes without any chance of recourse.

Our physical and psychological limitations and our neglected potentialities are all 'facts' of life that cause hardship and suffering for us. As our psychological strength expands beyond the boundaries of our physical lives, we may resort to mystical powers and search for enlightenment. Although such notions appear mythical, we usually find them a soothing alternative to our normal state of stalemate and suffering. This healing process boosts our ability to make effective decisions and live. But, more importantly, our sound decisions boost the process of healing too. When our decisions relieve other humans from hardship and suffering, help ecology, make someone happy, they turn into a natural process for healing our souls. So, making good decisions in a timely manner, when we still have a chance, is a major 'challenge' of our lives. They are particularly essential in the light of our extreme personal limitations and while we hope to embrace that mythical enlightenment in the process.

8. Personal Needs, Purity/Piety, Needs Gratification

We have become the subservient slaves to our rising artificial needs. We have a handful of instinctual needs that we must satisfy as a matter of *fact*. However, we have invented a large amount of artificial personal needs in the last century or so to pamper our Egos and we take them as a real fact of life too. However, this increase in our neediness about all these artificial needs has only caused us more distress and a lesser chance to attend to our authentic needs.

Our personalities evolve according to our perceived needs, and our attitudes and stress demonstrate the burden of those needs. Not only the characteristics of individuals, but also those of society and humanity as a whole depend on people's presumed needs. The types and intensity of personal needs that are prevalent within social superstructure establish our value systems. Conversely, our socioeconomic systems influence the nature and scope of our personal needs. Unfortunately, social values and superficial personal needs have become parallel forces infesting each other in a vicious cycle and destroying humanity in the process. This ominous energy is accelerating along a devastating path and only few people seem to even understand the scope of the problem or care about the doomed destiny of humanity.

Our culture is placing more emphasis on physical needs and pleasures, while our spiritual needs are misguided or have been further buried in our unconscious. Accordingly, our psychological needs are not adequately developed or satisfied either. For example, only a small group actively pursues and achieves 'self-fulfilment' as a basic psychological need. Instead, most people focus on shallow social norms, attempt to fake individualism, build a phony self-image, and turn into self-centred characters in order to compensate for their psychological shortfalls. Their boosted Egos manifest in the form of relentless urges of greed, power, sexuality, domination, and possession.

Creating a right balance among our physical, psychological, and spiritual needs is necessary for maintaining our health and stamina. Otherwise, we encounter chronic depression and psychological regression relative to the degree of imbalance. The other side-effects are limited mental growth and self-awareness and high gullibility, which many social organs depend on to fulfil their own agendas, e.g., getting elected as heads of governments or selling more useless products to the hypnotized public.

Our personal needs, regardless of their nature, type, and intensity, feel like necessities and 'facts' of our lives. However, most of them are superficial needs that we have built in our psyches in recent decades. These are more of the kind we adopt as part of learning and imitating social values. These shallow needs, driven by our Egos and physical needs, hinder self-fulfilment and purification of our souls. They merely cause more agony. Even some of our natural needs, like sex, are now abused and exaggerated artificially. They are brought to the highest level of consciousness as urgent superficial needs that we follow out of habit and obligation rather than a natural need satisfaction.

Contrary to the superficial needs driven by social values, we have some deeper (unconscious) needs, which are genuine and healthy. These needs have a kind of cleansing effect on our soul and for goading our self-realization efforts. Sometimes we feel the inner conflicts among our physical, psychological, and spiritual needs, and then we face a decision to satisfy one type of personal need (e.g., pleasure) at the expense of other types of needs (e.g., integrity). Yet, the purity and piety of our souls depend on our ability to identify *all* levels of our needs and reinforce the ones that lead to wisdom, growth and self-fulfilment. They are healing decisions similar to other life decisions discussed in the previous section.

Our needs, like all other 'facts' of life, mostly cause our suffering, as they compete with our natural urges knowingly or unconsciously. Even our lower level needs are satisfied through a great deal of hardship. The needs for food, shelter, sex, love, and belonging demand a lot of sacrifice and hard work on our part to get satisfied. And to the extent that some needs, such as love and belonging, are often hardly attainable, we suffer psychologically in a major way. On many occasions, we realize that our presumed achievements are not gratifying enough in the way we had imagined and expected them to enrich our lives. So we feel disappointed and discouraged. It is even harder to grasp and respond to our higher-level needs. In particular, understanding our spirituality needs, and finding a path to attain them, would be a difficult and enigmatic journey that requires patience and tolerance.

When we follow our inner urges to satisfy our deeper (unconscious) needs, we reach a state of spiritual gratification. This reflects the inherent purity and piety that resides within us—our soul. This purity and piety is a myth, as it is hard to grasp truly and maintain. It has been buried deep down in our unconscious after millenniums of human struggle for survival and domination. It has been buried deep underneath all our superficial needs in the new era. Nevertheless, exploring this myth, by fostering our psychological and spiritual needs, is the only way to relieve ourselves from life's sufferings. Thus, our 'challenge' is to understand, and attend to, our unconscious needs at least as much as we care about our conscious needs. The challenge is to facilitate the process of healing by creating some kind of balance between our urges for material (physical and sexual) needs and spiritual (non-physical) needs.

9. Perceived Reality, Real Reality, Health

The perceived and real worlds offer two opposing viewpoints for seeing and connecting to society and the universe. In the perceived world, we are mostly adapting ourselves to social rules and conditions. It is mostly the means of connecting with society and satisfying our external (physical) needs. The perceived world supposedly gives us the psychological security we need, as it provides a tangible meaning and rewards for our efforts. In this world, we are familiar with the variables and factors that we must deal with rather urgently in our physical lives. We have established some kind of relationship with various issues and aspects of this world, and we have contrived an alluring perception of this perceived world, which we now believe is the truth. Thus, it is hard for us not to see it as the real 'fact.' We accept the rules and conditions of the perceived reality world because we perceive them as 'real,' 'fact,' 'truth,' 'logical,' 'tangible,' 'rewarding,' and similar criteria that reinforce and symbolize the world of perceived reality.

In contrast, the real world is the means of connecting to the universe and our inner 'self.' It places an idealistic expectation on moral and mentality for some seemingly intangible rewards that are mostly one's imagination of transcendence based on one's limited (if any) inner experience. All these idealism and rewards feel abstract and fantastic—merely a myth—for our conditioned minds. Thus, the real world, the truth, and the universe outside our crooked perceptions appear imaginary (a myth) to us while all our imaginations (in the perceived world) appear realistic, practical, and 'facts' of life.

Turning to a real world where supposedly souls run physics is against the logic, values, and conditions that we are used to in our perceived world; it appears like an irreconcilable myth. However, the only possibility for us to redeem our souls is to resort to the mythical world of real realities. This transcendence can be accomplished by initially reconciling the facts and myths that separate these two worlds, without resorting to religions and superstitions. We must learn about the existence and supremacy of the real world, and then detect some aspects of this myth with the aid of our powerful, divine potentialities. We can awaken and use our potentialities in our dealings and encounters in a practical way and achieve inner peace too. We should stop rationalizing the wickedness and weaknesses of the perceived world that we have so readily embraced and believe to be the *truth* of our existence.

Our challenge is to transform our thoughts and actions, bypass the conditions and values of the perceived world, and excavate our divine potentialities and self-awareness for getting at least a glimpse of the real world. The realities and facts that we accept as truths in the perceived world are only the diseases that we have let into our bodies and psyches. The disease of wealth gathering and greed, which are the symbols of the perceived world, has penetrated every cell of our bodies and brains. Accordingly, our bodies and minds have not only stopped their normal functioning, but also lost the opportunity for normal growth.

We know that the most important asset for a person is his health, not wealth. Yet, we somehow ignore the immorality and the harms caused by our professions, sexuality, greed, anxieties and the stress of accumulating wealth. All these symptoms of social living, and the lack of spiritual motivations, are clear signs of a path to a definite and infinite self-destruction. Since the loss of health and the effect of psychological diseases cannot be observed or measured daily, we do not notice them until it is too late. We only realize the harm we have done to ourselves—by our futile deeds and greed that offer no value at the end anyway—when we collapse from a heart attack, ulcer, stress, or depression. Since our ultimate objective and challenge in life is to develop and maintain our psychological and physical health, we must assess and reconcile our understanding of the perceived and real worlds and distinguish their true factuality. We must ask ourselves why we ruin our psyches and bodies by all the nonsensical activities and thoughts we pursue in our perceived world with such childish passion.

The answer to the question, 'Why we inflict all these harms to our health?' brings us back to the same conclusion: that our perceptions of 'facts' are incomplete and distorted. We do not perceive and receive the important messages, such as the matters of our physical and psychological health, in a timely manner, but we quickly perceive many crooked features of the perceived world quite appealing, urgent, and necessary. We are thoroughly absorbed in, and have submitted to, the rules and conditions of the perceived world and we need a superhuman strength to pull ourselves out of this state of hypnosis.

The existence and power of the perceived world is a 'fact' and a major source of our hardships and suffering, which would continue to overwhelm us as long as we are not willing to challenge this 'fact.' The only escape from this superficial life of materialism is to transcend to the world of real realities, which we continue to accept only as a 'myth.' The process of healing our souls is the simple act of controlling our physical and psychological health. Remembering this vital message is a main 'challenge' by itself.

10. Death, Creation/Creator, Spirituality

Death is the saddest 'fact' of life. Our perception of a mortal life and our doubts about afterlife cause deep and sad feelings. Death of a close family member or a friend brings us a great deal of grief and pain, and the thought of our own dismal destiny is even more excruciating. With the death of a family member or a friend, we lose our connection with the person we love and the possibility of doing certain activities together. The thought of our own death also means losing touch with the people we care for, as well as all the pleasures of this physical world. Most importantly, however, the thought of *non-existence* per se is far more painful. These losses, thoughts, and pains are inevitable and devastating facts for all humans. Fortunately, we have the ability to ignore or undermine the finality of death for most of our lives and while we do not face a serious illness. This is fortunate in the sense that, by not concentrating on the fact of death, we minimize our sad thoughts. However, by ignoring it completely, we distort our perception of the real reality and forget how vulnerable we are. Remembering the fact of death on a regular basis and internalizing it would keep our thoughts focused inwardly in search of who we really are and what the purpose of our living is.

Whether there is an afterlife, and in what form, is something that we can only speculate on and wish for, in order to alleviate our fears and sadness of death. The religious beliefs, and personal convictions of some sort, with respect to the permanency of soul are the means of relieving ourselves from the anxiety of death. And the philosophical and theological ideas of man hint about the possibility and greatness of life after death. All these imaginations and hopes help us in overcoming our fears and sadness of the fact of death, but more importantly, they put us in touch with our inner 'self.' The questions regarding 'existence' and the purpose of life are derivatives of our thoughts about death. And from this platform we initiate our thinking and talking about the creation and the creator. We become inquisitive about the purpose of Creation and whether there is a creator. And then we find out that the idea of needing a creator for everything is only a figment of human logic that does not apply to the creation of the universe. Despite all the philosophies and scientific clues, we are still unable to make a valid judgment about our creation and creator, existence, death, soul, and after-physical-life. This whole issue remains a myth for us to doubt, contemplate, speculate, subdue our fears and sadness with, and keep our spirits high. This is the myth that we must deal with and continue to doubt throughout our lives, but also apply as a vehicle to know more about ourselves and awaken our unconscious needs and potentials. We might have even reached a sense of enlightenment that makes up for our personal limitations and satisfies our need for spirituality, but our doubts about the creator and Creation continue as another myth in our lives.

All the spiritual insights, philosophical notions, and scientific evidences lead to the conclusion that we are an integral part of the universe and creation. Physiologically, we are built of the same basic matter and energy that makes up the universe and which can be traced in every single subatomic particle and molecule. Some people go even one step further and believe that our minds, thoughts, and intelligence are an extension of a larger super-intelligence phenomenon, a universal consciousness, which is the substance of the universe and responsible for its creation. Keeping it at a mythical level, it might not hurt to have these kinds of superfluous beliefs. We can even believe that our creativity and insight flows from this universal source of intelligence, which we access through our awareness and souls. We are the creator and the creation at the same time when we attain a high level of consciousness. We are a minuscule manifestation of consecutive energy and matter transformation in the time-space dimension. We are necessarily a part of the whole energy and matter in both physical and non-physical forms. 'What we are' gives us the clue and ability to create a 'self' free from our Egos and in touch with our souls. We are able to see our real 'self,' which is immortal and becomes one with the creation and creator. And this is our 'challenge.' The challenge is to find the 'self'-fulfilling and actualizing creations that are within us. This is the process of reconciling between the 'fact' (and our fears) of mortality and the 'myth' of creation. The challenge is to discover how the potential ecstasy of personal creations surpasses the fears of mortality.

Maslow's findings regarding self-actualizers' emotions reflect the type of transformation that these people have been able to achieve. Self-actualization experiences are significant because they provide a more tangible and sensible set of evidences based on real experiments. These findings support the possibility of finding our spiritual 'self' under certain conditions. In particular, the following two quotes from Maslow's findings reflect how his subjects surpass the fears of mortality:

"One aspect of the peak-experience is a complete, though momentary, loss of fear, anxiety, inhibition, defence and control, a giving up of renunciation, delay and restraint. The fear of disintegration and dissolution, the fear of being overwhelmed by the "instincts," the fear of death and of insanity, the fear of giving in to unbridled pleasure and emotion, all tend to disappear or go into abeyance for the time being. This too implies a greater openness of perception since fear distorts." Towards a Psychology of Being, Abraham Maslow, Van Nostrand Reinhold, 1968, page 94.

"The emotional reaction in the peak experience has a special flavour of wonder, of awe, of reverence, of humility and surrender before the experience as before something great. This sometimes has a touch of fear (although pleasant fear) of being over-

whelmed. My subjects report this in such phrases as "This is too much for me." "It is more than I can bear." "It is too wonderful." The experience may have a certain poignancy and piercing quality which may either bring either tears or laughter or both, and which may be paradoxically akin to pain, although this is a desirable pain which is often described as "sweet." This may go so far as to involve thoughts of death in a peculiar way. Not only my subjects but many writers on the various peak experiences have made the parallel with the experience of dying, that is, an eager dying. A typical phrase might be: "This is too wonderful. I don't know how I can bear it. I could die now and it would be all right." Perhaps this is in part a hanging on to the experience and a reluctance to go down from this peak into the valley of ordinary existence. Perhaps it is in part, also, an aspect of the profound sense of humility, smallness, unworthiness before the enormity of experience." Ibid., pages 87-88.

At the same time, the challenge is to find the beauties of life that make our living so wonderful and joyful. Maslow reports a similar experience of self-actualizers, which may initially appear contrary to the previous quote about self-actualizers' willingness to die during peak experience:

"The person is more apt to feel that life in general is worth while, even if it is usually drab, pedestrian, painful or ungratifying, since beauty, excitement, honesty, play, goodness, truth and meaningfulness have been demonstrated to him to exist. That is, life is validated, and suicide and death wishing must become less likely." Ibid., pages 101-102.

Amongst all the other 'facts' of life, the perception of one's own death or the death of a dear is most painful. The only relief we may find for this pain and grief is to think of the possibility of some sort of non-physical life after death and that our souls are immortal. This is a 'myth' that we may cling to as a defence mechanism. The 'challenge' for reconciling between the fact of mortality and the myths of creation and immortality is to explore our inherent ability to actualize and fulfil our real 'self,' as a creator of ideas and art, as a self-actualizer, and as a builder of our spirit. We have a chance to achieve all these ecstatic moments in our short lives.

The Nature of Facts, Myths, and Challenges

The 'facts' and 'myths' discussed in this chapter comprise the most general and encompassing set, but definitely do not make an exhaustive list. Everybody can add and ponder other facts and the corresponding myths and challenges in the same manner analysed in Table 3.1.

As briefly noted at the beginning of Chapter Three, several interesting issues have come out of the discussions of facts, myths, and challenges. **First,** it appears that for every possible fact there are one or more corresponding myths and challenges. (We have not scientifically proven this, but there is no need or intention to do so. The only point is that our facts, myths, and challenges are highly interrelated.)

Second, it can be concluded that all the objects, ideas and events that we perceive as 'facts' lead to hardship and suffering, whereas the corresponding 'myths' provide a means of relief from these pains, and that 'challenges' are the means of cleansing our souls and healing our suffering. Our challenges provide the opportunity of reconciling facts and myths, and to transcend our 'self' through awareness and inner search.

Third, it seems that all the 'facts' are related to the physical aspect of existence and that they reflect our perceptions and contacts with the external world. That is, we look outside ourselves to find the facts. The moment we turn inward and look inside ourselves, we encounter all sorts of doubts and myths. Therefore, our internal world, the contents of our hearts, minds, and souls, have been grasped and treated as myth and unreal by us. We have conditioned ourselves to accept everything that is in the external world as real and as the 'facts' of life. And we are conditioned to undermine, doubt, and consider fantasy everything that exists or comes from our internal world of existence, our souls, hearts, minds, insights, and instincts. When we doubt the reality of our inner self, the only other way to deal with the inconsistencies and contradictions of 'facts' and 'myths' appear to be that of reconciling them somehow. We do this by creating some kind of balance between our factual and mythical realities. We examine the nature of all those 'facts,' which are mainly built upon our perceptions. And of course, this is only a compromise in the absence of personal wisdom to see, or courage to delve into, the reality that resides in our inner self. We might eventually do it and reach the highest wisdom deserving humans' dignity!

For now, we prefer to believe in, and insist on the accuracy of, our perceptions of the external (physical) world as undeniable 'facts,' while they cause our hardships and sufferings. Thus, we may ask, 'If our perceptions of the world are *real* facts, why do they have to be so painful? Why would God create a world around all these painful facts? Are these so-called 'facts' merely inventions of our imperfect perceptions and logic? Is it in our nature to only find means of paining ourselves and others instead of looking for salvation and peace?'

Accordingly, we insist on disregarding the reality (and the authenticity) of our inner world, because it appears abstract and a myth, when in reality it is the only source of relief from the worldly suffering. It seems that we not only are conditioned to perceive facts and myths in a distorted way, but also do not have enough courage to free ourselves from the ploy of ignorance we call 'facts.' We do not seem to get the message in spite of the constant tortures we bear within the realities of the presumed factual world.

The ultimate challenge for us is to recognize and act on a simple *fact*: That since we seem stuck in this formidable position with respect to our facts and myths, we might at least take on some special 'challenges' to reconcile the 'facts' and the 'myths.' The objective is to create at least a balanced position for them in our thoughts and actions—without confusing ourselves further, of course, or allowing another form of gullibility (like religions) hamper the foundation of our thoughts. Interestingly enough, we pause quite frequently and doubt the meaning and purposes of the 'facts' even though we have classified them as realities of life. Our deep doubts about all these seeming 'facts' of our lives make us ponder our lifestyle and choices pensively quite often. However, we never consider refuting their factuality. Granted, it is hard to do so anyway. How can we deny certain facts, such as birth and death? All other facts feel equally solid and irrefutable. Yet most of our doubts about 'facts' and symbols of the perceived world are warranted and useful, as demonstrated in this chapter.

At the same time, it is also perplexing why we have doubts about 'facts,' e.g., the purpose of living, even though 'facts' should by definition be inherently clear and indisputable? As an example, animals do not have the capacity and the instinct to doubt their existence or seek a validation for it. So, why do we humans have this obsession about the purpose of our lives and about the meaning of all the other facts? Why would our advanced brains make us doubt and challenge facts, which then lead to more confusion and stress? We like to challenge all the facts subconsciously. We struggle so hard to defy even the 'fact' of death by imagining an afterlife existence. Theoretically, however, facts are presumed to be unchallengeable. Thus, perhaps the only use of these types of (positive) doubts is to awaken our senses and come to terms with those facts, e.g., death, by accepting our mortality without trying so idiotically to fool ourselves about life in heaven.

Anyway, since we cannot grasp the meaning and the purposes of the so-called facts, and since we cannot change them, at least we may learn to live with them in some harmony (without putting too much meaning or emphasis on their importance in our minuscule lives). However, for reaching even this level of awareness about facts we must first ponder them rationally. Only then, we might learn to stop taking all the facts, especially our existence, so seriously and literally as undeniable phenomena. Instead, we might value our 'challenges' for reconciling so many facts and myths overwhelming our lives. This cleansing routine can soothe the pains of our existence while we learn to value our doubts too. We can do this by making intelligent and effective decisions, to create a synergy between mind and body, soul and physics, logic and instincts, and wisdom and Ego. The act of reconciliation would bring our Egos under control and consequently reduce both our dogmatism and doubtfulness. A main objective of our life 'challenges' is to relieve our tensions from our doubts by adjusting our views of the 'facts.'

At the same time, our understanding about the true nature of some myths can alleviate our stress due to our misperceptions of those myths. For example, one of the greatest myths occupying our minds during our entire lives is the myth of 'happiness,' especially when it is expected to be an absolute and everlasting one. We have crude personal imagination of what happiness means or should be. (This fantastical perception is a product of our efforts and mentality in modern society to seek happiness like another precious commodity.) Our perceptions and definitions of happiness result merely from our erroneous personal impressions and reactions toward 'facts' and 'myths,' as explained in this chapter. Our perceptions and the reality of happiness depend on how we see, interpret, and deal with the facts, myths, and challenges of our lives. This general background would be helpful in Chapter Six where a more elaborate discussion regarding the myth of happiness is offered.

PART III
Happiness and Depression

CHAPTER FIVE
Power and Personality

Personal power is reared and reflected in two ways: the inner power that gives us self-assurance and independence, and the outer power (charisma) that facilitates our relationships with people around us. The type and level of personal power that we possibly gain over the years remain mostly cluttered in our psyche, except for the portion that manifests through our exposed personality. Nowadays, particularly, the emphasis is on building our outer power for gaining popularity, participating in juvenile pleasures, and manipulating others. Even so, we go about it in a crooked way, mainly by creating phony personalities that lack enough roots and integrity to reflect even a small dose of character or charisma. We just keep boosting our Egos in hopes of reflecting our false pride, dreams, and confidence. Accordingly, people detect our shallowness quickly as we hardly appear natural. Meanwhile, our vulnerable personality consumes our energy throughout our lives without enhancing any kind of power or our sense of individualism.

This misguided approach and mentality is a product of social trends to feel important and love ourselves too much with no inherent qualities to match our arrogance. It merely reflects our neediness and struggle for social imitation and adaptation, which hardly help our outer power, but definitely erode the chance of building our inner power, too. Instead of finding confidence and independence, deep down we remain doubtful about our identity and feel more dependent on others and things to survive. We need more acceptance and approval from people every day to confirm our existence and we must surround ourselves with more friends, wealth, and pleasure to feel and prove our power. In the end, both our inner and outer powers remain shaky, while our superfluous needs and pretensions confuse us even more than they annoy others.

Conversely, if a person focuses on building his inner power, he finds no, or little, need for the outer power to maintain his identity and relationships, yet an aura of charisma surrounds him automatically already. His deep confidence and independence make him much less needy for other people's approval and reactions anyway.

The inner power evolves simply by strengthening 'self,' which is the neglected aspect of our personality as explained in the next section. The irony is that the inner power is easier to build, while the outer power normally grows during this process automatically, too. Furthermore, with an authentic identity and needlessness, a person gets a better chance of meeting the right people who share the same values and needs. Instead of seeking popularity among many phony people, he may find a few friends who really grasp his sentiments and thoughts. The only, rather harsh, drawback of focusing on inner power is that relating to the mainstream becomes rather difficult for the person, as well as for people who cannot figure out his rather stoic attitude. Not everybody grasps or respects that kind of quiet charisma, because it appears odd compared with the prevalent tendency to embellish personal power in society, i.e., in a showy and exaggerated way.

With our false personalities, nevertheless, we cause ourselves extra headaches by attracting people who are incompatible with us in terms of our needs and aspirations. Thus, we go through a long process of trial and error to finally accept that our relationships are only making us more depressed and desperate instead of enriching our lives. The lousiness of most relationships nowadays is due to our lack of inner power and integrity.

Personality Aspects

For building both our inner and outer power, we work on our personalities to acquire certain personal attributes and to portray a confident image to others. Therefore, a brief review of the main aspects (characteristics) of personality and its manifestation mechanisms would be useful here.

Analysing an individual's personality reveals three main dimensions or aspects in it, which we may refer to as Self, Ego, and Model. These aspects of a person's personality are not defined here in the same context of Freud's definition of the three divisions of psyche for psychoanalysis, which are Id, ego, and superego. While the latter classification emphasizes on the way personality is developed and retained inherently mostly in our unconscious mind, the former is interested in the way personality manifests mostly through our conscious efforts. Of course, some similarities and overlaps exist between the two models, but the classification of the three aspects of the personality, as defined by this author, is for a different purpose. It mainly explains the way we go about making our decisions, choices, and contacts with the aid of our manipulative personality aspects. (For interested readers, a more detailed comparison is provided in the Addendum, at the end of this chapter.)

The seven elements of Self are discussed in detail in Chapter Two of Volume II of this trilogy under the heading of 'Knowing Ourselves.' In brief, we may say that Self is the pure, unconditioned nature of man. Self resembles that aspect of man that is defined as Id in psychoanalysis in terms of being the unconscious aspect of psyche and the source of psychic energy. However, Self is also the unexplored and underutilized aspect of a person that entails his potentialities and spirituality dimensions. Self also contains the absolute and isolated aspect of a person untouchable by negative or positive experiences of social living. Ego, for our purpose in this book, is defined to be the conditioned personality of a man that reflects his lower mental qualities, subconscious needs and desires, vanity, self-centredness and high dependence on externalities. Ego represents the self-serving needs and intentions of a person, which are mostly hidden or at least not presented voluntarily. In general, Ego is the selfish aspect of a person's personality.

The 'model' aspect of personality manifests in the way a person tries to adapt to social norms and in the way he presents himself to others. It often ends up becoming the main feature of his personality and who he believes to be. We perceive and/or construct one or several role models (personalities) that appeal to us. We would then internalize and behave in the form of the model that we adopt overall or apply in particular instances. We do this for the sake of satisfying our conscious needs, or hiding those unflattering aspects of our Ego that we do not care to project in our daily dealings and relationships. We also adopt a Model when we do not have a set of values of our own, or when the elements of immaturity are present. Model becomes more prominent when Self and Ego are less developed and active.

Our personality is the combination of these three aspects of a person's identity at any instant. They are always present and interact constantly according to a rather fixed mix for each person. For example, an egoist is driven mostly by his Ego. Yet, the level of each aspect contributing to total personality at any point may vary and thus change a person's personality manifestation. Our mood changes also reflect the varying mixtures of the three personality aspects. (Of course, the concept of multiple personality is different from the tentative variations of personality aspects that lead to different presentation of personality and possibly mood swings, whereas multiple personality is a more permanent condition.)

Sometimes, Model may simply portray and reinforce the expectations of Ego, and sometimes Model may reflect a new feeling or role that it finds interesting and appealing. Sometimes, we can control our anger or frustration and present ourselves in a desirable format and model. And sometimes our basic honesty—a manifestation of Self—outweighs the other aspects of our personality and we say things that we might even regret later, e.g., when we tell the truth about something or someone.

Living in the highly structured and conditioning societies of the recent era has taught us to play the role of a Model extensively rather than revealing the natural person within us. That natural person (self) is subdued and lost at a very young age anyway. We use Model a lot because we do not want to portray the deceitful aspects of our Ego, and we do not want to show our gullibility and immaturity that usually radiate from Self. And we do not have the courage to be the 'self' that is not favoured as an acceptable model of success and passion in our cultures.

The varying mix of our personality aspects in particular situations and times makes us behave erratically and appear instable. Yet, a person's rather unique personality manifests according to the overall prevalence of one or two of the three personality aspects. We are usually dissolved in a personality that is mostly a Model, Ego, or Self, while we apply the other two in lesser proportions simultaneously as necessary. That would constitute our main personality. *That is the personality we strive to keep happy.*

These preliminary definitions of the three aspects of personality are elaborated further throughout this trilogy as various discussions about personality, especially Self, become necessary. Many other topics in this trilogy are also related to personality aspects. For example, the concept of happiness can be measured only in relation to the prevalent aspect of a person's personality. As soon as the topic of happiness arises, the immediate question is which aspect of his/her personality s/he is trying to keep happy. Our decision in this respect is crucial and determines the outcome, because the definition of happiness varies for each personality aspect. Normally, we associate the state of happiness with that aspect of personality that we are consciously placing an emphasis on. For example, the happiness of a Model oriented personality comes mostly from popularity and approval, which does not coincide with a general description of happiness. Someone whose depth of happiness is defined to him as, let us say, having the most amount of wealth or sex has a different point of reference compared to our general impression or formula of happiness. Yet even when a person is hoping to make the prominent aspect of his personality happy, his/her happiness remains shaky because the other aspects of his/her personality do not feel so happy at the same time. For example, when Ego feels happy (maybe because somebody expresses his/her love to her/him), his/her Model and Self might feel sad or even angry (maybe because s/he does not trust the sincerity of the person who has expressed his/her love). These crucial factors cause extreme complications in a person's psyche for feeling a real sense of happiness. These are some additional reasons that 'happiness' remains an abstract and mythical concept. Therefore, the question is, 'How can we compare people's happiness, and how do we define real happiness?' It is almost impossible, but the next chapter will tackle these questions somewhat.

Our genes, environment, and conscious efforts play their roles in the way our personality develops and manifests. While we cannot control their effects, we have some influence on the way our personality turns out, especially in the way it manifests. In fact, we often play a major role in faking a personality that is appealing and can serve our hidden and selfish needs and desires. We use different aspects of our personality randomly to achieve our immediate goals. Yet, the main purpose of our lifelong efforts to portray a certain personality is to maximize our power and appeal in the long haul. In particular, we use Model regularly in hopes of showing charisma and power. Unfortunately, however, the outcome of our efforts is usually more destructive than helpful. Many of us end up with shaky personalities that others can detect immediately, while we also keep struggling internally with the wrong self-image and a false identity that we are so keen to build and maintain. All these struggles and frustrations feel odd when we could instead use our potentialities and eagerness to create an appealing and powerful personality, which is natural too. That is, instead of trying so hard, and keep failing, to build a false personality in hopes of impressing (or fooling) others, we could direct our efforts into building a stronger identity and inner self. By doing so, we gain the needed charisma more naturally and better than it is achievable through superficial pretences. The main hurdle that deters most people from pursuing this option is that building a Self oriented personality takes time, and it takes even longer for others to recognize and respect it. We are usually not patient and strong enough to wait for all these natural developments.

The main role of our personality (and the mixed use of personality aspects) is to facilitate our communications and interactions, all for the final objective of maximizing our happiness in life. We try to be assertive, manipulative, and cooperative with the use of our personality aspects in order to get things done our ways and guarantee our ongoing popularity and satisfaction. Obviously, developing the various aspects of our personalities and manifesting them in certain ways also depend on our needs, intelligence, and perceptions of people and surroundings, all for the ultimate purpose of finding happiness. Sadly, we often choose to nurture a set of erratic personality aspects to serve our social needs and ambitions, instead of curbing our needs and ambitions within the parameters of a natural, healthy, and stable personality. Still we hope to find happiness too! Nevertheless, the role of personality aspects on creating happiness is studied in some detail in the next chapter.

Addendum

A Comparison of the Id, Ego, and Superego with Self, Ego, and Model.

The Freud's three divisions of psyche stir or influence the development of personality. In this sense, the emphasis is placed on sources and the course of development of an inherent personality. However, the final interface, i.e., personality manifestation, is of lesser concern in this model. At least two other questions can be raised about this model too. First, whether Id, ego, and superego completely explain the process of personality development. Second, to what extent a developed personality remains fixed and stable within the highly fluctuating and forceful external stimuli. That is, assuming a person has developed a certain personality, would he always use that personality or learn to fake different personalities that he finds either appealing or useful. Would a fake personality gradually influence the real one over a long period? Which one of the 'real' or 'fake' personality is more relevant for either psychoanalysis or the welfare of a person, and a host of other issues? It is becoming safer to assume, nowadays, that other than imitating the prevalent social patterns, people in general do not develop a strong, fixed personality to begin with. More importantly, however, they often prefer to hide their true personality behind a fake one that feels more useful for a person's special needs at any particular situation in social environments. Certain role models and values, e.g., pomposity, have become quite popular in society as a means of proving one's individualism and assertiveness. Everybody tries to portray a typical personality to gain acceptance from peers and friends.

In this author's definition of the three aspects of personality, the emphasis is on the final product, i.e., the manifestation of personality, rather than how and why it has developed in certain ways—or not—and often hardly used anyway. The manifestation of personality includes both the real and fake personalities, though the ratio of each of them in the final presentation varies among people. After all, the final product is most important for both the individual and people who perceive him according to a mix of real and fake personalities. (By the way, the ratio of fake and real personalities always remain hidden too and it is quite erratic as well.) In this sense, we can actually examine 'personality' in more details in at least three layers: 1) The true characteristics of an individual (the developed personality), 2) the way these characteristics are mixed with pretences and presented in public, and 3) how a person is perceived in totality by others. These details are not covered in this book.

Nevertheless, the two systems (i.e., development and manifestation) are interrelated and in many ways inseparable. They both need to be studied for the understanding of the other and for explaining and improving personality as an extremely important social phenomenon. In fact, both models start with the natural and inherent properties of man, which emerges from the basic reality of being (alive). That is, our instincts and urges, and perhaps our soul, comprise the foundation of personality and are included in Id (Freudian model) or Self (in this book's framework). Perhaps a point of distinction can be found in the negative properties of Id, which erupts in terms of disruptive urges and destructive drives. In 'manifestation' model, Self is relatively more stable, pure, and unselfish in terms of its nature and origin (how it is brought into existence) and how it would have manifested if human's nature were not corrupted by excessive Ego and Model mostly for adaptation purposes. In this sense, the negativity of any personality manifestation erupts mainly from Ego and Model, mostly due to severe external forces, and very little due to the basic instinctual urges that a human is born with. Mainly, our Ego creates superficial remedies and resistance, and negative personality manifestation, due to a person's unfulfilled needs and frustrations.

At the same time, it is plausible that Id or Self, as the intrinsic nature of man, contains some assertiveness and adaptation tendencies (Ego and Model) automatically. These tendencies are the inherent (basic) characteristics of humans as needed for their survival. Only to the extent that Ego and Model develop extensively beyond their elementary (natural) presence in Id or Self, they manifest as unique and prominent personality aspects of humans and thus warrant the studies like the one presented in this book. Model and Ego require a closer study and attention, as critical psychological developments of the newer eras. Model and Ego have become more complex and forceful, in line with people's rising superficiality and egotism, and they are affecting our interactions and social order in major ways.

The definition of 'personality' used in this book depicts the inner interactions of Model, Ego, and Self. What we refer to as personality is expected to reflect the characteristics of an individual in terms of his preferences, habits, and ability to express his feelings, needs, and goals. It has two main properties: (i) The potentiality and reality that exist within an individual regardless of how well he can utilize or demonstrate them, and (ii) the image he portrays to others of himself, which reflects how well (or deviously) he is able to express himself regardless of his true character.

CHAPTER SIX
'Self' and Happiness

The objective of knowing 'self' is twofold: To recognize its essence and keep it content—all in search of that elusive happiness. Without discovering the essence of 'self,' we would never find real happiness, and without a keen desire for true happiness we would never undertake the horrendous task of knowing our 'self.'

We often believe that a 'formula of happiness' is out there that we may eventually discover to live happily ever after. Despite our rational doubts about the existence of such a formula, after a lifelong of trying and failing to find it, we still keep looking for it because deep down in our hearts we believe that we really *deserve* it. We believe that life is inherently meant to be happy; and that if we do not grasp happiness, it is merely due to our weakness and misfortune. However, our only fault might be our intentional delay or laziness to know our 'self.' We must realize that a relative sense of happiness may emerge only when our means and methods of living satisfy 'self' fully and permanently. Otherwise, there is no evidence that life can be a happy journey. Not everybody deserves happiness, either, especially when we adopt a doomed lifestyle to begin with. In our contaminated social environment, reaching the state of selfhood becomes impossible, since people have rampant superficial needs, materialistic mentality, and low self-awareness. Nonetheless, despite these severe limitations, we still hope that some general ideas about happiness may be drawn from people's life experiences and philosophies. While we realize that there is no standard formula for happiness, the discussions in this chapter are an attempt to establish some general guidelines for finding at least a sense of contentment.

What is referred to as the formula for happiness in this trilogy is merely a crude rendition of personal opportunities that might render peace of mind and freedom. Of course, everybody has a unique set of needs and aspirations, which makes a common perception of life or a universal formula for happiness more whimsical. Genetics, family background, and rearing result in personalities that value things differently and make judgments accordingly. Yet, the idea is to examine the possibility of inventing a process or framework that might guide us build a relaxed mindset, regardless of our genetics and perceptions of life. After all, humans' inherent urge to find happiness may not be totally baseless or useless.

Description of Happiness

It feels strange that an ultimate (or common) definition of 'happiness' has not yet been developed and agreed upon in the long history of humanity. All we have after all this time is only sporadic speculations by some philosophers and gurus. A great collection of happiness definitions can be found in *Happiness*, Perennial Books, 2014. Still, finding the right formula, to contain the complex feeling that our wild imagination of happiness suggests, has proven futile so far. We can perhaps describe some of the characteristics and sensations of happiness, as presented in the next section. Though, even such general descriptions would be incomplete for different types and intensity of happiness that people experience on different occasions and situations.

Overall, 'happiness' merely represents the highs of an emotional roller coaster that our lives ride on. We have learned that happiness is not a steady state, but rather some exotic stances across the dynamic (transient) flow of feelings. We are happy for a short while, before losing our tranquility and looking for it all over again. An absolute and permanent happiness is a myth and fantasy, especially within the rough modes of social living nowadays. A lasting happiness is not psychologically feasible, anyway, due to all kinds of conflicting thought processes and chemical reactions in our brains. Human nature also restricts our capacity for happiness, as explained in detail in the *Nature of Love and Relationships*. (See list of books by this author.) Yet, we hopeful humans cannot accept our helplessness to seize happiness as a permanent state and purpose for living. We hate suffering and boredom, so we strive to conquer happiness for good, once and for all. In fact, it does not hurt to imagine that an *absolute* and ultimate happiness is possible under some conditions outside the normal boundaries of human thoughts and wisdom. That is, at some level of wisdom, an ultimate happiness, without ongoing emotional highs and lows, may become plausible. Similar to our impression of the 'afterlife' myth, we can keep ourselves amused with the myth of happiness too.

'Happiness' Attributes

To describe happiness, we should explore, i) What happiness is—the 'feeling,' ii) What generates it—the 'cause,' iii) What it does to us—the 'impact,' and iv) What we do with it—the 'effect.'

The Feeling: The ultimate happiness is a deep inner feeling of joy, relief, tranquillity, lightness, self-satisfaction, self-fulfilment, transcendence, completeness, freedom, mental pleasure, needlessness, mental strength, independence, love, and a sense of mind-body interaction. Our happiness experiences may not be as complete as described by all these feelings, but rather entail a good bunch of them in good proportions. Yet, a complete happiness potentially contains all the above ingredients and more, in large proportions. Overall, happiness is the sign and sentiment of a freed spirit.

The Cause: Happiness manifests in different ways as a result of an achievement or discovery, a new joyful experience, after some physical pleasure, at the end of a depression cycle, upon removal of a burden, through passion, sudden hopefulness about something, recognition and psychological fulfilment, compassion and support, spirituality, etc.

The Impact: Happiness brings us a high level of energy and rejuvenation, courage, humanness, and we become more forgiving and tolerant of others. We feel our spirits lifted and our outlook on life improved drastically.

The effect: In general, when we are happy, we enjoy life much more and maintain our physical and psychological health better and longer. We are compassionate and affect the life of others more positively by bouncing off rays of hope, joy, and humour. A truly happy person has a high level of energy, creativity, and humanness, and transmits his compassion and joy to others through positive attitude and taking on more activities and responsibilities.

A true happiness experience must entail all these four attributes in full. That is, happiness is not only a 'feeling,' and a feeling of happiness is not an end in itself. The 'cause' of happiness determines the depth and longevity of the feeling. And the feeling itself initiates a chain of internal and external reactions that impact the person's health and attitude and consequently affect other events, things, and people that surround him. Our happiness experiences often seem incomplete and short-lived because one or more of its four attributes are missing or weak. Possibly the 'cause' has not been strong or legitimate. Or the 'feeling' has not been deep and deserved. Or the experience has no lasting 'impact' on us. And perhaps the 'effect' of our happiness is not adequately transmitted to other venues or people. These types of presumed happiness experiences, or tentative pleasures, are nice to have, but they are not deep and effective enough to consider a real happiness experience. For example, when we hear a joke, have casual sex, or find out that someone we hate is hurt, we feel happy for only a short period. On the other hand, a real happiness evolves only upon the completion of a full cycle of cause, feeling, impact, and effect. The stronger, more authentic, and fuller the cycle of the four elements, the longer and more effective the experience would be.

Along with the completeness of the four attributes of happiness, the frequency of happiness experiences is obviously important, too. Generally, the feeling of happiness fades away when the 'impact' and the 'effect' are no longer present. When we forget the impact of our happiness, maybe because the 'cause' of it has not been strong enough, and when we lose our energy to 'affect' others or things, the whole cycle stops and happiness ends. Therefore, we need the continuity of the cycle—the cause, the feeling, the impact, and the effect. A 'formula' of happiness is merely an attempt to stress the necessity of keeping this cycle active and vibrant. Only the high frequency and speed of the cycle may guarantee a longer-lasting happiness. Self-awareness is required to feed the cycle properly and permanently in order to prevent it from leakage and exhaustion.

The causes of happiness by themselves consist of those experiences and events that happen to a person accidentally, and those that he specially plans for. For example, winning a lottery is a less effective 'cause' for happiness compared to a personal achievement resulting from diligent planning and efforts. The first kind of 'cause,' which is merely a fluke, leads only to a short-term happiness, because in essence, the cause is often not strong and genuine enough and usually not driven by authentic personal urges. Of course, a lottery windfall makes the winner ecstatic for a short while. However, it is not a legitimate cause of happiness because the person has played no effective role in achieving the rewards. The impact of happiness would wear off quickly too, since the same winning experience hardly happens again. Even if it kept happening every week, its impact would vanish after a couple of weeks. Thus, the person must find other causes to stir the sense of inner happiness in him. He may be able to use his fortune wisely to stir opportunities that cause full cycles of happiness, but the new causes would be the real sources of feeding the cycle, not the initial cause, i.e., winning a lottery.

Overall, the initial efforts and intentions of the individual are crucial for creating a fulfilling and meaningful 'cause' of happiness. Besides, since the 'cause' of happiness is under his control, he can extend his efforts more consciously to recreate the outcomes that would repeat the same experiences of happiness. In effect, by doing the right kind of stuff on an ongoing basis, the person contributes directly and continuously to the recreation of happiness experiences. Thus, the old saying that, 'We create our own happiness,' with our intentional involvement and awareness of the process, especially controlling the 'cause' of happiness. The potency of the 'cause' determines the depth of the other three elements of happiness, i.e., feeling, impact, and effect.

With this basic description of happiness attributes in place, the next step is to explore how happiness materializes for people, and whether and how the depth of their happiness may relate to individual's personality. Correlating people's personality aspects (Model, Ego, Self) with happiness attributes (i.e., feeling, cause, impact, and effect) helps us understand the myth of happiness better. We find that most happiness experiences are not genuine, deep, and effective because the four happiness elements react differently according to the personality aspects of individuals experiencing them.

The Happiness of 'Model'

The 'model' aspect of personality is the practical face of a person attempting to hide his gullibility, neediness, fears, selfishness, Ego, and his psychological defects from others. Model satisfies most of our *social and belongingness needs* by trying to adapt to the rules of society and becoming part of it. It is the aspect that justifies our *actions and decisions* within ordained social norms, which Model is expected to know and conform to. It speaks and acts to impress others and obtain the psychological support we crave so desperately. Thus, the more Model emphasizes on satisfying our shallow needs for approval, belongingness, and social status, the more our higher needs, including self-esteem and self-realization, remain neglected.

Ordinarily, moving up the 'personal needs tree' boosts the cycles of happiness, as long as the individual is aiming for the opportunity of satisfying his self-actualization and spirituality needs. So, finding real happiness becomes impossible when an individual stops at a low level and keeps striving for the same lower need satisfaction repeatedly. Remaining stagnant at a low level is against Maslow's theory that presumes people understand, plan, and strive for their higher-level needs intuitively. Stagnation is against humans' basic instincts. In reality, however, it happens quite often as people do not know or care about their higher-level needs—mostly because their Model and medium-range needs keep them on a substandard path of life. Even if Model was not so dominant and we appreciated the ultimate needs of our being, we do not find time, or know how, to aim for satisfying our higher needs, e.g., spirituality.

Persisting at lower personal (psychological) needs, e.g., for love or social status, actually results in frustration since no amount of love and social status seems sufficient; and a small breakdown in their supply feels disastrous. Like some kind of addiction, our tentative happiness comes from satisfying our mental or physical dependency. Attached to this urgent and short-lived need satisfaction are anxiety and self-pity, as this habit creates only more craving and dependency on others.

The 'cause' of happiness for Model stems from other people's recognition of his work or attitude. Thus, even his tentative sense of happiness breaks repeatedly while he remains at the mercy of others. It is impossible for people to understand an individual and give him enough credit regularly for who he really is, let alone who he is pretending to be as a Model. In fact, people would see the superficiality of the Model eventually and the approval pipeline starts leaking again. Thus, he now must strive to find a new group of people to confirm his existence. This mental conundrum is never fixed until the person stops the pattern of feeding his addiction and begins moving up the ladder of the needs tree to gain some sense of independence.

We could be rude and consider a Model dominated personality a phony character with no originality and authenticity. We could even take him as a charlatan or hypocrite trying to manipulate others by pretending to be caring or compassionate. However, at best, he is a simpleton eluding his real identity in hopes of impressing others or hiding his idiosyncrasies. He strives to manage a secondary personality, which only reflects his apprehension about his primary personality or inability to build one. These inner conflicts for Model prevent the development of a legitimate 'cause' for happiness.

Sometimes, Model adopts a personality stronger and healthier than his primary (flawed) personality for improving himself. This is an honourable exercise and a great achievement if he succeeds internalizing some of the Self's traits through the Model he has adopted. This high achievement would provide a legitimate 'cause' of happiness for him. In such exceptional instances, the Model might help a person proceed toward independence and a 'self' dominated personality through self-awareness.

While some moderate Model is useful for social adaptation, etiquette, and coping, Model domination shows either a person's deep neediness or his immaturity and insecurities. A Model driven by immaturity imitates a personality with needs that are neither in line with his own nor authentic per se. He simply pursues some inferior needs just for playing the role of a particular model, e.g., as a gang member.

The 'impact' of Model's performance and achievements would be at best a tenuous happiness and thus not heartfelt. Often, his conscience turns against the Model and perhaps induces an internal resentment and competition with this fake personality. We may recall those instances where we did not feel so proud deep down in our hearts when in fact our Model was quite satisfied with the performance and outcome. For example, as part of the initiation in a fraternity or sorority, we may engage in activities that are normally not quite a part of our real character. We do things to get the acceptance of others. Afterward, we feel down and confused as our conscience asks why? Role-playing a Model, we tell our kids not to lie, but then do exactly the same thing ourselves, sometimes even in front of them.

A Model feels excited and happy when he makes up stories about his wisdom or courage to get the respect of his family and others. However, the Self, observing the masquerade from inside, knows how cowardly he has twisted the facts to serve his Ego. Happiness of Model is thus shaky because the person knows that he is only serving his Ego with no Self respect or satisfaction.

The success in selling 'who one pretends to be' presumably constitute a Model's cause of happiness. If the outcome is effective enough and repeatable, it would only encourage the person to pursue the needs of Model and depress his own (ones that are more natural) even further. The 'cause' of happiness is weak, anyway, but still those repeated tentative happy instances encourage the person to reinforce the 'model' personality and thus accelerate the destruction of his real personality, or jeopardizes the possibility of growing a more authentic and independent character.

The tentative rewards that Model receives for adaptation and approval do not serve him in the long run anyway. A Model is always running the risk of being exposed to others sooner or later, often when he becomes most popular and attached to the incentives and causes of his happiness, which he is now quite addicted to and counting on. During this process, he continues to quarrel within himself—with his deprived real nature, which he is personally trying so hard to suppress. Like any actor that often loses his own identity by playing the role of a character continuously, a Model gets confused about who he really is. The more a person is successful as a 'model' personality, the faster he is detached and alienated from his inner needs and instincts. He often learns to like what he is, or is doing, as a Model, while he would increasingly feel anxious without knowing why.

A Model often transforms into a happy-go-lucky person, due to the effect of positive thinking propagandas and the social appeal to always portray a positive attitude. Yet, deep down, he often feels unhappy, frustrated, unfulfilled, and tired of playing games all the time. Constant doubting of one's identity subconsciously does not bring a healthy lifestyle for anybody. However, it is even worse for a Model, because his disguise becomes superficial and ineffective faster if he cannot portray the positive reflection of a truly happy person constantly regardless of how he really feels. Sometimes, we are bound to keep a happy face to pretend we like our jobs, are happy with our relationships, to appear tactful and respectful, etc. Perhaps there is not much harm in keeping a happy face as a gesture of mannerism and social behaviour to the extent that we do not get absorbed into this superficiality deeply. As another exception noted before, using Model to reinforce our inner needs and reach selfhood (and perhaps a natural sense of optimism) is an honourable and productive process.

Sometimes, a person keeps switching from one Model to a different Model, hoping to find his real niche. He usually switches when he does not get what he had expected from a Model or because he becomes frustrated after playing the role of that Model for a while. When a person fails to play a role properly, or when people detect his shallow personality, he must find a new mask. The mental health of the person switching from Model to Model suffers even more than the case of a person who has a more stable role to play, even as a Model. There would be no deep 'cause' of happiness in a cycle like this, as the person becomes highly confused about his identity and mission in life when he switches the role model and disappointments mount with every switch. A simple version of this situation is when a person cannot decide on a career and switches between jobs and every time finds a reason to quit. He cannot figure out his real vocational needs (and potentialities).

The 'cause' of happiness, e.g., getting approval and acceptance, not only undermines his authentic needs toward self-fulfilment, but also encourages him to become more phony and shallow every day. His time and energy are wasted on goals ineffective for his psychological growth or improving his idiosyncrasies. Of course, the underlying reason for being a Model is his insecurity and immaturity in the first place. Thus, he is unaware or careless about his other personal needs beyond the needs of the Model anyway. In fact, his urge to repeat the same experience to stay happy only reinforces his conscious or subconscious efforts to suppress his instincts even deeper and run away from his real needs faster. Accordingly, Model is less likely to ask 'who am I?', because he keeps justifying to himself why he likes to be somebody else.

In all, for a Model, the 'cause' of happiness is something or somebody, which he generally has no, or very little, control over. When the 'cause' of happiness remains so shaky and irrelevant for Model, the other elements of happiness, i.e., the 'feeling', 'impact', or 'effect,' always remain too tentative too.

The 'feeling' of happiness is shallow and usually offset by the constant, subconscious fear of losing the momentum when the effect of his pretensions wears off. The happiness cannot make a major 'impact' on him since the presumed rewards are irrelevant for realizing his higher psychological needs. And obviously, a

Model cannot 'affect' others (especially people with low Model orientation) positively as he cannot connect to anybody truthfully. Even when he does something for someone, it would be insincere and only out of fear of losing that person's approval, or for satisfying a selfish purpose, e.g., manipulating someone, or he is simply trying to conform to some rules just to maintain his status, e.g., his job. And, of course, the cycle of happiness itself is often impaired quickly in the case of a Model, when the approval and acceptance channels dry up even temporarily.

It is interesting, and sad, how our social values and environments encourage Model attitude (compliance and hypocrisy) in particular. And it is even more interesting how, in fact, Model personalities help satisfy the dependency needs of one another by promoting phony social values and norms, despite their knowledge of the low sincerity and integrity of the words they exchange. By giving and receiving compliments, Models support one another's psychological needs for external approval and social status as an end in itself. Like an addiction, a Model craves attention although he knows it is phony and perhaps even a means of being exploited. Salespeople know this weakness of Models (in the general public) and use it to the extreme. Models usually say things differently in the presence and absence of a person, which often is a sign of both their hypocrisy and desperation. Unfortunately, 'model' oriented personalities are increasing in society and they are pushing phonier social values and behaviour too. Therefore, we find more depression in society than real happiness.

The Happiness of 'Ego'

The 'ego' aspect of personality handles our value systems, judgments and punishments, senses of competition and superiority, desires and expectations. It reflects the *real intentions* of our words and actions, and our *reactions* to other people's words and actions. An egoist is self-centred with extreme expectations and narrow perceptions of others, and he is harsh in his judgments and punishments with a dramatically biased value system. Ego is an exact opposite to Model in many ways, especially frankness, impatience, and pomposity. Therefore, a person's Model and Ego often clash and cause extra headaches for him. However, they also help each other, e.g., when Ego uses Model as a strategy to manipulate another person.

Unlike Model, an egoist's needs often extend across all levels of the personal needs tree. In particular, he is too ambitious with a high need for achievement and recognition. He has an extreme need for control and doing things his way. Yet, his achievements remain non-actualizing because his self-serving objectives usually supersede the sense of purity and selflessness that self-actualization requires. Therefore, while an egoist may have many experiences of achievement and thrill, they are seldom actualizing and they hardly cause lasting happiness.

An egoist attempts to use a scheme or his charm (through Model) for attracting and exploiting others. However, an egoist does not have the patience and motivation of a Model to attract people merely for the sake of friendship. If his hidden intentions are not satisfied quickly through pretensions of Model, he gets frustrated and resorts to a different strategy, e.g., aggression, to satisfy his important and urgent need for self-gratification.

The Ego's 'cause' of happiness relates to the outcome of his selfish actions and intentions. He works hard to serve his Ego for the highest level of thrill and satisfaction. He must keep boosting his Ego to feel happy, mostly by getting things done in the *manner* he desires, which is often more important than the outcome itself. He can forget his failures and forgive himself quickly as long as he succeeds in making everybody follow his lead. He is convinced that his judgments are always fair, logical, and appropriate. When he seems to compromise, he is simply using Model for manipulation and exploitations.

An egoist is stubborn and certain about all the *facts* in the world. He believes he knows everything and has the answers for all the problems, while others are ignorant and inferior to him in logic and vision. His high expectations from others and himself usually remain unfulfilled because his goals are unrealistic, his expectations from others are more selfish than rational, his directions are too rigid, and individuals' Egos clash all the time. Simply due to his demanding personality, seldom an egoist gets satisfied with either the outcomes or the means of achieving them.

Egoists' inflated Ego and inherent drive for gratification push them to take risk and set tough (and often unrealistic) objectives. However, their needs for control and self-importance stop them from putting their guards down to find contentment and their Self. They have wrong perceptions about the means of satisfying their needs, especially the higher ones for which a true self-actualizer must depend merely on himself instead of exploiting others to get things done.

An egoist's 'cause' of happiness also relates to other people's reactions to his expectations. Often his happiness is at the expense of those whom he exploits. It depends on someone else's submission and willingness to play along with his game of exploitation and manipulation. Naturally, in most cases this expectation cannot last long and causes many frictions.

An egoist's 'feeling' of happiness comes from shallow short-lived gratifications, because his objectives are self-serving and often achieved by pushing others. Therefore, he must keep manipulating others and struggle for more signs and symbols of achievements to boost his Ego and maintain his shaky cycles of happiness. The more he depends on people to achieve certain goals, the more he must feed this cycle (by pushing others) to maintain the momentum. Even his tentative satisfaction from his achievements merely boosts his Ego rather than soothing his soul. He is *ruled* by his Ego and lives to satisfy it—a never-ending struggle to preserve his pompous identity.

His shallow feelings of happiness cannot 'impact' him, as he has no time or patience to stop and contemplate on his fulfilments and their true meanings. He often does not even know, or care about, the real purposes of his struggles while he follows certain routines aggressively. Artificial objectives, such as maximizing wealth and power, justify all his struggles. His triumphs have no relationship to his essential and inherent needs. And of course, when he is unaware of the relationship between his needs and triumphs, he can never internalize his achievements. Thus, the rewards and fulfilments cannot impact him deeply. The only 'impact' of his fulfilments is his eagerness to repeat his mischievous and exploitative activities that boost his Ego and give him some wicked feelings of satisfaction.

Accordingly, he has no ability to affect others either, except for the burdens of his manipulative attitude that intimidate others. Thus, for an egoist whose fulfilments come at the expense of hurting others, the 'effect' of his accomplishments is negative. Egoists' plans and actions are always calculating and self-serving for specific personal interests, either for an immediate benefit or future exploitation. Doing things for the sake of 'affecting' others positively does not mean anything to an egoist unless it has some advantage for him personally, and this scenario seldom happens.

The cycle of happiness for an 'egoist' is too short and thus s/he requires extreme momentum to maintain even a tentative sense of happiness. Otherwise, frustration and stress take over quickly. A tremendous level of effort is required to feed the cycle and still real happiness is hard to maintain.

Establishing a working relationship with others is extremely difficult for an egoist even when s/he tries to use his/her Model. Particularly, establishing a mutually acceptable marital relationship and teamwork atmosphere would be very difficult for egoists. Volume III of this trilogy discusses some of the implications of egotistical family quarrels and competitions between partners to keep the upper hand in their relationships. These kinds of games and attitudes are, unfortunately, prevalent and somehow even encouraged in our societies as a means of establishing partners' individuality. They lead to constant psychological struggles that hinder partners' communication and happiness. Work environments are becoming quite difficult to tolerate, too, due to the rising number of egoists and psychopaths running organizations nowadays. The negative effects of these people's managerial style have brought the level of social stress to a record high.

The Happiness of 'Self'

'Self' is that aspect of personality that holds our basic instincts, feelings, and needs, including spirituality. It holds our potentialities, genius, creativity, and psychic energy. This aspect of our personality also contains our innocence, conscience, and regrets. Self is our *real being* outside the conditioning rules of society, aside from the value systems that we have decided to adopt and adapt ourselves to. Perhaps a symbolic representation of Self can be found in Tarzan whose instincts and feelings are intact and pure. However, Tarzan is merely a raw picture of Self while his potentialities and spirituality dimensions remain untapped.

We all meditate in some form, either consciously or subconsciously, to get close to our Self, although we often know very little about the meaning of Self or the means of reaching that pure state of being. When we go to church, mosque, or a shrine to speak to our Gods, we are doing some form of meditation to contact our Self—our soul. We need to do this meditation, at least in private, in order to heal our physical and psychological hurts from living. We need to go somewhere in Nature alone and think, quiet our minds and understand what our inner voices are saying. These are the basic experiences of Self that most of us have enjoyed at least a few times. However, on most occasions, we do not recognize and appreciate them as a device for entering our most intimate, yet neglected, state of natural being and for finding some relative freedom at least. We bypass the opportunity to delve into our Selfhood after a short pause at the entrance every time we meditate.

Contrary to the situations for Model and Ego that require external stimuli for approaching some form of happiness, the happiness of Self is automatic. The only requirement is to acknowledge the Self that is within every one of us ready to be explored and nurtured. It is surely not a straightforward and easy task, but it is possible to get at least a little acquainted with Self. The first step is to believe in the possibility of being a better human being for our own sake at least and then learn how. Afterward, we can use the power of Self to overcome the negative influences of Model and Ego at any opportunity. Every time we let Self overcome the Ego's or Model's attempt to taint our deeds and decisions, we get one step closer to realizing Self. It cannot happen overnight, but with practice and active meditation, we can give our Self the power to overrule Model and Ego when they try to dominate our existence and behaviour.

How is the happiness of Self automatic? And how happiness attributes, i.e., cause, feeling, impact, and effect apply to Self?

The 'causes' of happiness for Self are several. The main cause, which is perhaps less tangible to people with no or little experience of Self, comes from the achievement of being a Self dominated personality per se. We can imagine how a caged animal feels once it escapes. We know how much risk and trouble prisoners are willing to endure to find a way to flee. Reaching Self dominance resembles these experiences of freedom, except that finding Self would be even a more meaningful and permanent experience. Once a person learns to recognize and free his Self from the captivity of Model and Ego, he enters the world of eternal peace and tranquillity in which happiness is automatic. There is no need to feed a cycle of happiness in order to maintain it, as long as one stays in the kingdom of Selfdom. The happiness of Self is inherent. Merely our superficial needs and the influence of Ego and Model suffocate this natural source of happiness.

There is no need to discuss the other 'causes' of happiness of Self when the main cause is so prominently adequate. Yet, some other elements of happiness for a Self-driven person are interesting to discuss.

A Self dominated person finds the opportunity and strength to realize humans' essential (but hidden) potentialities. By saving the energies normally wasted by Model and Ego, Self focuses on the means of actualizing himself. He concentrates on thoughts and activities that nurture the real nature of a person rather than the ones that hurt and destroy his physical and mental abilities. Generating valuable ideas, exploring the creative domains of mind, and maintaining the vision of a universal existence, provide happiness experiences that replace, or at least mitigate, the mundane tasks of living and surviving. The purpose of one's being becomes vivid and meaningful. Simple thoughts and activities derived from the energies of the inner 'self' turn into self-actualizing and spiritual experiences. Oneness with the universe that rules our being manifests as unique moments of ecstasy and experiences beyond the meanings of the worldly pleasures. These are some other 'causes' of happiness of Self.

A 'self' dominated person does not depend on outside world to induce a 'cause' of happiness. He finds the sources of fulfilment without exploiting others and expecting approvals from other people. He is not threatened by the punishments of the power-thirsty authorities of our world, nor does he care about the luring rewards of compliance. He is neither attached to the worldly values that control him, nor detached of the harmonic worldly relationships that complement his being and co-existence. The challenge for maintaining this delicate balance constitutes some other 'causes' of happiness for Self.

All these 'causes' of happiness are Self-directed and not controllable by outsiders. Therefore, the happiness generated through these experiences is manageable much better by the individual and remain more consistent and repeatable by him. He is in control of the 'causes.'

The 'feelings' of happiness, which are induced by self-controlled 'causes,' prolong rather continuously, and they are authentic and deep, with a lasting impact. There are hardly any interruptions in the 'causes and feelings.' In fact, for a Self-driven personality, the 'feelings' and 'causes' are usually the same thing, because the cause of happiness is inherent for Self, as noted earlier. This natural property gives the whole cycle of happiness more momentum, intensity, and continuity. Maslow's descriptions of self-actualizers' feelings provide great evidence of how deep those sensations are, and how they directly relate to, and connect with, the causes. (See quotes in the previous chapters, especially Chapter Four.)

The 'impacts' of Self-controlled happiness are fundamental and coincide with the 'cause-feeling' interconnectivity. The impacts are psychological, spiritual, and a source of deep tranquillity.

The 'effects' are also paramount and continuous. A 'self' dominated person has a different view of people, events and things. In particular, he has a great deal of compassion toward everybody despite his profound knowledge of people's inherent impurity and frequent malice. He feels connected to the whole universe and knows that he is an inseparable part of it, including all the badness within and outside him. Therefore, everything he does is automatically and directly affecting other things and people in a positive way, simply because they reinforce his own 'cause' of happiness. To him, the give and take are the same thing and have the same meaning and effect. In all, the four elements of happiness have an integrated and integral interconnectivity that drive a cycle of permanent and self-nurturing happiness experiences. This cycle accelerates even faster once one's ability of utilizing the potentials of Self are largely developed.

Personality Aspects' Role for Happiness

The above discussions of the three aspects of personality suggest that happiness can happen only to Self. The happiness of the other personality aspects is at best shallow and temporary. Usually one or two of a person's three aspects of personality overwhelm the other(s). We may remember many evidences supporting the dominance of a particular personality aspect over others during our interactions and relationships. Overall, however, we usually do not detect enough of our own Model or Ego the same way we notice them so quickly in other people. This low awareness about ourselves is in line with our general tendency to ignore our psychological defects unless we make a point of exploring them. We simply deny our Model and Ego despite the comments and clues we receive from others as well as our own conscience.

We do not believe or admit that we are anything but a pure Self. We do not like to admit that our prominent Model prevents us from understanding who we are and what our purpose of living is. We would never accept the idea of our strong Ego depriving us from sensing compassion and having a tranquil and happy life. Obviously, until we acknowledge these sad facts, we would not find the courage and incentive to study our Self. Unless we admit that we have become slaves to Model and Ego, we would never believe in any of the suggestions about Self and happiness.

We hate to admit that our weaknesses and unhappiness in life are the result of letting Model and Ego run our lives. Even if we get the courage to admit it to ourselves, we have a hard time taming these crooked aspects within us. How would a Model or Ego consider adopting a more 'self' controlled personality? Initially, he would not even have an idea what being a Self means, how it works, what it requires, etc. However, realistically, if he is going to give up, or at least tame, his Model or Ego, he would first require a tangible understanding of Self and the way he should act and behave from within this aspect of his personality. He is estranged to Self, and actually, his Self has never had a chance to grow. Without a relatively comprehensive grasp of Self, the switch would be impossible regardless of our efforts. Playing Self (e.g., as a Good Samaritan) without understanding its meaning is merely another attempt for building a different Model personality. To remain realistic, the switch to selfhood must be gradual and in line with one's appreciation and practice of a Self-controlled life.

This book talks about 'self' in different dimensions and from different angles. In essence, 'self' is one of the main themes of this trilogy, as it emerges frequently in all the topics and chapters. In particular, the seven basic elements of 'self' are discussed in Chapter Two of Volume II. We try in different ways to explain what 'self' really means, how we can find it in ourselves, and how we need to use its potentialities to make our lives tolerable and perhaps happy. Still, at the end, what this book can offer is only a general idea of what 'self' really is. Everybody must explore it individually and maybe find a personal interpretation of 'self' in terms of definition and application, though the same source of energy manifests and directs us through life. Therefore, an ultimate definition of 'self,' or how exactly it leads to happiness is somewhat personal. Just by trying to become a better human being would get us there. Detecting and defusing our Ego and Model bring out the Self automatically.

The degree and depth of our happiness depend on the varying prominence of Model, Ego, and Self at any time, and thus our happiness experiences find different qualities and properties. We have *a kind of* multiple personalities due to an aspect of our personality becoming more dominant in various instants. This also indicates that expecting a continuous happiness mood is almost impossible even for a Self dominated person. Although a Self-controlled personality has the highest chance of carrying a tranquil and happy life, still the other two aspects of his personality emerge occasionally in small doses. When Model or Ego takes over temporarily, even a 'self' dominated person thinks and behaves erratically. The firmer his Self-control, the less frequent

Model or Ego finds a chance to interfere. Nonetheless, the random dominance of Model or Ego is normal. We should expect moments of distress even when we have a genuine Self dominated personality. There are several reasons for these moments of weakness erupting.

First, our temporary switch to Model or Ego, as a requirement of coping and living, might cause experiences that ruin all our previous triumphs and thus lead to a sense of discomfort and delusion. For example, we might submit to adultery or some other mischief in a moment of weakness. This experience brings a cycle of depression that overrides an enduring cycle of happiness. Our conscience might bother us for a long time.

Second, it is possible that occasionally we neglect to attend to our Self. Although the happiness cycle for Self is automatic and self-nurturing, remaining a 'self' dominated person demands constant *awareness*. If we forget our need for ongoing meditation and development of Self, the 'self'-control process stops, Model and Ego take over, and the happiness cycle breaks.

Third, even for a 'self' dominated person, moments of doubts and questioning erupt, especially when it becomes necessary to adapt himself to social demands and get along with people. During those moments of self-doubt we question our choices and paths, we think about our sanity and philosophy of life, we think about our responsibilities and financial obligations, we suffer from our solitude and loneliness, we think about our relationships that we are hoping to 'self'-control, etc. Under these circumstances, we are psychologically vulnerable and undergo a state of mild depression, if not something more serious.

Nevertheless, some inconsistencies in the level of our happiness should be expected, even for a 'self' dominated person. Developing 'self'-control becomes important for managing these irregularities in our lives, too. The more we grasp and practise a 'self' dominated life, the better we can cope with, and defeat, the periods of temporary distress or doubts.

CHAPTER SEVEN
Personality and Depression

Understanding the role of personality aspects in creating happiness experiences is only half of our challenge. The other half pertains to our ability to endure depression cycles. Happiness and depression are contending forces that compete and clash in our psyches all the time. Therefore, our search for happiness is futile when some sneaky forces of depression bombard us. They are either generated internally from within us, maybe not even consciously, or imposed upon us by outside sources. We should understand the nature of these two sources of depressions and mitigate their impacts. However, our personality is responsible for creating most of our depression and suffering. While Self stirs happiness, personality causes depression.

Thus, depression should also be measured in reference to the three aspects of personality, i.e., Model, Ego, and Self even more closely than 'happiness' was dissected in the previous chapter. In particular, every aspect of personality plays a different role in creating self-induced depressions. They also have different strengths for fighting the forces of depressions from outside sources, such as social, financial, and relationships. Furthermore, the same elements of happiness, i.e., cause, feeling, impact, and effect, apply equally to depression. Therefore, we can evaluate the forces of depression from within the same framework, i.e., by gauging the effect of each aspect of personality on the four elements of depression.

We should actually study two issues about our depression according to the three aspects of the personality: First, we must find out how each of these personality aspects generates self-induced depression. Second, we must study how a person dominated with any one of these personality aspects deals with depressions caused by inner (personal) or outer sources.

The Depression of 'Model'

The self-induced depression of Model accumulates inherently from his inability to move up the 'personal needs tree' and fulfil his higher needs, including spirituality. He is not quite aware of those needs and that his neglect to satisfy them hinders his psychological growth and self-image. Yet lack of fulfilment creates boredom, which is obviously a hidden source of depression for everybody. Not knowing the real sources of his boredom, about his higher needs, and how to attend to them, are the 'causes' of his depression. Furthermore, his needs for approval, love, and sense of belonging cause him stress and self-pity when they do not happen enough in reality or he doubts their authenticity. He gets disappointed with himself and others, so he continues to develop new tactics to get the love and approval he needs so desperately. He tries to play his role as a Model more precisely and effectively and thus becomes phonier. He exhausts himself by wasting all his energy seeking attention and recognition instead of dealing with his authentic inner needs. All these strenuous efforts and reactions are hidden causes of self-induced depression.

The depth of depression is the highest for Model, as he feels too helpless without a large dose of external attention on a regular basis. His only sense of psychological security in life is given to him by outsiders. He must try hard to maintain this safety net.

Therefore, he ignores his other psychological urges in order to concentrate on these low-level needs. This incessant struggle (strategies and activities) for acceptance and love by itself reinforces the cycles of depression vigorously and frequently and makes the task of self-redemption too difficult.

With respect to 'externally induced' depressions, Model is quite vulnerable, because he is always extremely anxious to cope with external forces and fit within society rather like an obsession. The 'causes' of his depression relate to any of social, financial, political, or relationship problem that he seems unable to solve. When there is a problem in one or more of these areas, it means that there is a conflict between a Model's *urgent* expectations and what he actually gets. This conflict to Model usually means rejection or his inability to adapt. He takes the matter too personal, due to low self-image and high oversensitivity. He feels defeated, misunderstood, and ignored, especially considering all his efforts to be loved and understood. Somebody or some mechanism is not taking his efforts or his needs seriously. It does not matter how in practice he deals with these external sources of his depression. He may take a legal action, retaliate against his companion or spouse, try to become more accommodating, leave the company he is working for, etc. The important point is that internally he has to deal with the pressures of coping and possible rejections, which he has a hard time accepting as a reality of life.

Model's high expectations for being always understood and accepted hardly match reality, while he also naively over-trusts human nature. Thus, he faces a major dilemma often when people's reactions seem odd and unfair to him/her. A rejection, in whatever form, is extremely personal and unbearable for him emotionally, even more than it may hurt his Ego, and thus results in a deep depression. As expected, Model is mentally prepared to hide the setbacks and his emotions, instead of confronting his opponents assertively. Actually, Model develops a strong defence mechanism to take rejections lightly on the surface and jump to other opportunities to satisfy his need for acceptance and approval. Yet, every rejection brings him deep depression, plus the added pressures of hiding his frustration. Thus, he suffers for it internally longer than if he somehow dealt with his depression and people's aggression more assertively or just ignored it rather stoically.

The cause, feeling, impact, and effect of depression for both types of self-induced and imposed depressions follow the same pattern. The 'causes' of his depression are numerous as delineated throughout this section. The 'feelings' of depression are quite deep and devastating for Model, although he attempts to appear calm and collected for playing his role (as part of Model). The 'impact' and 'effect' of such depression are obviously harsh and harmful to him and other people around him. It is very likely that his oversensitivity and repeated rejections (two other causes of his depression by themselves) lead to low self-image, self-loathing, and passive aggression, which he would also try to hide and control as much as possible. Signs of his neediness for attention and affection also show in his sudden, occasional outburst or even his pretentious show of compassion. The irony is that, with spreading negative 'effects' on others, as a result of his neediness and smothered depression, he annoys the same people he depends on for love. He turns gradually into an oversensitive person who expects unconditional attention and love, but is often incapable of providing true compassion to others despite his pretensions. People usually have a hard time dealing with these ultra sensitive individuals and odd (uncomfortable) situations that emerge from such interactions. In general, everybody has difficulty finding the right level of Model to adapt and get adequate approval without becoming too needy and rejected.

The Depression of 'Ego'

The self-induced depression of Ego is caused by his inability to achieve enough of his goals and expectations, in terms of not only results, but also the *means* of attaining them. He becomes extremely agitated and depressed anytime his plans fall through or somebody resists, or forgets, to do what he demands. Furthermore, Ego regularly attracts conflict and contradiction. S/he likes to control everybody and every situation and gets depressed often because controlling others and events are both difficult and unreasonable expectations. There are always arguments and clashes of Egos among individuals, leading to frustrating situations and the loss of a great deal of energy and productivity. Ego does not forgive and forget. He does not accept even an occasional submission, i.e., blaming himself instead of others. Every discussion, competition, battle, transaction, and simple matter that he is involved with has to end in a 'win' situation for him, but more importantly a 'loss' for somebody else. When this is not the case, he gets anxious and depressed. In addition, since he is mainly preoccupied with 'winning and success' instead of 'learning and contribution,' he has a hard time exploring his self-actualization potentialities and needs. He may continue to win and feel successful, but also builds up a great deal of stress and anxiety, because he cannot internalize the meaning of a real achievement. He feels depressed and empty, in spite of all the symbols of winning and success surrounding him. His successes are not heartfelt and 'self' satisfying, because they are not selfless and authentic. S/he might hide or dismiss his/her inner conflicts and lack of deep satisfaction, but the depression of his/her psyche keeps building up. These are some of the major 'causes' of the self-induced depression for an Ego-driven personality.

The externally generated depression of Ego is similarly due to his expectations not being fulfilled and the clashes of his Ego with the demands, shortfalls, and Egos of other members of the society or organizations. He has a hard time having a simple conversation without the interference of Ego and an inevitable contradiction or clash.

Therefore, for Ego, the causes of both self-induced and externally induced depressions are also very much the same. They both result from expectations not met and competitions not won. His depression experiences are caused either when he is trying to exploit others and they resist (self-induced), or when others are imposing their own rules and expectations that do not appeal to him and thus become Ego-threatening (externally induced).

The 'feelings' of depression are severe and recur frequently due to the pressures on him/her to fulfil a wide range of his/her needs in peculiar ways through selfish schemes. Ego must make continuous efforts to push others for some (often unreasonable) goals, excel in everything, and win all the competitions, even when the rewards are not significant or the issues are not important. As these egotistical schemes and processes go on constantly, the rewards and disappointments are also recurring with a high frequency. The 'feelings' of fulfilment and depression are thus hitting him continuously based on the outcome of each experience. They are exhausting and depressing. It would be like a gambler becoming happy with every hand he wins and depressed with every hand he loses. At the end, the whole cycle of happiness-depression feelings becomes a nerve-racking loop and more of a stressful mechanism even when the cycle is at its height during a happiness experience. The psyche anticipates the depressions that may come tomorrow or the next second, and also remembers the depressions of yesterday(s).

The 'impact' of depression experiences and cycles on the person is obvious. The nervous breakdowns, neurosis, stress and heart attacks, which are sweeping us our feet in large numbers every day, are mostly the impacts of endless depression cycles and experiences caused by Ego. The 'effect' is also obvious. The amount of pressures we are putting on one another with our Egos continuously is simply killing our spirits, not to mention the stress and exhaustion they cause. In families, in work places, in our simplest transactions, and every time that we get into action or interact, our Egos interfere. What could we expect the 'effect' of a neurotic or overanxious person be on others, other than causing more damage to this vicious cycle of impacting self and affecting others adversely every day, to what disastrous end—only God may know.

The Depression of 'Self'

The self-induced depressions of Self are caused by his regrets about personal impurities that he is incapable of controlling while living in a chaotic environment. Self feels sad about the impurity of human nature, especially when friends and family members keep disappointing him more often than not. Self gets sad when he feels helpless in expressing himself and when his Model and Ego take charge temporarily, while Self feels obliged to keep them in check. We suffer, consciously or subconsciously, when Self, which is our conscience in this sense, fails to restrain Ego and Model. When our innocence is threatened, Self becomes depressed. When our potentialities are not effectively utilized, Self feels empty, unfulfilled and depressed. And when our spirituality needs are not satisfied, Self feels lonely, unprotected, helpless, and depressed.

The externally induced depressions come from the environments that Self is expected to adapt to. The realities of social living initially restrict the growth of Self. However, more importantly, these socioeconomic and political environments enforce the kind of value systems and conditions unacceptable to the integrity of Self. There is always a conflict between what these environments expect from a person and what his Self can submit to.

For both cases of self-induced and externally induced depressions, the 'causes' are merely the symptoms of social living that are mostly out of one's control. Yet, despite the limited power to induce change, Self has a much better capability to absorb the waves of depression without getting infected. While there are experiences of depression, the 'feelings' of depression are mild, infrequent, and manageable. This is because Self (that is perhaps partially aware due to a person's conscience) recognizes the 'causes' of depression as weaknesses of his personality (the Self in the process of development). Self realizes that these weaknesses are impossible to bypass and ignore completely due to the realities of social living. Self knows that these mild depressions are natural during the process of growth. During the transition from the *perceived* world to the *real* world—the process of cleansing our illusions—depressions are the results of our regrets for past mistakes and memories. We may never get the chance to become hundred percent purified as an absolute Self, which means some depressions always resurface due to our vulnerabilities and sense of human impurity. However, the intensity is low and Self is aware of its nature, cause, and healing effect. When Self knows the reasons of his depressions, he uses this information to heal itself rather than store it as a psychological hurt.

Therefore, for Self, even the impact of a depression experience is more of a learning and healing nature, rather than an obstacle along the cycle of happiness experiences. We may say that the 'impacts' of a depression experience for Self are more positive than negative. In fact, these experiences may help the growth of Self, as they reinforce the process of self-control, creation, and meditation. During these periods, we learn a great deal about our true potentialities and creativity in line with our finer impressions of the universe, Nature, and our existence.

The 'effects' of depression experiences are at the very least neutral for a Self personality. Usually, a depression experience leads to a temporary withdrawal and meditation. During this period, Self does not deal with others and issues, but rather concentrates on the 'cause' and 'feeling' of the experience and tries to learn a lesson and build more stamina and creativity. After a period of solitude, Self emerges with much more energy, compassion, and wisdom that can only have positive effects on others.

Depression experiences are too pervasive and powerful because they occur regularly to every aspect of personality separately or concurrently. We feel depressed too often because one or more of our personality aspects may be hurt at any time when its unique needs and urges are jeopardized. Depression experiences also have different implications for each of the three aspects of personality in the long run. Model and Ego depressions have extreme repercussions on both the person himself and people around him. For Self, however, a depression cycle is mostly a learning and healing opportunity that keeps helping the person achieve his objective of Self-control faster.

One danger of depression lies in the fact that people do not understand its nature and source and thus have difficulty analysing it. Therefore, they simply suffer more and accept depression as a reality of living. A depression attack should in fact be viewed as a warning signal to pause and find its source realistically by relating it to a specific personality aspect and the underlying message coming from it. Understanding its source, internal or external, is important too.

The Happiness/Depression Cycles

The cycles of happiness and depression clash regularly and lead to additional personal frustration and stress. Even small events, e.g., someone's simple whining, spoils our mood and often even ends a happiness cycle prematurely. We feel these mood swings regularly and yet do not stop to grasp the important life lessons they offer. For one thing, we ignore the simple fact that controlling the sources of our ongoing, self-induced depressions is more important than looking for that elusive happiness. We forget that our own raw ambitions, obsessions, idiosyncrasies, phobia, and uptightness prevent us from feeling peace and happiness. We look for shallow pleasures to suffocate our depression instead of learning to understand the real source and message of any depression.

In Chapter Six, we set out to explore the possibility of finding a meaningful and lasting formula of happiness. We are going to conclude here with the single note that, "Unless we build a 'self'-control mechanism to at least monitor our ongoing cycles of depression and assess their causes, the idea of finding happiness is obscure and unattainable."

The four elements of 'cause,' 'feeling,' 'impact,' and 'effect' of a happiness or depression experience determine its nature and longevity. Happiness experiences last when 'self' is dominant and we are free from our wicked thoughts and urges. Conversely, depression comes more often when we are serving the needs of Model and Ego.

Nonetheless, we face a major dilemma all our lives: On the one hand, we are limiting our chances for real happiness experiences by empowering Model and Ego beyond the minimum role they must play in a healthy lifestyle. We just do not see or care how they are keeping us from achieving happiness while we struggle with our greed-laden ambitions and fantasies. On the other hand, overcoming the urges of Model and Ego, especially in a crooked environment like ours, is definitely not easy. We cannot grasp and revive the obscure, weakened Self quickly to fight off the wicked Ego and Model. We need self-awareness first and then patience, practice, evaluation, and growth. Only when we recognize Model and Ego as obstacles, we have a better chance of defeating them and revamping their roles in our lives and decisions.

Finding the ultimate happiness is an idealistic objective, anyway, and yet, we may get at least a glimpse of it if we can curb the incessant cycles of depression. This is a huge challenge, which makes ultimate happiness an extremely high expectation for common people who are driven mainly by their Models and Egos. We need an absolute 'self'-driven life and personality to escape the perils of the socioeconomic and political environments, and even so, it would be an impractical and imprudent practice. We cannot remain unaffected by the inefficiencies, ineffectiveness, corruptions, and abuses of socioeconomic systems and authorities that we elect to run our countries and communities. The entire democratic process is screwed up even in developed countries while the rich rules the means of controlling people's minds and votes. We have to get involved and we are eventually forced to play their games to defeat them when necessary. We cannot confront Model and Ego driven individuals merely by our Self. Our bureaucratic systems and organizations are also the exact replicas and representations of the 'model' and 'ego' personalities (the executives) that are running and controlling those organizations. We will be crushed quickly within the Ego-driven mechanisms and destroyed under the influence of Model oriented societies instantly. At best, we would be isolated and rejected. It is too late to be a Mahatma Gandhi or Nelsen Mandela.

Choosing and maintaining the right balance of personality aspects is a daunting personal issue and choice. We need to use as much of the 'self' aspect of our personality to attain some level of happiness, and at the same time, we need some 'model' and 'ego' aspects to help us survive in this chaotic social order. What is the right mix? How much should we be threatened and feel insecure by our basic survival needs, i.e., financial and economic pressures and organization demands, etc.? And how much happiness can we really bring to ourselves by leaning more toward our Self? These are major life decisions that we must make, particularly at the younger age, for building the foundation of our thoughts and life philosophy. We face these dilemmas throughout our lives, anyway. All along, we change our minds, preferences, and criteria regularly to adapt, and thus become more confused as we grow and learn about the meanings of survival and pleasure versus happiness.

The objective of happiness (peace of mind) is an integral part of our thoughts about life and living. Our discussions of happiness show how fragile the whole issue of life philosophy can be, considering the major contradiction between the path to happiness and the path of survival. It appears as if 'happiness' and the 'practicality of living' are opposing ideas that cannot be easily reconciled into a meaningful philosophy. Nonetheless, the possibility of happiness through 'self' exploration is a reality that we can depend on for developing the structure of our life philosophy. We must stop doubting the fact that happiness is an intrinsic virtue of 'self' and that it is the only place we should look for happiness. We may then focus only on doubts and decisions about life practicalities, since they are stopping us from reaching a state of 'self'-hood and happiness. Within this framework, we can even entertain our deep belief (expectation) about deserving happiness as our legitimate right of being a *being*. Deserving happiness is perhaps a true claim if we can deal effectively with both our idiosyncrasies and the practicalities of living that create too many cycles of depression.

It is interesting to study our *mood* when we are neither happy nor depressed and thus appreciate its value for our welfare. What kind of a state is that? Contentment? A normal state? This study is beyond the scope of this book, although it seems that we live in that state more often than we are either happy or depressed. However, if somebody asks us how we feel at any moment, we suddenly lean toward a sense of satisfaction (happiness) or boredom (depression). This shows the deep state of our psyche regardless of our superficial feelings. Overall, maintaining a sense of contentment and mental stability over the long period would be blissful, but rather abnormal for human nature in general. Thus, as we move between the moods of happiness and depression rather frequently, we cause so much turmoil for our psyche. We overuse our nerves and drain our spirits. We cause our sufferings.

The Formula of Happiness

The discussions in Part III show why prescribing a particular 'formula of happiness' would always remain a tentative attempt at best. It is difficult to establish a standard or criterion for real happiness due to many factors. For one thing, individuals' perceptions and unique mix of personality aspects (i.e., Model, Ego, Self) make their expectations and approaches in life different. Accordingly, their definitions of happiness vary based on their needs and deprivations. Moreover, happiness experiences are unique in intensity and length, too. These obstacles and many other factors make the practicality of finding and applying a fixed 'formula of happiness' questionable. Yet, we all hope to unravel this mystery, too, along with many other life puzzles.

In the final analysis, happiness is an abstract perception that eludes a comprehensive definition. The best definition that we can invent for common purpose is that 'happiness' is the outcome of profound experiences that impact a person's soul deeply, improve his outlook on life, which then affect others positively too.

Nonetheless, the following general guidelines can be derived from the discussions in the last two chapters regarding the characteristics of happiness:

1. Happiness is not a phenomenon out there that can be defined and accessed independent from the personality of the person experiencing it. An individual cannot pursue a path of happiness outside himself and without making substantial changes to his/her own personality and outlook on life.
2. Contrary to common perception, we do not deserve happiness as long as we expect to find it within our pervasive, crooked lifestyles and shallow mentality.
3. Pleasures can at best replicate only a tentative sense of happiness. They do not cause happiness or eradicate depression.
4. Happiness is an intrinsic property of 'self.' Thus, it can be automatically generated from within us, without too much effort. All we need is a simple knowledge of how the principles of happiness work within 'self,' and how they can be nurtured in our minds. The first principle, of course, is to minimize the roles of Model and Ego in our lives. The challenge is to believe in, and activate, as much of the 'self' aspect of our personality as we are capable of accessing and us-

ing. We must monitor every one of our actions, reactions, communications, and encounters to gauge the influence of Model, Ego, and Self, as well as the motivations behind them. Ultimately, we must learn to become a better human being.

5. We should view happiness as a flower blossoming from the plant of personality. The same way a plant must be observed and fed with nutrients to support its flowering properties, a person's personality aspects must be constantly monitored and balanced to enhance one's capacity for happiness. A mature personality has the properties of a year-round flowering plant, where everlasting happiness manifests as an intrinsic property of one's unique personality. Thus, happiness is automatic when the personality is well groomed. Yet, explaining any happiness experience is like describing the beauty of a particular flower that has its own unique properties and fragrance.

6. Happiness requires high self-awareness. Not only the prevalence of 'self' is required for cultivating the plant of happiness, but also special attention to the properties of the flower itself is necessary. We should train ourselves to be aware of the happiness of our 'self,' the same way we look at the flowers of a particular plant consciously and enjoy it. If flowers are not healthy and strong, we assess the situation and adjust the watering, fertilizing, or change the environment (the soil) of the plant. In the same manner, the happiness of 'self' has to be monitored and personality adjustment be made to correct any signs of lethargy in the intensity of 'self' happiness. The awareness of 'self' is discussed in several parts of this trilogy. It simply means remembering 'who we are,' 'what the purpose of our living is,' and the whole vulnerability of our lives leading to the inevitable death. Being conscious of our physical health as well as our psychological growth are other means of 'self'-awareness. We also need to have 'self'-control over our physical and psychological needs

(i.e., social and inner temptations) to avoid mental deprivation or stagnation.
7. A real happiness experience has four attributes. It has a legitimate and worthwhile 'cause,' it generates authentic 'feelings' of inner joy and completeness, it 'impacts' the person in a meaningful and deep way, and as a result, the person can 'affect' other individuals, events, and things in a positive way as well. For lasting happiness, we should pursue mostly those experiences that can entail all these four elements fully. Accordingly, the cycles of happiness should be continuous and deep.
8. Happiness cannot rely on external sources and whims. The events and experiences causing happiness are only important to the extent they can create the four attributes of happiness regularly. Therefore, small experiences that can be attained quite readily are potentially more powerful in steering and generating happiness experiences. For example, the joy of gardening is something that, once appreciated, can become a major source of real happiness and 'self' growth. When we explore the details of a good piece of music, especially classical music for those who like it, we discover simple and small notes and creations every time we listen to it. For music and art, even though somebody else has done the creation aspect of it, we still appreciate and associate with the genius that has gone into it and enjoy it with high intensity. We can repeat the experience of listening to the music or viewing the arts that reinforce the cycles of happiness experiences in our lives. We can make a habit of producing those simple experiences that keep the cycles of happiness running perpetually and smoothly. When it comes to our own creations, the intensity of happiness caused by these achievements and self-actualizing experiences is ten folds higher. It makes a lot of sense to score individual achievements, i.e., arts, inventions, and other ventures that enrich our lives and propagate the in-

tensity of our happiness experiences by affecting other humans too.

9. Happiness runs parallel with the level of personal potentialities realized. Following our dreams, when they are supported by our realistic recognition of our potentialities and abilities, has a good chance of leading to happiness experiences. Conversely, following some erratic dreams, solely based on false pretences, hope, positive thinking, or according to our misleading perceptions of our potentialities, would most likely lead to stagnation and depression experiences.

10. Happiness experiences are much more frequent and rewarding once we choose and follow a path of wisdom with a fixed life philosophy. Abolishing the sources of our gullibility, e.g., our blind submission to religions, positive thinking gimmicks, or unfounded spirituality regiments, is the first step toward wisdom and happiness. Through our search, we learn about the other dimensions of our 'self,' including our spirituality urge. Accordingly, we would not only learn about our ignored potentialities, but also access inner energies that would free us from the limitations of a mere physical existence. The path of wisdom gives us the power to reject the imposing and conditioning value systems, while remaining realistic about our relationships and responsibilities in society.

11. Happiness cycles are less frequently interrupted when we learn to recognize and avoid the traps of depression cycles. When 'self' induces depression, e.g., our sadness about human impurity, the experience should be used for learning, healing, compassion, and creating.

12. Happiness cycles are intensified when we learn to pause and ponder our rational doubts about objects, people, and events. Through this awareness process, we develop a personal life philosophy to deal with reality, make the right life decisions, and fulfil our responsibilities effectively.

PART IV
Philosophy and Reality

CHAPTER EIGHT
Social Conscience and Philosophy

'Philosophy' explores ideals about individual and society in terms of values and rules of morality. Yet, the reality that we have created for ourselves, and feel so proud of it too, would never come anywhere close to those philosophical ideals. In fact, 'philosophy' often appears like an opposing picture of 'reality,' merely for teasing our severe gullibility and shortfalls as humans. Our societies and the general public have difficulty grasping and implementing even some basic principles for relating and living harmoniously. Thus, after such a long history of humanity and deep contemplations, philosophy still remains only an impotent symbol of social conscience. It reflects our good intentions and a bunch of far-fetched ideologies for speculation and dreaming, but not something to realistically depend on for correcting ourselves.

On the other hand, we would never stop humouring the public and ourselves about the possibility of eventually gaining the capacity for a better humanity somehow—perhaps after a few more millenniums of hurting one another and suffering. We hope to find an idyllic means of living that fits humans' nature, dignity, and needs. We hope to generalize the ideas and rules of morality and find a social order and political system that can inhibit all the chaos and tyranny everywhere. We realize that these objectives are somehow naïve and elusive, but we like to accept them as our ultimate, noble goals. Thus, our lasting search for a global philosophy to goad a more practical and harmonious social living would continue and probably get nowhere. Or maybe we succeed by a fluke! Meanwhile, perhaps we could place some emphasis on developing our personal life philosophies within a narrower dimension. We could attempt to at least build our own convictions and beliefs for defining our life outlook, find wiser purposes for living, and choose simpler lifestyles.

Personal Philosophy

Everybody has a perception of life intuitively, which grows into a subtle personal philosophy, though not consciously or in an elaborate form. We build our tastes, preferences, ideologies, and general guidelines, which collectively constitute a raw personal philosophy. Yet, our views and outlook on life are usually scattered and fluid, because we do not have a systematic approach or method for developing them more actively and purposefully. Furthermore, we have constant doubts about the validity of our choices and life outlook.

Many political, religious, and social groups have hoped to create a new culture and thought process to embrace a more plausible set of human values. After all, the main purpose of philosophy is to make a better sense of our erratic reality—the perceived reality—and explain it to the public for general knowledge and better communication. However, it appears that human character hinders the development of a sensible philosophical platform to share for communicating among ourselves and resolving our rising dilemmas of social living.

One option for better living and raising self-awareness is to study and formulate our personal philosophies a bit more seriously and objectively. It can help us cope with social values and structure, survive, and relate to others more effectively with the least amount of friction. The ideal would be to build a personal philosophy that can best guarantee our independence and integrity within society in a consistent manner and reduce human sufferings too. However, not everybody has the time and mindset to formulate a personal philosophy, never mind adopting a rather stoic one.

As an alternative, some scholars could offer a handful of personal life philosophies applicable to any particular era for living more peacefully. It must be comprehensive and sensible though. We have enough scattered philosophies that advocate simple notions such as positive thinking or living in the now, etc. For example, the discussions in this trilogy can be streamlined into one type of personal philosophy that is plausible and practical. The objective is to study and suggest several practical philosophies that people can choose according to their needs and personality for the ultimate goal of gaining their individualism and a relative happiness. Then they can set out to understand its principles and significance for making their daily routines more sensible. These basic philosophies, which are developed gradually based on collective thoughts and analyses, could at least help people cope with life better and grasp the dangers of their erratic whims. The whole idea is to offer a simpler and more practical way of living based on common experiences and convictions related to the values and structure of society at any particular time. This may be a better approach than depending on our dogmatic leaders and shallow social values for setting our life objectives and paths. It would be a better option than trusting our raw personal dreams and erratic expectations, or waiting forever for some idealistic philosophies, which are hard for people to understand or practice anyway. After all, while a generalized philosophy with ethical norms may be hard to implement in our rigidly controlled societies, we could at least develop a basic guideline, to depict actual life limitations and demands. It could provide some general notions for healthy living and building our fundamental thoughts and beliefs.

Eventually we might even be able to incorporate solid individual philosophies into a general theory, perhaps as a simple *guideline for social conscience and relationships*. During this learning process, we might also realize the folly of our present life. Overall, it seems plausible that personal philosophies and plans, once studied in congruity, eventually find practical common grounds, at least for general dialogue and easier communication. But first, we must develop some personal philosophies that seem sensible for the present era.

Our Habits and Life Routines

Sometimes it appears that we are simply living randomly from day to day, chasing wild dreams, merely making a living, maybe accumulating wealth, and seeking pleasure. We do things that make sense only today and are meaningless the next day. We do things out of habit without knowing our real purpose for doing them. We may have some kind of financial and career development plans, but have no idea what our life is all about and what we want to do with it. Sometimes it appears that we are not aware of our true beliefs, needs, or convictions for building a basic life philosophy. This is a *random living* existence. Often we are too naïve when we wait for someone else, perhaps our companion or soul mate to come along (hopefully soon) and tell us what would be good for us as a life plan or the means of finding happiness.

Philosophy is customarily developed by thinkers and theoreticians. And *reality* is shaped in our mind by the ideas and suggestions of our parents, governments and powerful groups and individuals who manipulate and exploit the rest of the population. The hypothetical expectation that the ruling government protects the public's best interests is only an idealistic theory that would never actualize. In the final analysis, we are left out in both fronts, i.e., philosophy and reality, helpless and estrange to the rules imposed upon us. We have not learnt to create our own personal philosophy, because we have never considered it important, possible, and necessary. And we do not know how to participate in the shaping of the reality of our own life by resisting the global 'reality' that is forced upon us in our soulless societies. The point is that if we do not show initiative to create our own philosophy and a plain reality of life, we would be at the mercy of others who would force one upon us. Instead of a moralistic life philosophy, we have adopted a materialistic living ideology and pursue it passionately. We have developed biases, prejudices, and superegos to get ahead in all the competitions and challenges of life. And instead of expanding our vision and definition of a reality that fits us, we conform to social norms—which we privately believe are invalid anyway—just for being accepted as a loyal member of society and to stay popular within the circle of friends.

A personal life philosophy serves many purposes. However, mainly, it helps us rise above our random living to a level of 'self' control and 'self' induced life. This would bring us more in line with the 'self' aspect of our personality, while reducing 'ego' and 'model.' The random living life is a product of the imposed and illusive reality that we have known and accepted. 'Self' controlled life, on the other hand, is one in which we listen to, and honour, the vision and wisdom of 'self.' In the *Quantum Healing*, Bantam Books, 1989, Deepak Chopra states the followings:

"We all have the power to make reality. Why make it inside boundaries when the boundless is so near?" Ibid., p. 234.
"There is no more beautiful experience than when the world expands beyond its accustomed limits. These are the moments when reality takes on splendour." Ibid., p. 235.

Not everybody may find the power to make reality or feel the splendour that a more insightful reality can bring us, but we can at least try to escape the boundaries of the perceived reality that is screwing up our brains and causing us so much hardship. We may expand our minds and make our reality boundless by developing our personal life philosophy that supports our thoughts, actions, behaviour, decisions, doubts, and depicts the way we see things and live, according to the rules of 'self.' We can at least develop a little integrity for our being and in our thoughts. This is the main purpose of a personal life philosophy. Other purposes of a personal life philosophy become clear in the following discussions.

Basic Plans and Ideologies

Most of us put our ambitious dreams on hold to attend to our immediate needs and to devise practical plans with the highest chance of securing our future. We realize the need to adapt to the chaotic socioeconomic environment somehow, especially to job market demands and increasingly complex format of family relationships. Everybody, especially youth, faces this normal adjustment process. Throughout this process, we establish the relevance (practicality) of our *plans* to social environment, but also in relation to our deep beliefs and *ideologies* (e.g., our definition and means of happiness, life purposes, reasons for working, objectives of accumulating wealth, the purpose and hassles of marriage and family, etc.). We also assess our potentialities and limitations when we develop and pursue our specific plans. These basic plans must coincide with and support our personal life philosophy. We must be clear and careful in terms of the purposes of our plans in the long-term.

On the one hand, being too ambitious or passionate about our ideals and dreams often obscures our sense of reality and practicality. It merely undermines our chance and efforts to adapt to the harsh realities of life. In fact, without quick adaptation, we increase the risks of a lifelong isolation and possible headaches and regrets in the future. On the other hand, ignoring our dreams and true potentialities, just for the sake of a quick adaptation and survival, has its own risks and regrets. Nonetheless, we must make a decision according to our personality and needs, and then live with its consequences almost for the rest of our lives without whining or feeling defeated. We also need some timetable and criteria for achieving certain goals within specific life stages regardless of our ambitions and the kind of plan we choose for our future. By the way, personal ambitions not supported by both a sound ideology and a refined plan should be placed on hold, especially during the early stage of life when everybody must build a plan for his/her future according to some sensible life philosophy. This basic element of our philosophy must make sense even when we are quite sure of our potentialities related to our ambitions. It is always important to pass the practicality test first according to valid criteria. That is, while we do not need to worry about, or adopt, other people's criteria of practicality, we must remain objective about our own criteria when we set out to assess our raw ambitions and put our life plan together.

The above basic steps are merely for balancing our ultimate goals in relation to our beliefs and capabilities. We may naively assume that our personal goals match our beliefs, potentialities, risk orientation, and a realistic 'life vision.' Yet, finding our true niche and temperament is not an easy job nowadays. Furthermore, even our most diligent plans have at least fifty percent chance of going sour and producing unsatisfactory results. We must be prepared for these unforeseeable outcomes too. How realistically we set our plans and how seriously we pursue them is a personal choice, which at the end reflects the strength of our beliefs and convictions too. Only we are responsible for the outcome of our choices, while extending our best efforts for setting our life plans and implementing them. One thing is certain, though: If we lack either (or both) life plans and personal beliefs, do not establish a sound, meaningful criterion for assessing them, or keep deferring our major life decisions, we face many disappointments in life at the very least.

Our life vision or personal plans do not need to be elaborate or aggressive, but only practical. Making a conscious decision to have a simple and humble life is as good—and often better—as any complex, greed-ridden plan. Any plan is a good plan when built on healthy, thoughtful personal beliefs, which reflect our honest and true representation of who we are. It must also be realistic within the parameters of the socioeconomic environment. Having all these plans and convictions are mostly important for maintaining a consistent level of motivation to withstand unforeseeable obstacles and inevitable disappointments along the way. Meanwhile, we must also remember that laziness and pessimism do not bring anybody any sense of existence and accomplishment.

A main purpose of self-analysis is to ensure that our life philosophy and our socioeconomic plans match. If not quite sure, we must stop and reassess all the variables again. We must first come to terms with ourselves, delineate our beliefs honestly, and distinguish them from our naïve aspirations before building our life plans. Youths, in particular, must remain careful about the practicality of their aspirations and ambitions. We should avoid the temptation of trusting our guts or assuming we know why we are choosing certain plans. We should overcome our pride and stubbornness and instead admit to ourselves at least that we have no supporting convictions for the way we are, feel, or the things we do. Often, it is merely our erratic passion that is making us so restless and reckless. Our first reaction and response to the question of who we are in relation to our plans is usually misleading. Instead, we must invest a great deal of time and become honest with ourselves in terms of our convictions and beliefs—to really grasp whether we have any meaningful life plans or not. We must truly know the level of risks we are willing to take for maintaining our relative independence, draw a list of personal beliefs and ideologies, and then attempt to match them with our plans more objectively and critically.

Most of us have life plans, or at least we think so. If we also have strong beliefs and convictions about who we are, how we like to live, and why, then our personal philosophy can be easily drawn by ensuring those plans and beliefs coincide according to reliable criteria. This sensible coordination of our plans and beliefs constitutes a simple definition of a personal philosophy. Yet, we must test the soundness of our plans and beliefs concurrently. Usually our shallow beliefs or thoughts invent impractical plans. And often our convictions are only naïve justifications to support our crooked or fanciful plans. We should fight the temptation of assuming that our plans are based on objective judgments, valid criteria, and reliable convictions. Those of us who have no plans, are not seriously pursuing them, or cannot find any beliefs or resolutions to support those plans, have even more work to do. Trusting some raw, half-hearted convictions and beliefs (often by imitating social norms and teachings) would be quite risky. It might prove more wasteful than doing nothing while the elements for a long-term plan, according to some personal beliefs and life philosophy, are under scrutiny. It is always better to act only when we are ready and reasonably doubtless. However, we should stop struggling aimlessly with a bunch of ambitious dreams for a long time, or procrastinating in hopes of devising a right plan. Sometimes, taking on tentative plans while working on the long-term plan is sensible, while we strive to finalize the latter within a reasonable timeframe.

Sadly, devising practical life plans is getting more difficult every year, as our societies face more uncertainties and imbalance. Therefore, we should work harder and think deeper about our life philosophy and plans to live rather peacefully within this hectic environment and for whatever end that can justify our efforts. Everybody must develop both short and long-term practical plans, at least for satisfying his basic needs and building certain relationships. The outcome of such plans must fit his ideologies closely and fulfil some meaningful life purposes within a certain period, e.g., five to seven years if he is in his twenties. The main goal of our plan is to attain at least a sense of contentment and peace of mind in life, which becomes mostly possible by learning about the characteristics of an ideal personality.

The Ideal Personality

The ultimate purpose of developing a 'self' driven personal life philosophy is to mitigate social hardships and maybe even find happiness (peace of mind). Chapter Six discussions about happiness indicate that any personal philosophy must start with a deep alignment of Ego, Model, and Self. Of course, our general life plans and ideologies are also significant for developing our personal philosophy, as they reflect our personality and outlook on life. All along, we envision the characteristics of an *ideal personality* in search of happiness. Not that everybody can hold such high standard of personality, but rather we can use this model of an ideal personality for gauging our character and detecting our possible shortfalls for attaining happiness. Our search for an ideal personality resembles the attempts of conventional philosophy to define, or maybe even create, 'pure humans.' But the *ideal personality* noted here is merely for the purpose of coping with social needs *practically*. For that end, we already agree that human nature is not pure, nor can such high qualities be promoted within the crooked standards of new societies.

From the conclusions in Chapter Six, we expect an ideal personality to somehow emphasize on Self. Though, he utilizes Ego and Model in small doses, too, for practical purposes, only to boost his relationships and maintain his identity in society without being completely isolated or dominated. Therefore, developing a personal life philosophy requires a study of one's three aspects of the personality, especially the right mix for creating the ideal personality.

In the desired personality, the domination of Self is, let us say, around 60%, which is an arbitrary but reasonable estimate. We can assume that Model and Ego each make up about 20% of the ideal personality. With this kind of mix, we can say that the needs and motivations of the individual are 'self'-directed and 'self'-controlled. When the needs of Model and Ego compete with the needs and motivations of Self, it is assumed that they are not too conflicting and excessive, and applied only for practical purposes. In fact, this low portion of Model and Ego emerge only as a defence mechanism, and not for offensive or dependency purposes. They are only tentative measures for adaptation and assertiveness, anyway. We must remain a good judge in deciding how much of Model and Ego we use, how often, for what purpose, and whether their use is almost absolutely necessary. Maintaining the right balance is a big challenge, but a definite necessity for developing a plausible personal life philosophy and finding tranquility. The Self, Ego, and Model attributes of an ideal personality are explained below, while various characteristics of an enlightened man are discussed throughout this trilogy.

The 'Self' Aspect of the Ideal Personality

'Self' has the lowest ambitions amongst the three personality aspects, and ultimately becomes needless. The higher the level of a person's self-awareness and transcendence, the lower would be his/her neediness and attachment to worldly values. Accordingly, an ideal personality with a mix of Ego, Model, and Self puts little emphasis on materialistic or egoistic desires. However, he sometimes needs Ego and Model for coping, defending himself against biases and prejudices of others, or becoming assertive to protect his dignity and relationships.

The physical needs of Self are also minimal and only for running a healthy life while facilitating his psychological and mental growth. The challenges of a 'self' driven person are for inward gratification and not external rewards. Even the love and belongingness needs of 'self' are unselfish and global, instead of possessive and focused. While enjoying the blessings and happiness experiences of social living and loving, he disallows these needs overwhelm him or derail his plans. In particular, s/he learns how to deal with the love-deficiency syndrome that most people suffer from nowadays.

Of course, gaining all these divine qualities and reaching even a relative 'self' orientation is difficult. We all depend on other individuals, groups, and organizations to satisfy our basic needs, including love and belonging, while they place their own needs and rules on us through this interdependency. This rising level of interdependency in society, especially for dealing with personal insecurities and psychological deprivations, inhibits people's chance of exploring their Self. They feel obliged to use all their energies on coping and finding external acceptance. Thus, they find little energy and motivation to attend to their higher needs that support the intrinsic aspect of Self. We prefer to remain needy than becoming needless!

A *personal life philosophy* aiming for 'selfhood' and real happiness starts with a commitment to free ourselves from the temptations of, and dependencies on, the lower needs that society nurtures in us. The goal is to develop the means of understanding and striving for mental freedom and satisfying our higher needs. By developing a personal life philosophy and a personal plan, we hope to minimize our reliance on external sources beyond some minimal limits that are essential for survival in society. Instead, we plan to gain self-reliance and self-control, while satisfying specific personal needs that support a 'self' oriented life philosophy. Our personal life philosophy's motto largely says, "My needs are 'self' generated, 'self' controlled, and 'self' satisfied."

The self-reliance and self-control traits do not mean or lead to selfishness, however. On the contrary, self-reliance is based on a belief that everybody has his/her own modest abilities to think and act independently without too much reliance on society or others. Guided by this fundamental belief, Self is incapable of assuming self-superiority. A 'self'ish person cannot be selfish. A desired personality is self-reliant, because he values his 'self' objectively. He does not need to exaggerate his being and beliefs to attract the approval of others, although he knows the inherent value of 'self.' In fact, self-reliance is for living more practically, since Self knows that reliance on others is doomed, especially in our highly egotistical societies. Of course, the experience and knowledge of Self are personal and not in his ability or interest to advertise them. The 'ideal personality' generates a humble sense of 'self'-approval to replace the need for external approvals. It is interesting, and depressing at the same time, to see how we sometimes even pretend to be humble and submissive as a Model in order to manipulate people or receive their approval to feed our egoistic needs. A self-reliant individual does not need to go through this humiliating hassle of playing games all the time to feed his Ego.

The concept of 'self'-value is also crucial for developing a personal life philosophy toward an ideal personality. Our societies suffer largely from the imbalance of personal 'self'-value. Only a small portion of us really understands our 'self'-worth. The majority of us are either overvaluing or undervaluing ourselves. This confusion is not solely our fault, but rather, it is the symptom of an epidemic transmitted to us from our parents, culture, and society. They are responsible for creating this false image of us in our minds, whereas our true self-image must be based on our 'self'-worth after a careful self-analysis and lengthy self-development. When we ignore or undermine our abilities and potentialities, we are deliberately undervaluing ourselves. And conversely, when we exaggerate in our minds about the role we play in this universe, and when Ego dominates our personality, we overvalue ourselves. Both conditions hurt mostly the person, but also people close to him. False self-images created by erroneous self-valuation have destroyed the superstructure of our societies. They have hindered personal communication, mutual respect, and our sensitivity to each other's needs. Even some of our efforts to help people, such as positive thinking propagandas and self-image development seminars, increase the burden of this recurring cycle of self-destruction and self-alienation as they advocate erroneous self-image and 'self'-worth.

As a way of encouraging positive thinking, our social norms appear to dictate that 'we are what we think (we are).' This implies that if we think of ourselves as some invincible, know-it-all person, we would in reality turn into such a personality. Thus, we imagine a superficial superiority, which is created by our twisted minds when there are no other viable criteria for measuring the real value of Self and not even knowing what Self is like. As a result, we have become the most arrogant humans in the history of mankind. Ironically and sadly, we humans have become least trustworthy and pure than ever. So our arrogance only reflects how far off the chart our personal self-images are.

A useful personal philosophy, therefore, requires an objective 'self'-valuation for building a positive self-image without becoming arrogant, or conversely losing confidence and faith in our abilities. Comprehending and refining this fine balance of 'self'-value is another important dimension of our personal life philosophy. This valuation process starts with a conscious belief and decision for exploring our needs through self-awareness. In the process, we learn more about Self and develop self-acceptance and self-approval. This would be a part of the process, or state, of awakening, as we acknowledge that our Self can be in charge of our lives. Thus, we set the stage for 'self'-awakening and 'self'-control.

The concepts of 'self'-value and 'self'-approval are admittedly much easier to discuss than practice. When we do things—let us say write a novel—we normally assess our success by external results, e.g., the number of copies sold and the amount of money made. Without such feedback, most of us have difficulty accepting the value of our contribution. We become doubtful of our achievement. The problem with 'self'-approval for our achievements is that we must not care about external results or receiving outside recognition. Yet, it is ordinarily impossible for us to *really* ignore the feedback, even if we learned not to care about a definite reward for our accomplishments.

The words 'value' and 'approval' inherently refer to comparison, judgment, and agreement by several individuals rather than one person. The 'value' of every thing is usually established by the price that several people are willing to pay for it after judging and comparing it with similar things. 'Self'-value, however, is more like personal and sentimental judgments that are non-negotiable and most likely are not valued in the same way and equally by others. As practical persons, we underestimate our personal and sentimental values and instead emphasize on the materialistic values that are universally judgmental and negotiable—which we assume reflect the objectivity of jurors. The reason is clear. We like to spend our time and thoughts on achieving or creating things that have value in the eyes of others, because we often doubt our own judgment, while expect to gain a tangible reward from our efforts. In real life, we need to create only those items that help us sustain our costly habits and lifestyle. Cashable creations are more useful in our minds than personal integrity, 'self'-acceptance, and 'self'-approval.

Conversely, 'self'-value is an inner assessment and hard to gauge. It is not expressible nor can it be measured in terms of equivalent cash, assets, or people's respect. It takes a lot of courage to depend merely on 'self'-value to judge our accomplishments. A similar kind of argument can be made for 'self'-approval compared to external approval. While the latter gives us confirmed love and acceptance, 'self'-approval requires solid personal criteria to make objective judgments and set tangible values for our efforts. Still, we often doubt the validity, usefulness, and relevance of our 'self'-imposed criteria (e.g., integrity and 'self'-approval) in a society with such a vast superficial orientation.

It would be interesting to study the concepts of 'self'-value and 'self'-approval within the contexts of the needs hierarchy model and self-actualization sensations. History is full of high-achievers like Van Gogh and Mozart who have had difficulty satisfying their basic needs for food and shelter, while creating masterpieces that others did not value sufficiently at the time. Yet, they seemingly had the highest degree of 'self'-value for their creations. Nonetheless, we wonder how their creations could generate real actualizing experiences for them when the lack of external values, love, and approval deprived them from satisfying even their basic mental needs. It is interesting to know if and how Van Gogh and Mozart might have avoided self-doubt and appreciated their real 'self'-value while constantly worrying about basic life demands. Judging by the size of their achievements, one would expect that they, and many similar artists and high-achievers to have climbed up to the highest levels of the needs hierarchy and felt fully actualized. However, most likely they did not truly, despite their tremendous potentiality for self-actualization. They might have had a homogenous level of 'self'-control to ignore the absence of external valuation and approval, while needing love and financial support so badly too. Yet, it would be hard for most of us to feel actualized when our self-actualizing efforts cannot help our dependent family sustain a basic life.

The needs hierarchy theory appears to break down in instances when the accomplishments of a person bring him to the verge of self-actualization without his lower needs being satisfied. The person may feel actualized or not, depending only on his approach toward 'self'-value and self-doubt, and his ability to deal with normal social pressures. Or conversely, his ability to set his ambitions aside, get practical, and move down the personal needs hierarchy.

In short, developing a 'self'-oriented and 'self'-motivated personal life philosophy is an inherent objective of an 'ideal personality.' It gives the person the highest chance for finding happiness or at least minimizing life hardships. By elaborating on the purposes of life philosophy, we learn about many traits of the ideal personality, which is guided by Self. The list of fundamental human thoughts presented in Table 1.1 of Chapter One, and the detailed discussions of those fifteen thoughts, provide a solid platform for building a typical personal life philosophy. Readers may go back to that part of the book to review those topics again.

The 'Model' and 'Ego' Roles for Ideal Personality

A small amount of Model and Ego is desirable for helping us deal with Model and Ego-driven people, as well as the rules and expectations in our societies. We need to establish relationships with people in order to exchange services and emotions with one another. Without some Model, we may appear rude and uncaring to those who are used to judging others based on their appearances and pleasing etiquettes. Self may appear cold and uncaring in the showy and supposedly tactful social interactions of our time. In all, our presentation of the 'self'-induced ideas and facts are better received and understood in a 'model' format, if at all. This aptitude helps us merge, communicate, and get along with others more effectively, while maintaining our private identity.

A small amount of Ego can help us assert and defend ourselves rather than remain passive all the time when we face people's offences and pressures. Self advocates patience, forgiveness, and tolerance as the main traits of the ideal personality. However, there are times when the ideal personality has to protest and perhaps even rebel against the excessive cruelty and unfairness that are symptoms of our modern societies. It is with our managed and controlled Ego that we judge and oppose when it becomes absolutely necessary.

Volume III of this trilogy deals mainly with the realities of our lives, critical decisions, and relationships that we must maintain with others and society. From those discussions, it becomes clear that, for practical purposes, we must engage in some activities and role-playing that are directed by Model and Ego. Many examples are offered in Volume III where these three aspects of the personality converge to create a best possible decision, action, or reaction. Our ideal personality emerges and takes control of our lives effectively. The important point, however, is that we ('self') should not allow Model and Ego exceed their shares of contribution in the ideal personality. During the course of life, as we struggle with life hardships and dilemmas, it would become a big temptation and easy for us to forget the essence of the ideal personality and allow Model and Ego to gradually take charge of our lives. The ideal personality has to remain 'self'-controlled at all cost and prevent a takeover by Model or Ego. This constant awareness and resistance constitutes Self's most challenging task.

CHAPTER NINE
Thoughts and Wisdom

Our thoughts are boundless and intriguing as we experience many facets of existence. However, the main purpose of thinking is to plan and control our lives. We hope our thoughts can help us build our life philosophy and *primary wisdom*, which we need for coping within society, making good decisions, and getting a deeper grasp of subjects and ideas. Thus, our philosophical thoughts find much more value for directing our lives compared to our mundane thoughts, which merely waste our brain cells and energy. Naturally, the soundness of our thoughts also depends on our level of consciousness and self-awareness, while we should know (and justify) the cause and purpose of our thoughts, too. Our thoughts are supposed to bring us wisdom, not stress and confusion. They should help us develop our self-image and self-worth, not depression or a sense of loneliness. Yet, unfortunately, our thoughts are seldom devoted to the right stuff of life. Thus, most of our decisions and actions remain a matter of habit and personality instead of reflecting a thoughtful life philosophy and primary wisdom. We let our thoughts derail our lives and deflate our spirits, instead of helping us control our erratic emotions and see life's essentialities.

The complexity of social life and our relationships force us to waste so much time and mental energy on shallow thoughts mostly for solving our problems and dealing with stressful facets of life. Our thoughts are often scattered and skimpy merely for responding to our urgent needs to compete, win, and get richer. We often ponder our options, solutions, or ideas merely to fight with others or manipulate them for some devious purposes. Thus, we seldom find the motive and time to contemplate and build a simple lifestyle, which could potentially eliminate the need for all that painful thinking about trivia or worrying about life issues, which nobody can solve, nor deserve so much of our attention. If only we understood the vanity of our naïve desires, we might stop our unrelenting stressful thoughts and suffering. We might let our thoughts and imaginations elate us beyond our erratic reality to the sphere of tranquility and freedom, instead of dwelling on issues promoted by our Egos as matters of life and death.

Unfortunately, most of us do not know the best way of using our brains. Sometimes, we think too much and too long, to the point of losing our sanity or major opportunities of our lives. Sometimes, our thoughts are sporadic and meaningless in the form of a daydream. And sometimes they create some theories and techniques that are enormously perplexing and amazing. Sometimes our thoughts goad evil actions, and sometimes we embrace the most humanistic and humble thoughts. Sometimes they are formidably destructive, and sometimes they create the ultimate sense of beauty and value. We can also learn to relax and meditate by thinking in certain ways, or by stopping the process of our thoughts for a while. The amazing vast scope of our thoughts reflects the complexity of human nature and hints the possibility of reaching a higher level of humanness only if we understood our naiveté, sentiments, brilliance, arrogance, and ignorance that contain us, all at once or in rotations. We only need to know the right thoughts to make our lives meaningful.

Obviously, the *extent, content,* and *intent* of our thoughts depend on a person's primary wisdom, personality, mood, and motivation. Yet, we all share the same fundamental thoughts about life intuitively. They are the most primitive and instinctual thoughts, and questions, that we reflect upon regarding our existence. They are the underlying thoughts behind the whole philosophy, process, and actions of life. And they are the unique thoughts that are specifically posed, and become relevant, in line with our evolving priorities and perspectives in various phases of our lives.

The Fundamental Questions

There are three main phases in our lives, i.e., i) childhood/ adolescence, ii) middle age, and iii) old age. During these life phases, three prominent and related thoughts (questions) occupy our minds as follows:

During the first phase, i.e., childhood/adolescence, our fundamental thoughts centre on the question of, *"What is my life going to look like?"* In this phase of our lives, we are anxious, doubtful, and inquisitive about our future and fate, but our thoughts still do not focus on, or reveal, our deeper needs and concerns. Despite our curiosity about our future and life, we do not question or focus on the main dilemmas and purposes of life per se. We become involved with the so-called life 'practicalities,' which seem to require our immediate attention as basic matters of survival. We are driven by social values and thus forget that certain life 'essentialities' also exist, which need as much or perhaps more thinking and understanding.

Although all the thoughts listed in Table 1.1 of Chapter one circle in our heads occasionally during the first phase of our lives, we remain unclear and passive about the purpose of life and our objectives. During this period of confusion, we mainly try to learn about social norms and means of adaptation. We find some clues about how we would like to shape our future and then make specific plans to get there. Nevertheless, we are uncertain and apprehensive about our decisions, the life that we must lead, the resources and results, our abilities, and the opportunities that may be offered to us, fate and luck, etc. These are the years that we have the highest level of doubts about our future and success, and, at the same time, *success and future* is our whole definition of life. We have little notion or concern about the purpose of life and the meaning of the things we do, as long as we pursue the expectations and teachings of our parents and society. We assume that the definition of life is there and it is correct. We assume that by now humans have figured out what the purpose of life is and what they tell us or show is based on millenniums of proper thinking and experimentation. We naively trust history and social values. Even worse, we trust our emotions and our friends' mentality about the youths' needs. We assume that it is our duty to set our actions and decisions in line with those definitions. By doing so, we also believe that success and happiness would follow automatically, and that this process would make a complete life.

In the second phase of our lives, i.e., middle age, we start to question the purpose of the life we are leading. Our thoughts centre on the question of, *"What is this life?"* During the first phase, we seem to have many objectives that make sense and have special value to us. Despite our many doubts, we have some inherent hope and optimism about future. We strive to achieve those objectives as if they were the main purposes of life. In the second phase, although those childhood objectives might have been achieved, we question the value of the outcome and the content of life itself. It seems we keep doing the same things over and over without getting an inner, deep satisfaction from life. It is not merely the boredom, but rather a sense of deficiency and failure that besieges our thoughts and feelings. This becomes the phase of reflection. Our hardships to survive appear to surpass the value of life experiences resulting from them. We work hard, tolerate injustice and unfairness, accept socioeconomic pressures, play along with people's erratic Model and Ego, and fight constantly with our families with no sign of relief in sight. Therefore, we question the whole purpose of the life we are leading. Sometimes, we think that a drastic decision is needed to free ourselves from this suffocating trap. However, we also have many doubts about the alternatives, our options, and solutions. It seems we have no choice but to continue to struggle and postpone all those risky choices or actions that might change our present life path. And before long, we arrive at the third phase of our lives, still hesitant and doubtful about our options and decisions.

During the third phase, we project the end of our lives and remember all the struggles, thoughts, and doubts that we have endured in the earlier phases of our lives. At this point, we question the value and purpose of it all even harsher in **total disbelief**. Our thoughts centre on the question of, *"What was this life (all about)?"* We regret many things we have or have not done, and we regret the things we spent so much energy and time on, not to mention all those useless worries and all those abuses we endured. Even at this phase, some of us may still question the purpose of life just out of curiosity or anger. However, most likely we have given up on finding an answer, or believe that it would be too late to do anything about it now, even if we could define a purpose for life. We can finally feel the sad 'conclusion' clearly and regret all the wrong things we did because we trusted life, society, culture, value systems, our family, and our lifestyles.

The Main Philosophical Questions

In a nutshell, the underlying philosophy of life is reflected in the three questions we ask ourselves in the three phases of our lives.

Phases of Life	Underlying Philosophical Questions
Youth	What will be (my life like)?
Middle Age	What is this (that is happening)?
Old Age	What was it (all about)?

There it is! The story of our lives as portrayed by the wisdom of our thoughts. Some precious lessons lie in this simple story. Each question may not reveal as much as they do together. They offer the gist of the deepest thoughts that engage any intelligent person as s/he matures. They are our ultimate visions, conclusions, and valuation of life experiences. Therefore, these simple questions can offer a great source of potential lessons and wisdom.

Once we grasp the gist of these philosophical questions, we can develop the foundation of our thoughts properly and pursue our life plans smoothly with lesser stress. We can lay out a more meaningful life for ourselves and find a more reliable path to happiness if we remember these philosophical questions and use them as our primary wisdom.

If we are lucky to live a long life, we would surely arrive at these questions in due time. At any of the three phases, we sense and live through the corresponding philosophical questions daily, but we seem unable to find a suitable answer for them at the time. Only when we arrive in the next phase, we can see the absurdity of the question(s) in the earlier phase(s). We get a tentative and awkward answer indeed. On the other hand, if we intelligently consider the questions we would be asking in the future life phases, as shown above, we automatically get the answers for our questions today. We simply realize that all the stages of our lives would be questionable and paradoxical, no matter how hard we try to make sense out of life and how diligently we plan our actions.

For the first question, 'What my life will be like?', there is the opportunity to anticipate our most likely answers in the future phases. That is, regardless of the degree of success and presumed happiness, we would still doubt the value and meaning of our lives even when we are in the prime of our lives, i.e., the second phase. Unfortunately, the third question implies that we would not find any relief or satisfactory outcome regarding the second question either.

Of course, we are not aware of the depth, effect, and importance of the upcoming questions when we are in a lower life phase. Our egoism and arrogance would not allow it. In phase one, we do not know and believe that a more fundamental question is awaiting us, which by the way negates the importance (validity) of the first question (What my life would be like?). That is, no matter how our lives turn out, we still question its meaning and value. Similarly, we would not expect the question in phase three to be so harsh, nor expect such deep sense of helplessness despite all our wisdom and wealth. That is, no matter how much we try to make sense of life and our plans and pleasures, no intelligent person would find a plausible answer for the question, 'What was it all about?' Some radical carefree people might resist this conclusion and insist that life is full of meanings and pleasures. Well, everybody is best capable of judging his/her deep senses and existence.

Perhaps it is in our nature to believe only in what we can feel or expect *now* (in this very minute) regardless of all the philosophies and prophecies that are out there about life. However, for the very same reason, it seems that we devote our lives to things and thoughts that at the end would prove to have no substantive value or meaning. All our lives we worry unnecessarily about things that are trivial and immaterial when we view and review them retrospectively in the future phases of our lives. This conclusion also suggests that perhaps we have all been 'living in the now' too much all along, more than what we like to admit already. That is, we judge our future needs only based on what we feel urgent today, instead of using our imagination and realize that our perception of life (according to the values of the NOW) is erroneous. We need the wisdom of foresight to make our lives simpler and stop our needless struggles and desires.

Many of us who pass through the three phases of life would admit that these three questions have come upon them in a profound, and often shocking, manner. They have struggled with those questions during the whole period in each life phase. Some of us may be less enthusiastic to admit this or have lived a life of less thinking for whatever reason. Some of us may be carried or absorbed by our Egos, self-gratification, or social pressures to the extent that thinking has been forgotten. Finally, there are those individuals who would not face these three questions, in particular the last two, because they have found a path of wisdom that directs them through the phases of life smoothly. Their life experiences are rather unadventurous, but definitely more peaceful and complete. These people have come to terms with the three questions, especially the last one, very early on in their lives.

The lessons we can learn from these questions are drawn from a projection of our state of mind and thoughts in the upcoming life phases. These questions should serve as hidden clues about the futility of submitting to the common processes and standards of life. The lesson is that, sooner or later, we would find out about the emptiness of our egotistical objectives. The lesson is that if we understand what would, and would not, matter when we are in the second and third phases of our lives, then perhaps we would focus our thoughts and actions in the right direction. The lesson is that the standard formula of happiness that our parents and society teach us is not viable. The lesson is that perhaps we should contemplate and find a basic path of wisdom that prevents our future shocks about life's futility, to prevent our mind and energy being wasted on shallow desires and social struggles. If only we knew what we would be thinking torturously in the future phases of our lives, it would be easier for us to sort out our priorities and establish a personal philosophy that is more sensible.

We learn a lot from our experiences, except that they do not pose or answer the three main questions of life in a timely manner. Unfortunately, we do not get the opportunity to reverse past situations and conditions, or to relive the lost years. The old saying that, "Everybody should have two lives: One to experience, and one to live," finds its prominence mostly during the last phase of our lives. We are willing to give up everything we have, all our wealth and worldly attachment, just for a second chance to think properly this time. We would do some (or many) aspects of our lives differently if we were given a second chance, simply because we now suddenly think differently at this late stage of our lives. Alas, we never get that chance. Alas, we hardly learn any lesson from the wisdom of foresight either.

We need a unique mentality and courage to understand and believe in the significance of the questions we would eventually ask ourselves in the future phases of life. If so, we could start *thinking forward* indeed. By thinking deep about the ultimate and eventual question of, 'What was it?' as early in our lives as possible, we can change our vision of life. We may appreciate the wisdom of this (third phase) question when we are in the first or second phase of our lives. Putting ourselves in a future state of mind is very difficult. Yet, only through forward thinking (the wisdom of foresight), we may invent an 'escape scheme' now, because in the third phase, it would be too late to escape the suffering thoughts of, 'What was it?', or the regretting thoughts of, 'What could be!' Later, we cannot do anything with these questions other than getting ourselves more depressed.

It happens that an 'escape scheme' (relief) can only be found in a path of wisdom. To become immune against the question of, "What was it?" in the third phase of our lives, we need two things. First, our fundamental thoughts should help us develop a philosophy of life by which we may assess and profess our purposes of living honestly and practically. Second, we must apply these thoughts and philosophy to our actions and decisions consciously and carefully in light of *forward thinking*. This full awareness of our authentic needs and purposes in life would prevent the question of, 'What is this life?' from materializing in the second phase of our lives. We should plan properly so that we would not have to ask this question from ourselves, at least not as a lingering reality of our lives during the entire middle age.

'Forward thinking' and possible escape schemes will be discussed further in Chapter Twelve. We intend to adopt forward thinking as a philosophical principle in developing the foundation of our thoughts and actions. Forward thinking suggests that the three questions of, 'What will be?', 'What is this?', and 'What was it?' should be contemplated in a package within a proper perspective. Accordingly, we may succeed in transforming our 'perceived' world into 'real' realities that have different emphasis and significance in our lives. This approach may relieve us from the excruciating self-induced problems that we have helplessly accepted as our inevitable destiny.

The Foundation of Human Thoughts

The issues and concepts discussed in this trilogy circle in our heads intuitively as we try to learn about our existence, find some truth about the world and people, and perhaps lead a reasonably purposeful life. We might ponder some fundamental thoughts more consciously and actively when some nagging questions about our existence and plans hit us occasionally. Nonetheless, similar thoughts run in our subconscious regularly when life dilemmas challenge us. Unfortunately, many trivial thoughts also distract our minds quite often. They cause stress and limit our chance to ponder the more fundamental thoughts, although our curiosity about existence and happiness cannot be avoided. In fact, we do not get enough chance for developing our fundamental thoughts because our brains are almost totally preoccupied with trivia. Our needs and sufferings cause an enormous amount of thoughts too.

Some people may eventually find the wisdom and willpower to curb their erratic desires and thoughts in order to think deeper and feel freer. They try to maintain their integrity and sanity by defining life more realistically. However, the rest of us struggle with our unrelenting, torturous whims and thoughts all our lives, unable to decide on a meaning for life. We suffer from depression and must consume a large amount of antidepressants to go through another day. Some resort to all kinds of crimes and self-deceit to elude reality inside their shallow identities. Ironically, our deep urges and sufferings regularly trigger many spirited thoughts in our heads about 'life,' anyway. We cannot avoid our inherent curiosity about life, which are regularly raised by some fundamental thoughts. We lose our sleep and peace when our thoughts demand real justifications for our artificial needs as well as our ego-ridden ambitions and lifestyles.

Nevertheless, we know intuitively about our need for some *fundamental* thoughts to define life, grow our convictions, and develop some kind of a personal life philosophy. Only then, we believe, we can justify our existence as an intelligent person somewhat. At the very least, we like to feel some basic senses of compassion and love and a bit of peace.

We may think of our foundation of thoughts as an intelligent engine with many complementary (but also clashing) parts that should work together for the ultimate objective of running a volatile machine called human. Making an efficient engine for running an instable cranky machine is not easy but necessary. Obviously, when the engine is not balanced and strong, it would not provide adequate efficiency and output. Some parts may not function well from time to time, like when we have our doubts or face sudden dilemmas. Yet, we have the responsibility of identifying the problem and repairing the part, so the engine can return to full efficiency. The engine requires regular checkups and tune-ups, like the times we need to stop our thought processes and quiet our minds. The engine might boil sometimes like the times when anger and egoism dominate us. In those moments, we should just slow down and stop for a while to let the engine cool down.

The foundation of our thoughts, as laid out in Volume I of this trilogy, will serve as an engine in pursuit of special objectives and decisions of life, as presented in Volume III. These fundamental thoughts, in conjunction with our real life experiences, make up our 'primary wisdom,' which includes our outlook on life, personality, and the means and methods of handling life matters, including our major life decisions and actions. An efficient and sophisticated engine is needed to drive our decisions and actions in the journey of life. We need a solid engine to withstand life turbulences and get us to our destiny as smoothly and safely as we deserve. We do not want any major regrets or breakdowns because of our naive mishandling of the engine.

This is how we envision the operation of our thoughts. Yet this is only one function of our thoughts. The foundation of our thoughts is much more complex and we cannot consider it solely an engine to run our decisions and actions. Beyond its application to our worldly affairs, the foundation of our thoughts should also help us find a true vision of life and our spiritual link to the universe. We have realized that our thoughts help us run our lives, but more importantly, it should transcend us beyond all the worldly decisions and actions. It should help us understand, believe in, and find a path of wisdom deserving the dignity of human beings in the form we have evolved. We may even reach a higher morality considering our intelligence and the long history of 'thinking humans' looking for salvation. We need a strong foundation of thoughts to help us transcend to other domains and territories not sketched on the one-dimensional maps of the perceived world. These discoveries are the most important functions for our thoughts, but unfortunately, we have so far failed to use them for mitigating human suffering as a whole.

Managing Our Thoughts

Most of our thoughts are mechanical, mundane, erratic, daydreaming, and often stressful. They are caused by hallucinations, paranoia, misperceptions, and personal idiosyncrasies in general. However, we also strive intuitively to manage our thoughts in order to be effective, happy, objective, and avoid the stress of

needless musing. We would like to manage our thoughts for three purposes:
1. To better understand and support our inner needs, life decisions, and actions.
2. To develop and maintain a personal life philosophy and find a path of wisdom to reach peace of mind.
3. To stop all thoughts in order to give our minds a chance to rest and our souls an opportunity to heal.

Managing our thoughts implies our ability to manoeuvre effectively within the above three states regularly while minimizing our preoccupation with all those mundane, liquid thoughts (the 80-90 percent portion). Our success depends on our character and background, but also personal efforts to control our thoughts at least thirty percent of the time. Even this minimal awareness of our thoughts is helpful for maintaining a healthier lifestyle. We spend a reasonable amount of time on decisions and actions related to our normal daily activities (purpose number 1 above). But aside from that, we merely waste our lives on soft thoughts like daydreaming, reminiscing our past experiences, and struggling with our paranoia and other psychological defects, including jealousy, spite, and competition.

With these types of raw and liquid thoughts, we develop more untenable expectations and unauthentic needs, which lead to further psychological deprivations and defects. We suffer unnecessarily and worry uselessly. Sometimes, we even create disruptive thoughts with no foundation or relation to our physical or psychological needs, but rather driven by our anger, spite, paranoia, or desire for vengeance. These futile thoughts directly inflict us with pain and confusion and sabotage our nervous system that explodes eventually. So most of us need a plan (consciousness) to re-distribute our thinking habits and energy to minimize the soft thoughts and instead cover the purposes 2 and 3 noted above in a more balanced and routine manner.

Managing our thoughts means controlling the types of ideas that we allow into our heads. We restrict troubling thoughts that have little or no consequence in the end. We rely on our primary wisdom to set our life priorities and make our major life decisions effectively away from personal whims and the pressures imposed on us in complex socioeconomic environments. The time we spend on enhancing the foundation of our thoughts through meditation and reading is never too much. Studying the ideas and prophecies of thinkers and philosophers enforces and supports personal thoughts and individual creativity.

Finally, we must learn how to meditate and create the moments of no-thought, and how much. A no-thought state also occurs by consciously freeing our minds from musing. We could instead amuse ourselves with life experiences (hobbies) that do not require serious decisions and thinking, but provide only feelings of joy, discovery, and satisfaction.

We may alleviate the repercussion of futile thoughts in two ways: First, we could build a general life philosophy to direct and harmonize the content of our trivial thoughts, and to limit those activities that induce such confusing thoughts. Second, we could attempt routinely to give ourselves a break from thinking and allow our minds to only feel things, or on some occasions stop thinking and feeling altogether—like the time we do a deep meditation. Forcing a right balance between the above two approaches (i.e., sustaining a life philosophy and creating regular no-thought moments) provides the best results, of course.

A 'no-thought state' can be reached once we learn to relieve our minds from trivial thoughts, which usually revolve around our needs, plans, and all the mental pressures of our suffering. In a no-thought state, we find peace and freedom, which is the same goal we have for sustaining our life philosophy with a diligent (active) mind. Therefore, the question is how often we should force our minds to relax partially or totally, if we can control it, instead of thinking more actively and deeply for building or monitoring our life philosophy.

On the one hand, we expect our minds to be always sharp and alert for defending ourselves, and to be in constant control of our actions and decisions. We also need a sharp mind as part of our ongoing self-awareness exercises. On the other hand, too much thinking and worrying is driving most of us to the verge of insanity in a society where hardly anything makes sense anymore. Thus, it becomes essential to find the right timing and ways for subduing our thoughts and quieting our mind as often and prudently as we can.

This paradoxical situation (i.e., keeping our mind in full alert versus total quiet) follows the same pattern that has surfaced throughout our discussions about our irreconcilable doubts, dilemmas, and inner conflicts, as integral characteristics of living. The foundation of our thoughts is formed around similar dichotomies, such as destiny versus planning, doubts versus decisions, facts versus myths, perceived versus real world, challenges versus suffering, life versus death, 'self'-control versus practical personality, independence versus dependence, socializing versus solitude, etc. Nevertheless, we must somehow learn to use the right meaning, mix, and balance for each of these dichotomies. Subsequently, we must find a philosophical framework to reconcile all of them collectively when necessary, too. This total paradox seems to be the underlying property of life and thus the foundation of our thoughts, as we navigate in the ocean of uncertainties forever.

The Significance of No-thought Experiences

At one extreme, J.K. Krishnamurti has commented that:

"Only when there is no movement of thought, life is full of significance." Truth and Actuality, Gollancz London, 1977, page 70.

A mystical truth lies behind this philosophy only in the sense that no-thought moments are not the means of forgetting ourselves or losing our senses. On the contrary, we actually understand ourselves better during such moments with a feeling of selflessness within a divine sphere, and thus sense the significance of our existence too. That is how some no-thought moments produce the highest level of significance in our lives, merely due to the opportunity of becoming more in contact with our 'self.' Wandering leisurely in a beautiful garden or a field, occasionally the glory of Nature manifests and absorbs us. In those moments, we become conscious of our existence within eternity as we stand in awe appreciating and admiring such grandeur and order. In addition, we feel an inherent relationship with Nature. In those moments, at the height of our conscious awareness of this heartfelt existence, our thoughts are silent, yet our subtle feelings are deeply serene and meaningful. We simply get absorbed in the depth of the real reality and feel delighted. And sometimes even get enlightened.

No-thought moments do not include the moods created under the influence of alcohol or drugs, when one loses control of thoughts, awareness, and self. Even going to the movies or similar recreations may result in forgetting our problems and stopping our thoughts, which have limited benefits. However, they do not constitute a true no-thought moment. These artificial no-thought conditions do not create the energy that a natural no-thought state causes. Meditation and no-thought states entail full awareness and conscious efforts for self-control. Yet, most importantly, the value of a no-thought state lies in the high energy and freshness it induces, and not lethargy or ignorance of self. Instead of getting high with drugs or suffer the hangover of our regular drinking we could depend on more precious means of creating our no-thought moments. We all know how much we need these moments, but we go about creating them in our wrong creepy ways, again as another phenomenon of our modern culture.

We may induce or capture no-thought moments in many ways. Music has special power in creating such moments. Without the need for an artificial substance, such as drugs, music by itself can penetrate our senses extremely deep and touch our souls. Gardening or strolling in Nature and similar experiences revive our sense of being and connecting to our souls. All these simple experiences, music in particular, have been proven to stir brain hormones, create serenity and vigour, raise our spirit and awareness, and enhance our health. Such experiences are precious, as they relax (and also connect) our body and mind. They help us recreate and prolong our no-thought moments.

Furthermore, no-thought moments release a tremendous amount of creative energy through deeper perceptions. For the person who knows how to appreciate and create no-thought moments, this energy turns into significant thoughts, deeds, or creations subsequent to a no-thought experience. In fact, this transition turns into a natural cycle when a person rotates between no-thought and thoughtful moments automatically. This is a phenomenon of the real world. And strangely enough, we are all subconsciously aware of it and apply it occasionally, like the times we withdraw from people and normal living environment to sort out our life issues in a quiet corner personally. Yet, we neglect using this device more consciously and frequently, because we do not know how to delve into a state of full awareness. And because we are afraid of loneliness even for a few hours to achieve a no-thought moment effectively. While the cycle of 'no-thought, focused-thoughts' sounds quite useful for developing our philosophical principles, it can also help us deal with our stress as well as major life issues and decisions.

Enhancing our level of awareness about the process and purpose of no-thought moments enables us to benefit from these experiences more systematically and fully. Managing no-thought experiences is another step in finding the path of wisdom and healing our depression. No wonder we get attracted to gardening, music, artistic expressions, and other types of no-thought experiences to reach our inner energy. We choose and pursue these activities and hobbies subconsciously to relax our thoughts and overcome our depression. However, we have not learned to become aware and appreciate the significance of these no-thought experiences and understand why we seek them so intuitively. Thus, we do not absorb the whole energy that resides in a no-thought experience.

At the same time, moments of full significance also arise when there is a movement of a significant thought. Certain thoughts are significant in themselves and also give significance to our existence when we embrace them. These are thoughts of new creations, thoughts of humanitarian actions and decisions, thoughts about our 'self' and authentic needs, thoughts about our relationships with Nature, and thoughts regarding our souls and existence. These thoughts make life full of significance. All other thoughts are symptoms of life necessities or deficiencies and do not particularly give any significance to our being.

Significant thoughts give special significance and meaning to our actions and enrich many aspects of our lives. In parallel, no-thought moments offer certain experiences that are by themselves full of significance and glory, because they bring us the inner peace and freedom that our souls require away from daily encounters, thoughts, and our efforts to adapt.

In essence, life is full of significance when there is a significant thought as well as when there is a conscious no-thought moment. Self-actualizers' feelings of completeness, when their significant thoughts create a new concept, meaning, or value, show how significant life is for them in those moments—and they express it excitedly to the extent that explaining such exotic experiences is possible. Equally important, moments of no-thought signify our existence, too, when we closely sense life beauties and values. These are the only two ways we contact the real world. In fact, these two ways of 'significant life experiences' are related. Our significant thoughts and consequent discoveries lead to special and intensified feelings that push us into no-thought experiences and tranquility. Conversely, we get inspired during no-thought moments, which trigger new significant thoughts. Self-actualizer are more aware of their 'self,' soul, the universe, and the spirituality aspects of life and humans. They are attracted to Nature and simple life experiences that induce many no-thought moments regularly. The person with significant thoughts has a special appreciation of no-thought moments and experiences, and seeks these moments with high passion and anticipation. Significant thoughts and no-thought moments complement, as much as induce, each other.

CHAPTER TEN
Thoughts and Sufferings

While philosophical and purposeful thoughts enrich our lives, even they cause disappointment and stress when answers are rare and life's reality keeps getting harsher, especially when compared with our sacred desires. In all, a large amount of our thoughts (both fundamental and trivial) causes stress and depletes our energy and spirits. We spend almost all of our waking hours wondering about our needs, sufferings, and remedies, either consciously or subconsciously. We resort to all kinds of pleasures in hopes of eluding reality or subduing our sufferings. Eventually, mental pressures get overwhelming, as we do not know how to go about controlling the content of our thoughts. Especially when our thoughts are not pleasant, motivating, or purposeful, they only hamper our ability to assess our decisions and actions sensibly. They only cause more doubts about the meaning of our actions and the purpose of living altogether.

Our psychological needs, in particular, get quite complex as our Ego and Model strive to make judgments about things and people, adapt, seek attention and acceptance, etc. As these needs are hardly ever satisfied, we agonize with our thoughts wandering in all directions to find a way out of these never-ending, depressing conditions. Actually, our needs and sufferings are usually the cause and effect of one another. Our unsatisfied needs create suffering, and our suffering induces particular psychological needs (mostly the need for compassion). Everybody demands a lot of attention nowadays to help him/her through the healing process or at least maintaining a minimal sanity. When we suffer, we *need* something to distract us or somebody to guide us.

On the one hand, our needs and sufferings create unsettling thoughts, which cause more illusions and pain. On the other hand, only through our thoughts (valid reasoning) we can contain our shallow needs and vain sufferings. Only significant thoughts can revamp our niggling thoughts. Friendships and consoling can also help a bit, sometimes. Yet, ultimately, we must come to terms with our sufferings on our own through rational thinking. Carl G. Jung says:

"Suffering that is not understood is hard to bear, while on the other hand it is often astounding to see how much a person can endure when he understands the why and wherefore. A philosophical or religious view of the world enables him to do this, and such views prove to be, at the very least, psychic methods of healing if not salvation." Psychology and the East, Art Paperback, 1978, pages 210-211.

Thus, building our foundation of thoughts is crucial also for enduring and curing our sufferings by grasping their sources. On the other hand, J.K. Krishnamurti suggests that a no-thought state can transform suffering into passion and compassion:

"When you suffer, psychologically, remain with it completely without a single movement of thought. Then you will see out of that suffering comes that strange thing called passion. And if you have no passion of that kind you cannot be creative. Out of that suffering comes compassion. And that energy differs totally from

the mechanistic energy of thought." Truth and Actuality, Gollancz London, 1977, page 85.

Both approaches offered by Jung and Krishnamurti are important for mitigating our sufferings and facing life's hardships. Regardless of our success to attain the high passion suggested by Krishnamurti, quieting our minds in a no-thought state periodically gives our brains a break and enriches our spirits. It mitigates the effect of insignificant thoughts and activities overwhelming our lives and causing our sufferings. However, before getting into a no-thought state or meditation, we should decipher the causes of our depression and suffering through a thoughtful self-therapy, as explained in Chapter Seven. In that regard, Jung's suggestion is more essential in the long run, at least until we master 'self'-control. In fact, without self-awareness and high consciousness, a no-thought state cannot heal our suffering permanently. Only significant thoughts and insights with full consciousness can provide a platform for gauging and halting insignificant thoughts and desires, which can lead to salvation and solace. We must learn to distinguish between significant and trivial life issues and how to use the former to defeat the latter. Then, we can assess the nature of our suffering through wisdom and self-awareness.

Our suffering intensifies when we cannot grasp its source or insist on creating foolish rationale for it. Often we create some imaginary reasons or excuses to justify our suffering and our feeling of self-pity, perhaps hoping to attract other people's sympathy too. All along, we only cause our suffering for no reason other than the weakness of our convictions and souls, out of laziness in general, or not taking proper actions for getting out of our self-imposed mental slump. Often our suffering is due to our high expectations from life and people. Sometimes, we doubt or deny the causes of our suffering and do not admit that our stress is a symptom of a more fundamental problem. We ignore our inner feelings (conflicts) that signal the vanity of our lifestyles, or quickly turn them into the feelings of defeat and uselessness.

Sometimes, we suppress our thoughts and the symptoms of our hidden problems, e.g., neediness or greed. Sometimes, we allow some elusive concepts like love and happiness ruin our grasp of reality. When we doubt our inner feelings and instincts about our suffering, we dampen our interest or motivation to adjust our approach to life. Not knowing our reasons for living, or adopting erroneous purposes, cause our sufferings too. We are often too stubborn to accept the fact that our shallow mentalities are causing all our suffering, and instead keep pushing the same values and methods that have proven impractical and stressful. A good example is our erroneous approach in marital relationships, while continuing with the same methods and expectations. We cause our own sufferings through our idealistic and whimsical thoughts.

We all have personality issues and psychological defects, which create pain and problems for others and us. These personal idiosyncrasies differ according to our unique needs, interests, and willpower, of course. Yet, the healing can begin only when we stop doubting the fact that our peculiar defects and obsessions are causing most of our sufferings. We must acknowledge our paranoia and hang-ups, and learn how to view, defuse, and cure them. We need the courage and commitment to overcome the main barrier, i.e., our denial of the depth of our insecurities and eccentricities. We have some lingering doubts about our identity and purity, but fail to stop and analyse them.

We must admit that nobody out there in society is going to change to accommodate us and reduce our sufferings. The chance of finding our soul mate or even a reliable companion is also quite low. The odds would not rise if we keep imagining otherwise or dreaming. We must learn to accept, and live with, all these painful facts. Actually, we should expect the matters to get worse and pressures to mount in the years to come. We must accept the hard reality that no one understands and cares about our sufferings and real needs the way our imagination desires. Life hardships would hit us all our lives with very limited, if any, compassion.

Enough clues and warning signals are often around us about our misunderstanding of life, but we insist on ignoring them. Our frustration and anxiety often reflect our inattention or misinterpretation of the causes of our suffering. We feel helpless, as our struggles do not even bring us relief, let alone happiness. Instead, we feel desolate and lonely, and we get more exhausted and stressed out every day with our search for love and happiness. We try to correct the whole world and to make everybody understand our concerns. We like to inform our friends and family about our failing relationships and our needs. However, it seems, the more we try, the less we succeed to communicate with the rest of the world. Our frustrations and anxieties keep rising and we look in the wrong places for remedies.

A major problem is that we look externally for the causes of, and the cures for, our sufferings. We look for the faults of others, things, and systems. We ignore that mostly our own defects, and our persistence to take the perceived world too seriously, produce our sufferings. Our ignorance of our inner powers inhibits our real potentialities to manifest and energize our existence. Our thoughts and primary wisdom are lacking a strong foundation. Grasping these concepts is difficult for a person who is trying hard to find an honest job to meet his financial obligations, but keeps failing due to discrimination or job shortages. But if he finds the wisdom of living in the real world, realizes his inner powers, and looks for his few real needs instead of many superfluous ones, then perhaps he would stop caring too much about finding a job altogether. He learns to create his own job, accept a lower paying job, or maybe even ponder the possibility of living without a job if he has the psychological power and resources to do so. The bottom line is that *ideally* not even joblessness should become a cause for chronic stress and suffering. It should *ideally* induce more creativity to explore other options and opportunities for living.

Life's inevitable struggles become a bit less painful and overwhelming if we learn to manage our thoughts mostly by adjusting our expectations and attitude. Only we can feel and defeat these self-induced causes of our sufferings. We must learn to ignore those insignificant life events and expectations that enforce our erratic thoughts and break our spirits. Just a mere acknowledgment of our defects that cause our sufferings can mitigate the feelings of frustration and helplessness. Then we can use this awareness to subdue these known (deep-rooted) causes of sufferings gradually. Only we can adjust our mentality and adopt a more practical life philosophy. We can change our lifestyle and attitude to subdue our sufferings, and maybe even remove our personal defects and desires causing them.

We can build a profound foundation of thoughts upon personal experiences, through studying the visions and prophecies of great thinkers, and by making a finer judgment about the truth of existence. We can weed out the influence of social conditioning on our thoughts and crippling our power of reasoning. We can refute common perceptions and ideas that are senseless. We can resist the temptation of living and thinking for external approval, sexuality, greed, and power—as they are the direct sources of our sufferings. We can learn to manage our pains and paranoia better by pinpointing the insignificant thoughts behind them. And we can refuse to comply with superfluous standards and expectations propagated in society.

Common Sources of Suffering

Despite our unique personal reasons and remedies, most of our sufferings have common sources. Learning about the nature of epidemic social sufferings can heighten our awareness and lead to faster recovery. Of course, the intensity and nature of our suffering varies according to individuals' sensitivity, insecurities, weaknesses, surroundings, and life outlook. Yet, the common sources of mental sufferings relate to some kind of personal needs deprivations, such as:

- Financial burdens and worries
- Social burdens, sexual deprivations, and loneliness
- Paranoia, greed, jealousy, spite, etc.
- Psychological defects and chemical reactions in brain
- Lack of social recognition, insecurities
- Personality imbalance due to excessive Ego or Model
- Stress, fears, physical issues, unfulfilled dreams, etc.
- Incomplete or problematic relationships
- Lack of self-actualization and spirituality
- Boredom
- Etc.

Often a few of the above sources mix and cause niggling thoughts and sufferings. The fact that our sufferings are creations of our thoughts does not mean they are not real. Yet, their intensity is based on our perceptions (thoughts) about their importance, causes, and effects. Remembering this fact and controlling our thoughts help us mitigate our sufferings, mostly by redefining our long-term purposes of living. Furthermore, solutions are found easier for most of these causes if we unlearn the conventional methods and criteria of assessing our problems. We must become a bit more creative in circumventing social inconveniences and pressures. What we perceive as a problem might not be a real issue at all in a new perspective. Of course, suffering is mostly an emotional reaction, which is hard to measure quantitatively or set a rigid criterion about. Normally, our minds evaluate a recent situation in reference to past experiences or erroneous expectations (as a criterion) to gauge its impact and intensity. Our conditioned brains do some tricky and hasty assessments that instigate the feeling of suffering. Thus, we must discard the patterns and directions of our conditioned minds, and instead, depend on self-awareness to assess the causes and effects of a recent painful experience in a compassionate manner.

We have the option of 'self'-therapy or seeking the assistance of experts to overcome the depression caused by our psychological defects, or Ego and Model. All we need is an initial awareness and honest assessment of our weaknesses, which cause our suffering. We can help ourselves if we really believe that some *adjustments* are necessary. However, most of the time, we really do not see our deficiencies or believe in our ability to overcome them.

Obviously, some sources of sufferings are more difficult to control. This usually happens when external forces create or reinforce the sufferings. For example, financial burdens are always tangible and possibly due to no fault of our own. Even when caused by our defects such as laziness or extravagance, we still suffer, maybe even more, though at least we could try to do something about it. If we are reasonably aware, and make use, of our potentials to make a living, and do not waste our resources on unnecessary habits or ideas, then our financial hardship is probably not our fault. Or when we have difficulty with our relationships, it is often hard to adjust the situation. In most cases, it is also difficult to get out of them without causing a different kind of suffering for ourselves and others. Still, some alternatives may exist to alleviate the suffering. These kinds of unsolvable relationships can be worked out with some *adjustments* in our mentality and attitude when the situation itself cannot be rectified. Usually couples must find a more practical relationship model to help them interact more productively, even if it would have be a rather passive relationship.

We can choose a personal life path and develop a sensible mentality away from the influence of our lifelong biases and prejudices. A sound foundation of thoughts definitely shows us the need for passion and compassion, flexibility, stability, strengthening our beliefs, grasping 'self,' understanding the true means of happiness, and a life philosophy that inhibits sufferings. During this process, as our wisdom grows, we might gain some insights about life's mysteries, too, which would be only a sacred personal achievement, but never a definite and universal interpretation. Nobody can ever develop a comprehensive meaning for life.

Our sufferings, their causes, and our incessant search for a more peaceful means of living are merely the symptoms of our negligence to strive for self-awareness and the wisdom of a *'self'-control* life. Once we learn to live under the guidance of 'self,' according to the simple rules of the real world, we would not face as much suffering in our highly demanding societies. In the real world, beyond our demented illusions about life, our wisdom would be sufficient to void the sources, and avoid the thoughts, of suffering. We would be able to anticipate the situations, thoughts, and feelings of suffering. We may even be able to turn them around to our advantage in the form of passion and compassion, which are usually the main keys for discovering a few basic things about the big mysteries of life.

We can readily grasp and relate to the common sources of our sufferings. However, some deep causes of sufferings are due to the deprivation of our inner needs, including spirituality. This happens when we neglect to place sufficient emphasis on significant matters of life and to relinquish the majority of nonsensical desires, ambitions, plans, thoughts, actions, and decisions that we have been emphasizing on uselessly.

Our psyches are burdened by many sources of suffering from early on in our lives when we grow within, and adopt, many crooked social values. For example, a child may show frustration and suffering when one of his grades is not high enough or if he is not getting enough attention at school from his classmates and teachers. His conventional thinking (and sense of competition) makes him feel inadequate when he feels unappreciated or when he gets any grade lower than 'A,' because he has established it as a criterion for self-worth. These kinds of experiences feel like major failure or rejection and valid excuses for suffering. Only through some kind of mental rewiring and creativity, he might unlearn the condition of giving the matter of competition such significance. He needs a better criterion for success in order to avoid unnecessary sufferings all his life. Instead, we all absorb and apply these crude criteria for the rest of our lives so naively.

A fundamental cause of suffering is loneliness. The impression of loneliness hurts many people all by itself, even if they are only slightly ignored or when they are alone just a few hours. They are simply not prepared to bear even temporary loneliness, or even the impression of it. Obviously, many options exist nowadays for groups or individuals to work together to alleviate their sufferings due to loneliness. However, learning about the positive side of loneliness can reduce our fears of it, too, at least partially. During our no-thought experiences, we learn how moments of solitude (loneliness) could be relaxing and peaceful. Naturally, loneliness on a long-term basis is more complex than occasional ones. However, we can create some no-thought experiences to inhibit loneliness sufferings, learn some self-reliance, and perhaps induce higher consciousness and exceptionally divine feelings.

Drawing upon the sacred energy and passion that a no-thought state or loneliness creates, we can satisfy our deeper needs, which automatically generate tranquility and freedom. In those moments and conditions, we can create beautiful things and thoughts that override the feelings of loneliness many folds. The only problem is that our fears and conventional view of loneliness do not allow us to test and appreciate the advantages of solitude. We have become so desperately attached to things and other people, and, as a result, developed this tremendous paranoia and phobia about loneliness. Yet, in the real world, in fact, we are alone and stay lonely, even if we have a house full of friends and family. This does not mean that socializing is unimportant, but rather to recognize the merits of solitude early on in our lives. A more important point here is that the fear of loneliness can be cured only by discovering the joy of many life experiences that erupt only from loneliness and are extremely beautiful and full of passion.

Sufferings due to boredom relates to the lack of self-fulfilment. It reflects our negligence to find our niche and developing it. We all have some hidden potentials that press us subconsciously to emerge. They demand our attention or else we feel unfulfilled and empty. Exploring and nurturing our potentialities is difficult. However, once developed, they provide a chance for both 'self'-actualization and personal growth, which are the best antidote for sufferings too. These adventures are merely for internal gratification with no other ulterior motives. These experiences fill our lives with joy and creative energy, which would subdue our stress and banal sufferings due to boredom.

If our suffering relates to greed and jealousy, then it should be obvious how we can get rid of it. Why do we continue to look for more of the same things, which we cannot consume in our lifetime anyway, is difficult to grasp. How much wealth and power is enough? We can only ask our Ego! This only shows the absence of a reliable foundation of thoughts to guide our lives.

A solid foundation of thoughts is also the engine that drives our decisions and actions in the journey of life. In this journey, we follow a main path, loaded with social norms and values, which we may call 'The structure of life.'

The Structure of Human Life

We have different lives and destinies. Yet, in the larger scale of the universe and social order, we all travel the same road and reach the same destination. Like other species, we have a life expectancy, a range of strengths and weaknesses, special habits and defence mechanisms, certain habitats and existential characteristics, etc. Our relatively higher intelligence goads our drive for individualism and a variety of goals and lifestyles. Yet, a natural process defines the boundaries of our existence, while we proceed within certain social parameters, mostly driven by our genetic inheritance. After all, we are still only one infinitesimal part of the whole existence, in spite of our amazing initiatives, all the skyscrapers we can build, and the technologies we have mastered. Both the natural laws (our instincts) and social order drive us to follow a rather uniform path of life hypnotically. However, for building the foundation of our thoughts and life philosophy, we must establish how sensible following the guidelines of this shallow life structure is.

We all go through certain life phases and do similar things to prepare ourselves to live, multiply, raise our offspring, and die. In the process, we hope to satisfy our physical and psychological needs, both the instinctual ones and those we have developed artificially throughout the history. We have created things and thoughts that we believe are useful to us, although we can never be sure about that. We have already demonstrated how some of our demented thoughts make us capable of destroying our cultures and lives. We kill each other directly, or engage in life activities that would eventually destroy our societies and human existence.

Nonetheless, all these human attributes have evolved into a peculiar life structure according to our perceptions of our identity and needs and now *it* directs us uniformly within globally predefined parameters, although some of us are richer or happier. Within this ordained structure, everybody participates in similar processes and activities, instinctually or habitually, and pursues similar ambitions as a matter of social expectation. We entertain similar thoughts and do similar things to survive within this structure. This framework also imposes a rather fixed mentality and a common set of goals for us to follow. It imposes major decisions and doubts on everybody to dwell upon within an inherent order during three definable life phases. However, does this life structure make real sense? We must answer this question to our 'self' and soul.

Like a tree that has roots, a trunk, branches and fruits, the structure of human life is also constructed around some *foundation, purposes, activities, and outcome* during three life phases. In the first phase, we prepare ourselves for the life that lies ahead of us. We spread our roots and develop our strengths and primary wisdom to get ready for the challenging and demanding phases awaiting us. In the second phase, we develop our careers and family lives, which, similar to the trunk of a tree, comprise the main body or purpose of our lives. In the final phase, we expect to reap the fruits of a lifetime of efforts and growth. This common vision and approach to life feels natural to us all, but are our thought foundation, purposes, activities, and life outcomes sensible for a thinking human or are we still living soullessly like a tree?

The definition of a structure is significant for identifying the nature of the main decisions and actions needed in life. The intention is not to generalize life. Similar to a tree that has many branches and somehow signifies its uniqueness, individuals' distinctive dimensions are very interesting by themselves. They influence our progress, preferences, and mentality in making decisions and behaving. Our decisions and actions vary, because we see the same things differently, and because we judge a situation or person according to our personality and beliefs. However, despite our differences in judgment, values, decisions and actions, we all must follow the same road—a general life structure fitting our social values and culture. This life structure reflects the eventual commonality of human thoughts and actions in pursuit of their personal goals, for the purpose of survival, adaptation, and for getting other people's approval and cooperation. Our needs and struggles to adapt create a uniform structure for human life, though it has become a rather dysfunctional mechanism nowadays.

We cannot challenge this inevitable truth about humans' life and their perceptions. The only problem is that we follow this life structure rather blindly according to our presumed facts and myths. We have learned certain things about life and ourselves, but the unknown reality is getting wider in scope and affecting the structure of our lives significantly too. We know that our physics (and existence) is only a by-product of an accident, when one *particular* sperm luckily finds its way to a *particular* ovary in a special moment. But our souls? We do not know where it comes from and where it returns to. As long as our physics is healthy and conscious, we have a personality and a set of characteristics that contain both our physics and soul. Some of us know better how to envision and combine these two features of humanness, whereas a great majority of us can only understand, and stagnate mostly at, the physical level.

Understanding the features and values of our prevalent life structure is essential for developing our foundation of thoughts, but also as a main source of our suffering. Volume III is devoted to a study of humans' life structure, its characteristics, and the way we helplessly follow its guidelines rather robotically. Many questions can be raised about the validity of this structure and our hypnotic attachment to it. At the end, we may still believe that it provides the best option for living despite our inability to justify its meaning and purposes. However, by learning more about this dull life structure, we might be able to perceive and change at least a few aspects of it for ourselves for getting a bit more sense out of our existence. Most people are hoping to figure out the meaning of their activities and ambitions within this frivolous life structure when they say they want to 'find the meaning of life.'

Life's Major Decisions

Most of our decisions are simple automatic reflexes, such as walking, observing, listening, etc. They are mostly habits performed subconsciously with no substantive thought. The second group of our decisions requires some thinking, yet are considered mundane duties of living, such as shopping, cooking, eating, choosing a movie, going on a vacation, etc. They recur within the same frame of thoughts regularly. These two groups of decisions have no long-term effects on our lives, other than satisfying our basic needs and keeping us alive. As long as we stay rational, their outcomes are not too consequential. A wrong choice would not change the course of our lives.

The third group, however, holds high risks and requires conscious, significant thoughts. These major life decisions are essential due to their severe impact on our lasting welfare and happiness. They involve other people and external factors that we cannot control. Thus, their outcomes are quite unpredictable, yet have serious impact on the quality of our lives. They change one's life direction and they may cause lifelong agonies and depression. Indeed, they often result in irreversible consequences (e.g., a bad marriage) or loss of precious opportunities (e.g., regarding our career plans).

The problem is that we often fail to recognize the importance of our major decisions until it is too late and we face many disappointments and regrets. We do not know the right factors and do not realize the gravity of our decisions when we must make a good judgment, especially when some sort of infatuation infects us. Instead, we choose to be optimistic and adventurous. We just get sloppy or merely ignore the potential risks, especially when we do not have a proper decision criterion and a life philosophy to support our analyses. To measure the risks, we follow almost the same basic, shallow approach we apply to our mundane decisions, except perhaps we get more obsessed with some misleading factors (e.g., sexual attraction) that we find most urgent and valid all of a sudden. Our idealism, emotions, fears, genetic qualities, personality, and other reasons, make us lose our alertness, patience, and sensitivity to distinguish the long-term effects of some decisions. For the same reasons, in fact, we often emphasize on wrong factors naively when we make our major life decision. Often our decision criteria are too superficial and influenced by the perceived world's idealism, e.g., a chance for happiness, success, or having a companion. Most of us are emotional, driven by our sexual urges, and 'live in the now' too much already. We are too absorbed in our illusions and phony personalities to appreciate the real life essentialities or the importance of certain life-changing decisions. For example, when we marry a person for his/her money, love, or other superficial reasons, we get ourselves entangled in a situation with high potential for disaster.

Sometimes, we ignore or casually undermine the risks, hoping for the best instead of the worst; or we assume that dealing with the consequences later, if necessary, would not be too difficult. We cannot anticipate how differently we would feel and think in the future and what new criteria would all of a sudden make us look foolish for our past sloppy decisions. We are usually obsessed with our lousy justifications and false assessments, so we also ignore everybody else's advice, or our own inner voices that attempt to caution us. We simply do not care what would happen later, as long as we get something we crave so badly now, e.g., a companion or a taste of love. Laziness is another factor for our indecisions or ignoring the risks of our emotional or hasty decisions today.

Another factor for our sloppiness toward major life decisions is that people interpret life's essentialities differently according to their personalities, ambitions, and outlook. Some pursue life for pleasures only, some seek power per se, some emphasize on wealth accumulation, some crave constant approval and love, and some become stoics or idealists. Each group has a different standard of 'essentiality' for similar decisions, although they all have a somewhat similar understanding of the overall nature of our life structure. Overall, people have very peculiar life outlooks and insecurities that make them rather careless with their important life-changing decisions.

At the same time, youths' frustration with social chaos is another (sort of understandable) reason for their reckless decisions and behaviour. TV shows like American Idol reveal the vanity of social structure and youths' struggle to fit in. Their naiveté and lack of preparation for facing the sad reality of our shoddy culture is astonishing and worrisome. It is disheartening to watch the huge wave of dreamers coming for an audition and to hear so many of them insisting that singing and fame are their only goals with no plan B for their futures. That is their final decision!

The main point is that unless we plan our lives extra carefully nowadays, we must prepare ourselves for major disappointments and suffering throughout our lives. We normally do not have a good appreciation of major life decisions in terms of their complexity, or how deeply they can spoil our lives, usually forever. We do not know that we are too vulnerable and bound to make bad mistakes in today's chaotic social environment. Therefore, we create all kinds of self-induced causes for a lifelong suffering.

Even when we realize the deep lifetime effects of certain decisions, decision-making process and requirements are nowadays too complex all by themselves, as explained in Chapter Sixteen of Volume II. Even governments and corporations have major difficulty in making proper decisions in the present social structure. They do all kinds of feasibility studies for business purposes based on economic and financial data and forecasting algorithms, yet the world economy is in such disarray. Even these sophisticated economic models and studies have proven to be full of flaws and used only for justifying governments' agendas and giving the public the impression that they know what our officials are doing. Some of our personal decisions have much severer consequences on our lives, but are even less analysable than economic data, while we do not have proper decision criteria or models to aid us, either. Instead, a great deal of emotional factors always interferes with major personal decisions both before and after we take an action, as we lose the control of many factors and people involved in the implementation of our decisions.

Nevertheless, we must remember that for every major life decision, we must understand its risks totally and be prepared to face the worst possible consequence before making the decision. As a basic example, someone quits his job to accept another one, without doubting the possibility of not being happy in the new job. He is either naive to think that things would definitely work out as he plans, or losing the new job and looking for a third one is not of a major consequence to him. If he is confident to find another job quickly, then, of course, the consequences of quitting his present job is not substantial. As a result, the decision itself would not be a major one, assuming that his assessments of the future events and circumstances hold true. However, in most cases, even when we feel certain about the outcome, still things often turn out contrary to our expectations. Our decision criteria and social circumstances often change frequently without any prior indication. So being too optimistic or adventurous might not be a good strategy for many people. Again, trusting our naïve view of social systems or people's promises is a personal responsibility and if we are not careful, the matter is only our negligence. That is how we cause our self-induced sufferings. If, in the above example, we were talking about a prospective marriage partner, instead of a job, the gravity of such decision becomes even more apparent.

Although we usually sense most of these basic requirements for planning our lives, we often do not scrutinize on them seriously with enough patience or let our emotions or insecurities make us ignore their importance. Volume III of this trilogy is devoted to these important decisions due to their significant risks and impact on the quality of one's life.

'Life' and 'Self' Decisions

Based on this book's discussions, we can divide essential decisions into two major types. The first category of decisions relates to the requirements of living in society, maintaining our relationships, satisfying our economic needs, etc. Let us call them 'life' decisions. The second type of decisions relates to our eagerness to learn about our personal identity, spirituality, and real inner needs. Let us call them 'self' decisions. In this regard, we make decisions to adopt and pursue a specific life philosophy, build a solid foundation of thoughts, and take specific actions to maintain a high level of awareness and 'self'-control. The objective is to satisfy our self-actualization and spirituality needs by understanding more about our 'self.'

For people who do not grasp, or care to realize, the essence of 'self' and its unique needs, no decisions or actions regarding the second type seem necessary, let alone considering them 'essential.' This group, which holds a majority in society, has no patience or interest in these kinds of questions and efforts. Thus, they concentrate solely on 'life' decisions, i.e., socioeconomic matters and relationships. On the other hand, in the eyes of the minority who believes in understanding 'self' and leading a 'self'-controlled life as an essential guide and philosophy, placing emphasis merely on socioeconomic decisions and actions appears ridiculous. They believe the other group is not only missing the real meaning of life, but also causing their own agonies and pains merely out of their naivety—not to mention their high share of irresponsibility for creating the chaos in society.

For a prudent person, it is essential to at least understand the implications of, and relations between, 'life' and 'self' decisions and actions. We need this awareness for creating some form of harmony between social life and personal enlightenment. It is hard to imagine how we can go through life without some notion of 'self' included in our foundation of thoughts to support our decisions and actions. It seems that our personal problems and social pains are the outcome of our shortsightedness, and the lack of a good foundation of thoughts and 'self'-control. Nevertheless, this is the reality that many of us have chosen as our only option. Thus, we continue our lives in vain without understanding the reasons for our living and suffering.

On the other hand, only a small group can concentrate solely on 'self' questions and decisions, e.g., self-awareness and divinity. They find the strength and courage to break away from the mainstream and pursue seclusion and enlightenment as their sole path of life. This mentality and approach is not something that many of us can understand or attempt, so we do not spend much time explaining it.

For most of us, adopting a middle ground or moderation seems perhaps the most sensible approach. We just hope to combine the benefits and wisdom of both 'life' and 'self' decisions and actions to attain the highest level of personal fulfilment and peace. At least, we may be able to regain some relative freedom and curb some of our sufferings. At a middle ground, we can learn about ourselves and our life options without giving up so much of our regular life commitments and pleasures. At the same time, we can apply the wisdom we earn from 'self' decisions and actions to our social life situations directly.

The Substance of 'Self' and 'Life' Decisions

A right mix of 'life' and 'self' related decisions and actions can enrich our lives and reduce our sufferings. Our occasional encounters with our spirituality urges, while pursuing our normal lives, might raise our interest for 'self' awareness and possibly making our life decisions more in line with non-materialistic values. For example, we may consider devoting a part of our lives to some humanitarian causes. Building the foundation of our thoughts and choosing a life philosophy require learning about 'self' too. These moments of awakening happen to many people. Some pause and pay attention to those profound thoughts (because they soothe their minds). They discover something new about themselves and their inner power. They may take these signs seriously as a guide for exploring the seven basic elements of 'self,' as discussed in Chapter Two of Volume II. However, most of us bypass these callings quickly and impatiently, or do not follow them up seriously. Thus, we never get the chance to at least explore the alternatives to our mundane lives. We continue to suffer when we never get a chance to discover our real essence of being and free our souls.

Realistically, we do not know how to deal with the inner voices and questions circling in our heads, especially if we do not have the time, or when the messages contradict our lifestyles and values. However, with some patience and practice, we can learn to absorb these messages and give some benefit of a doubt to the possibility of a more serene life outside the prevalent social structure.

Transcending to the real world sphere and realizing our 'self' occur gradually, of course. We must learn the basics first, and then mature by getting deeper into our unconscious mind and 'self' personality. During this slow process of transcendence to a new realm and realizations, we learn more about our inherent identity, including our weaknesses and potentialities. Only through sacrifice, reserved apprehension, and wisdom, we may climb the mountain of the truth and reach the summit. Only through patience and conviction, we can achieve selfhood and feel the results of our meditations and beliefs. Nobody can jump beyond his/her *primary wisdom* (which evolves slowly) for a higher vision of life—not even with the use of drugs or artificial stimuli. Unfortunately, the majority of us fail, because we look for a quick solution and salvation, or at least a sign of wisdom, when we have not even learned how to do a basic self-analysis or create a no-thought experience for ourselves.

The secret for finding a relative peace of mind and happiness lies in our ability to develop a flexible mentality, in which both 'life' and 'self' choices are simultaneously and continuously interactive, and justifiable too. Both 'life' and 'self' orientation are important within the structure of human life and require our scrutiny and right decisions. As noted, however, our emphasis on 'life' decisions, has limited our ability to bring meaning and serenity to our daily routines.

Discussions in this book have revealed a long list of 'major decisions' we must make as we face major dilemmas about:

- The purpose of life and means of happiness.

- The kind of life philosophy that fits our personality, needs, and plans.
- Our values, beliefs, and convictions.
- How to manage our thoughts and create no-thought moments.
- Our authentic (versus superficial) personal needs and how to go about curbing or satisfying them.
- Our long-term objectives and a plan to achieve them.
- The risk oriented opportunities and timing of them.
- Our real potentialities and limitations.
- Monitoring our three personality aspects and finding 'self'-control.
- The career we should choose.
- Gaining our financial sense and living within our limits.
- The means and criteria to choose a spouse.
- Having children or not, how to nurture them, and what our role should be.
- Etc.

The above decisions and actions also raise many basic questions such as the followings:
- Why do we feel, act, and choose in certain ways?
- Why do we educate ourselves or learn things?
- Why do we need friends and companionship?
- Why do we work?
- What are the sources of our fulfilments?
- What are our financial resources?
- How should we set our life priorities and expectations?
- How do we feel about our relationships with people and Nature?
- Etc.

We ponder these questions regularly, but only superficially within the context of our mundane busy lives. They appear to surge from our subconscious mind, more in a form of an inner voice (or conscience) that requires profound, philosophical answers. In fact, these questions reflect the inherent urgency of 'life' and 'self' decisions in some combination, depending on how deeply we view them or act upon them. We cannot avoid them even if we are the most pragmatic 'life' oriented person. These questions, and our corresponding decisions and actions, inherently construct the structure of life. We face them regardless of our emphasis on certain inner needs, and whether or not we have a profound foundation of thoughts to draw upon. However, we do not pause adequately to contemplate these questions in some depth in relation to our purpose of living and for being a better person. Volume II of this trilogy discusses 'self' decisions and Volume III deals with 'life' questions and decisions in some detail.

For those devoted to 'self' and in search of a profound foundation of thoughts, a different concern may also exist. The challenge for this group is to transform those profound thoughts into practical actions. We may have been successful in preparing a sense of 'self' commitment and some kind of foundation of thoughts to guide us through life. But then, when it comes to act upon our commitments or convictions, we fall short of our objectives and standards. When the time comes for us to act with integrity, we fail to adhere to our 'self'-control discipline and we get tempted by money, love, pleasures, greed, sex, and other personal weaknesses that often take over our profound commitments and character. Or sometimes, we simply become lazy in pursuing our commitments and objectives. Or we lose our patience and conviction.

For many reasons, we often fail to implement the ideals and standards we have set in our foundation of thoughts. We may then take this failure as a sign of irreparable personal weakness. We give up our idealistic vision of 'self' and a commitment to delve into the depth of our being. We just adopt a superficial, phony, or passive/aggressive personality to plough on through life. The means of building our spirits to overcome these obstacles is addressed in Volume II.

The 'Self' and 'Life' Impasse

Ironically, 'life' and 'self' appear like two opposing poles on the mysterious realm of human existence. The more we emphasize on 'life,' the more we lose sight of our 'self.' Conversely, attending to 'self' requires letting go of 'life' drastically, at least in the form we perceive and live it merely according to our desires and ambitions. Our struggles to find 'self' within 'life' (or 'life' within 'self') only increase our inner conflicts and we get more impatient and frustrated with people and ourselves. Both life and self feel like abstract mysteries that we can never grasp, let alone integrate. We try hard to at least find a meaning for life. However, it persists to remain a mystery, like a vague notion only teasing and confusing us. We feel the same way about 'self,' too, which appears to be an ambiguous concept beyond our reach. Yet, we know that both 'life' and 'self' are real, as inherent features of human existence, even though we are unable to define or find them. We suspect that 'life' would reveal its true meaning only if we find our 'self.' And we suspect that 'self' would emerge only within the context of the true life, which is pure and simple, unlike the lifestyles we are pursuing nowadays. These facts suggest that 'life' and 'self' are actually complementary (instead of opposing) poles for signifying human existence. They are the prerequisites of each other and only together reveal their meanings and significance.

Fortunately, many of us believe that our curiosity and struggles to find life and self are justified. Many clues show that our seemingly vain attempts to find the essence of our existence, the 'self,' within 'life' is not an ambitious or naïve adventure, but rather an instinctual urge that might be the key to our salvation. And our seemingly futile struggle to find the essence of 'life' within 'self,' the free being, is not a passing romanticism, but rather a natural calling.

We must live with this paradox throughout our lives while we hope to make the right decisions for living, too, at least for stopping our naive or egotistical choices that cause us too much suffering. It gets difficult to build a reliable life philosophy when we seem to have difficulty understanding even the meanings and contents of life and self as two main pillars and puzzles in the realm of our mysterious existence. Still, in spite of this paradoxical barrier, we must find a means of developing a solid personality and foundation of thoughts for making those major life decisions listed on pages 265-6. In fact, the difficulty of making such vital decisions stems from our failure to figure out the meanings of life and self at some basic level at least. After all, it is not easy for most of us to create a right balance between 'life' (our worldly desires) and 'self' (our spiritual aspirations).

CHAPTER ELEVEN
Actions and Adjustments

While hoping to discover 'life' and 'self' all our lives, we try hard to fit within our complex and showy lifestyles. We strive to build our convictions and adjust our attitude to make ourselves acceptable in society. We want to be open-minded and flexible, while we dream that our actions would eventually have some meaning and value.

Yet, the prospect of our endless struggles often appears doubtful. Even our sensible decisions and actions lead to no tangible outcome, if not disaster and disappointment. It hurts, especially, when we cannot find peace with others and within ourselves after making so many tough, heroic adjustments in our mentality and attitude. It seems like we are staggering on a wobbly path of life and hoping for some kind of magic and enlightenment to save our souls.

With such busy, agitated state of mind, our personalities also form around some naïve beliefs and expectations from 'life,' with little regard for 'self' realization. We just pamper our Model and Ego in hopes of capturing happiness and success, but become only more needy and greedy, without getting any lasting rewards. Thus, we wonder about the value of our actions and planning our lives so diligently to no avail. We doubt our decision-making ability altogether—now or when we had a chance to plan our life better. We wonder whose fault it is that we do not get the right results from all our efforts. Nevertheless, we blame one or a combination of the following factors for our failures and disappointments:

1. Social Disorder
2. The Role of Destiny
3. Personal Negligence

Coming to grips with these three bottlenecks can help our alertness for personal decision-making. We might even admit our normal sloppiness and naiveté in handling life's main challenges. We might doubt our objectivity for drawing our life plans and taking worthy actions. In all, our failure to grasp the impact of the above noted three bottlenecks would in fact be only another evidence of 'Personal Negligence.'

1. Social Disorder

At work, in our families, or during our routine socioeconomic activities, we must deal with other personalities and depend on their cooperation. The problem is that most of our life's major decisions and actions require the participation or knowledge of one or more individuals. Therefore, we seem helplessly at the mercy of society and too many people to plan and follow a rather smooth life. Unfortunately, the present social disorder driven by capitalistic values and low morality has made everybody too self-centred and careless about other people's needs and plans. So, even when we do our life plans diligently and take timely actions to secure our future, there is always a good chance that other individuals, and social disorder in general, sabotage the outcome either deliberately or ignorantly. There is a lot of ignorance and deliberate malice in society, and the situation would only get worse by the way our social values and structure is designed. We cannot avoid people's role or interference and all the bad information in society that affects our life plans somehow. The best we can do is to keep this major bottleneck in mind when tackling our major life decisions regarding our jobs, marriages, investments, etc. We must be ultra vigilant even for maintaining a simple life, if we wish to avoid being shattered within this horrendous structure and lose our integrity and identity. We should be neither influenced nor intimated by this chaos. Most importantly, we must make sure that our mentality and actions are not already infected and we have not become another promoter of this disorder, e.g., as a pushy salesperson selling useless or shoddy stuff to people.

Our role for coping in society is discussed in different parts of this trilogy, especially in Chapter Two of Volume II when the seven elements of 'self' are studied. Particularly, read the 'Individualism' element.

2. The Role of Destiny

Is destiny something we can affect even slightly with our actions and decisions, e.g., when we perform all kinds of analyses and make timely decisions for living well and happy? Our basic knowledge and common sense dictate that we should try to play a role in forming our future. Yet, we realize that no matter how diligently we plan and decide, the odd outcomes of our decisions and actions often remain beyond our control. Sometimes, things keep going wrong no matter how hard we plan and decide. And sometimes things happen in our favour no matter what stupid decisions we make. We all have felt the existence of some strange (maybe playful) power that either blesses or punishes us for no reason at all. Scientifically, all these coincidences are attributed to the randomness of the universe and people's irrationality. But some of us cannot stop feeling that there is something more fundamental behind these coincidences.

So, are we at the mercy of destiny, or we could take some control over the outcome of our actions and decisions? Is there any sense to overly concern ourselves about our major decisions and actions beyond hoping for the best and leaving everything to destiny? 'Just take the risk and do not worry,' could be one type of personal life philosophy. If the consequences of our major actions are unpredictable and unanalysable, then what is the point of trying to measure or even fuss about some imaginary outcomes too much? Should we admit our severe limitation for building our lives or still believe in having absolute control, or something between these two extremes?

These fundamental doubts and our curiosity to resolve them have constituted the need for all the discussions in this trilogy. The goal is to explore our doubts, including the role of destiny, and develop a reliable belief system for ourselves. It would be a personal matter and decision as to how much faith we should have in fate, and that should constitute a major chapter in itself when we write our unique life philosophy. Yet, one thing we can always remember is that, regardless of the type of our life philosophy, the outcome of our major life decisions could potentially ruin our lives forever—or conversely, guarantee a tranquil outcome.

We have concluded that, since the consequences of major decisions and actions always remain uncontrollable, we need a strong foundation of thoughts to make the right decisions in the first place. But then, we also need a high spirit to face all the inevitabilities and deal with our possible failures more patiently. This does not merely suggest that we should be more thoughtful or spend more time on thinking. Rather, we must learn to accept all the risks associated with our choices and decisions, including our choice of a life path and philosophy. We must learn about various elements within our foundation of thoughts, including spirituality, in order to build a plausible personal philosophy of life toward a relative sense of happiness. We can build a superior foundation of thoughts based on an appreciation of what those means of happiness are. We can try to understand what really matters at the end and not only today. We can set our priorities around those values and thoughts that become valid in the third phase of everybody's life. Yet, some people may argue, quite validly, 'Why should I even believe I would reach the third phase of my life?' "I might die tomorrow. Let's be happy now," they could suggest. Nonetheless, the important point is that the way we would measure the consequences of significant life decisions cannot be, and would not follow, the same criteria we use for mundane decisions. We should also remember that the way we would measure those consequences, when (and if) we reach the latter phases of life, cannot be, and would not follow, the same criteria that seem relevant and important to us today. So, for this reason alone, we cannot simply 'live in the now,' and according to the perceived world values and criteria. Instead, we must apply the criteria that would make sense in the third phase of our lives, and perhaps more in line with those authentic human needs within the real world context. We can use 'self'-control to mitigate the demands of Ego and Model for compliance with prevalent social norms and making life's major decisions. It would also be wise and more prudent to believe in reaching the third phase of our lives. If we live healthy, we will have to face the reality of life in all three phases of life.

3. Personal Negligence

All the topics in the remainder of this chapter reflect our personal negligence for the shoddy outcomes of our actions and life plans. We are at fault when we are lazy, remain naïve about social chaos and peoples' intentions, have low morality, ignore 'self'-awareness, or do not care about adjusting our attitude and mentality to get along with others more harmoniously.

The Morality of Our Actions

Many of our actions and reactions could turn up to be hazardous to others and us. This is not a big surprise considering humans' enormous quirks and poor nature. It would not be too much of a crime, either, if our actions have been mostly due to our mistakes or ignorance and not intentionally too malicious. However, we are guilty if we ignore our mistakes. Our reluctance to adjust our wrong actions, especially if it has harmed other people, shows the inferiority of our character. It is a big 'personal negligence.'

Sometimes, we might even have valuable thoughts and intentions, yet our shaky moral and character prevent us from turning them into worthwhile decisions and actions. A good example is the promises of political leaders to do all sorts of services for the helpless and desperate public (which are significant thoughts and intentions), but they eventually fail to act honestly. Even when they start with sincere thoughts to help people, their actions turn out mostly egotistical and self-serving (with hardly any selfless motives for their actions). They only cause us more doubts and desperation when they lie and abuse democracy to manipulate voters with their luring propagandas and shoddy promises. Even worse, we elect them to save a few dollars on our taxes perhaps, instead of worrying about all the corruption and the collapse of the entire social system in a few decades.

When our leaders all over the world behave so greedily and irresponsibly, as puppets and agents of conglomerates, how can anybody expect the rest of us, we commoners, ever think and act a bit more honestly and compassionately for our own sake and possibly saving the doomed destiny of humanity? We have difficulty transforming even our few significant thoughts into actions, because it requires certain personal qualities such as confidence, integrity, and perseverance, which many of us have lost during our dealings and encounters within the crooked socioeconomic environment. After all, a great deal of character and morality is necessary to avoid the luring social incentives for compliance and instead focus on some worthy thoughts, plans, and actions.

It is hard to judge our negligence or mistake quickly, but we can learn to do so if we keep monitoring the outcomes of our actions and relationships more consciously and conscientiously. If we stop being so self-centred and careless, we acquire a sense of awareness about our actions, especially when other people are involved.

Nevertheless, we must feel obliged to control regularly the morality of our actions and the way we deal with other people's reactions even in our basic relationships, let alone for discharging our social responsibilities. It always pays off, at least personally, to stay less selfish and more ethical.

Awareness and Actions

Low 'self'-awareness is another serious 'personal negligence' for decision-making. One main benefit of 'self'-awareness is to become proactive and take the right actions in life, instead of procrastinating or depending on destiny. Actually, the goal is to be prepared for destiny interfering for better or worse, usually the latter. 'Self'-awareness is also for gauging the value of our actions for us and its possible impact on others. Furthermore, 'self'-awareness reminds us of the high significance of some life decisions and actions, so we begin to discern life questions and choices clearer. Accordingly, we gain more control over our actions and their outcomes, along with a better perception of their meanings and importance. We gauge the causes of our failures and success more realistically. Through self-awareness, including our reserved trust in destiny, we feel in charge and full of confidence with less concern about so many issues in the world that we had taken so seriously as matters of life and death. We relax and take life easier with our simpler needs and expectations.

Awareness does not refer to a mythical (supernatural) state or wisdom. Awareness is not the same thing as awakening, which has a higher divine source, although they evoke each other within a person gradually. Awareness is merely the degree, depth, and longevity of our attention to every important thought or life experience—a high level of consciousness and comprehension of factors surrounding an issue leading to full 'awareness.' Using an example can perhaps help.

We listen to music with different degrees of attention. This is true even when we listen to our favourite type of music and particular pieces that usually give us a special feeling. Sometimes, we listen to music in background while running our errands or read a book. We hear it, enjoy it somewhat, and relax, etc. In these instances, we are aware of the music, but our degree of consciousness and comprehension is low. Sometimes, we make a point to listen to music per se, by going to a concert hall or in seclusion at home. In these cases, we pay more attention, understand, and appreciate the music much better. As we prevent interruptions, the span of our attention increases and therefore we get carried by the music. Occasionally, we may lose our attention and fall into a daydream, get distracted, or even fall asleep, perhaps by the romantic feelings that the music itself is creating. This is an average awareness level, even though we mean to pay attention and money (if we go to a concert) to listen to music.

At a full awareness level, however, we simply follow every single note. We anticipate the approach of the next note, receive it, absorb it and get ready for the next note to arrive. In fact, many notes are emitted simultaneously at every tiny instant, yet in full awareness, we can distinguish them and synthesize them instantaneously. We not only follow the notes, but also comprehend the relationships between consecutive notes and bars in harmony with the overall orchestration. While partially absorbed in the music, we remain more conscious of each moment and note, and in the way we relate to the whole tune. This is almost like a conductor's job leading the orchestra, with full attention to every note and instrument that should emerge in a fraction of a second.

In the awareness mode, we do not forget ourselves or fall asleep, but get dissolved in the process of following the notes that are pouring out at an extremely high speed. In fact, we become extremely conscious and alert. We become the carrier of notes. Our mind is capable of receiving all the notes at high speed, while blocking any other thought or distraction that may try to interfere with our level of concentration and attention. The span of attention must be long enough for full comprehension and grasping the depth of the message completely, or else we must start all over with still higher attention. With a piece of music, we hear the first note and continue to focus for the length of the music for a complete appreciation of what it really means. Long intervals of full attention, which is required for major pieces of classical music, can increase the level of awareness and enjoyment once we learn to do it. This is, of course, only one aspect of the classical music that makes it attractive to some people. A conductor's or a soloist's long pause at the end of a performance shows his/her attempt to return to the normal awareness level after spending a long time within the realm of full awareness.

The value and depth of an experience or thought increases substantially when it is fully comprehended. That is why awareness can introduce us to such divine dimensions of life (and 'self') that are not visible or sensible under normal conditions and regular levels of awareness.

These simple principles of awareness apply to all our encounters in life. For awareness, we simply ask ourselves some basic questions and then draw upon our foundation of thoughts to find the answers objectively in a peaceful process of meditation. By these questions, we like to find out whether the decision or action at hand is significant or not, and if yes according to what criteria. We like to gauge the criteria we use to validate our decision and action too. Are the criteria based on family and social conditioning or 'self'-control principles developed through our life philosophy? We like to know which aspects of personality are in charge of judgment about this decision or action. If it is Ego or Model driven, we like to find out why we cannot resist or avoid them. We like to know how to distinguish worthy actions from unimportant and irrelevant ones. Many shallow activities (such as obsession for fashion, shopping, travelling) have now been taken as the necessities of living, but they are merely distracting us to attend to more fundamentals of life, including our understanding of 'self' for becoming a better human being. We should reduce our concentration on such trivia beyond the minimum level of attention that is practically required for relaxation. The idea is to save our precious energy, nerves, and time for more significant thoughts and productive decisions of life. And conversely, by learning to use the right criteria, we like to acknowledge, and place more emphasis on, those major life decisions and actions that we have so far handled so casually. We want to stop dwelling on our obsessive needs and life patterns.

Through 'forward thinking,' we learn how trivial some of the things we do in life would prove to be. Conversely, we can learn how to build a fulfilling life by doing certain activities that are real sources of inner satisfaction, which we have neglected all along. High awareness about important things, and relinquishing insignificant ones, is simple and practical, once we put our 'thoughts' into it and when we find the right criteria for making these distinctions. One simple test is that almost all Ego driven activities and thoughts are unessential. The same thing is true of a great majority of Model motivated thoughts and actions. Through awareness, it becomes easy to detect Ego and Model oriented thoughts, and thus reduce their significance in our lives when we must make decisions or when we have doubts.

Significant things in life are so by their own natural existence and manifestation. They are not the creations of our fantasies and naïve values. And they are not urges pushed by Model and Ego. However, we cannot make this simple distinction as long as we are entangled with mundane and trivial matters we have chosen as our biggest challenges and problems. The test of significance lies in the genuine feelings of joy and a lasting inner satisfaction that comes from some experiences, such as watching a sunset with full awareness. These authentic feelings are never found in other experiences, which would necessarily reflect the insignificance of most activities we do. Furthermore, significant experiences release a large level of energy that is heartfelt and continues rather consistently throughout our lives. They lift our spirits, whereas trivial experiences only consume our energy without giving back anything in return, other than perhaps some short-lived pleasures and egotistical satisfaction.

As we eliminate unauthentic things and feelings from our lives, our senses become sharper gradually for finding those significant things in life that enhance our authenticity, make us feel our souls, and make us feel the whole world with our souls. From these experiences, we build up a high level of awareness to differentiate all the significant things in life even more diligently. The discussions of facts and myths in Part II revealed how all those things we accept as 'facts' indeed cause our sufferings, and all the things we view as 'myths' can become the sources of inner joy and significant facets of our being. Those discussions can provide a starting point to heighten our awareness of the significant stuff of our lives.

Another reason that some life decisions are considered 'major' is due to their prominent potentials for mapping the path of our lives and preventing lifelong disappointments and sufferings. Thus, adopting the needed 'self'-control principles and adapting ourselves to the requirements of that unconventional, and rather lonely, lifestyle are major life decisions. We must be prepared for the inevitable hardships of adjusting our mentality to live closer to the boundaries of the real world, rather than within the illusions of the perceived world. This mental adjustment is another *major* life decision by itself. Although we cannot expect to attain 'self' awareness easily, we can approach it gradually with honest efforts and beliefs. We must be truly convinced that pursuing a 'self'-controlled lifestyle is a viable option for us in the long run. But how can we adjust our mentality to achieve 'self' awareness?

The Capacity to Adjust and Act

We may have strong beliefs and profound thoughts to build our standards and decision-making criteria. We may even be a great philosopher and an advocate of certain worthy causes in society, and yet often fail in our encounters because we cannot refine our simplest attitude. For example, our Self may induce the soothing thought of forgiving someone, for our own sake, despite his/her proven guilt. However, we hesitate to go to our friend or spouse and tell him/her how we feel, and our willingness to move on. Our spoiled Ego keeps resisting and preventing us from actually doing something a little different for a change. Or, we might have realized, through our rare 'self'-driven thoughts, that we have made a mistake. Yet, when we must admit and express it openly, again our Ego or Model stops us. Our false pride, or the idea of, 'What others may think about our passivity (or admission of some guilt),' prevents us from doing the right things for our own sake at least. These types of inner resistance and mental conflicts hinder the transformation of our significant thoughts (e.g., forgiveness) into actions. Our muddled mentality is ruining our chance of looking outside the box and perhaps freeing ourselves from the hold of the ostentatious social norms and our spoiled personality. In all, our shallow personalities usually stir merely vile thoughts and decisions, and in return, our trifling thoughts warp our personality further. Only Ego and Model thrive and drive our actions. Thus, the value of our thoughts and decisions become questionable, too, if not futile altogether. Only occasionally, when Self happens to get a break, our thoughts become significant and we initiate some worthy actions.

Fear and insecurity are other causes of our failure to adjust our mentality and turn our worthy thoughts into soul-cleansing actions. We get intimidated and invent juvenile justifications for our inaction. Often, we even doubt our earlier profound decision to adjust our attitude and we revert to our old judgments and habits. The sources of our fears are numerous and too complex to discuss here. However, we all have hidden insecurities that overwhelm us when we least need them. They are often justified, too, for coping in society and staying practical in life. For example, we may not like our boss or job, but the fear of losing our source of income and not finding another job forces us to compromise our integrity and beliefs and accept our boss's intimidation or selfish expectations. Another example is, when we are lonely, we compromise on the quality of the person we may accept for friendship or marriage. Now just imagine the humility of feeling obliged to work in a debilitating job only to keep a nagging wife and a bunch of unappreciative kids happy—perhaps for a few more years before they leave us anyway with all kinds of accusations and ingratitude.

As if reality is not tough enough to deal with every day, sometimes we witness our paranoia paralyse our thinking and decision-making abilities. Our erratic perceptions of reality turn into bizarre illusions that overwhelm our whole existence. Our paranoia and illusions become inescapable 'facts' of life in our heads and cripple us completely at the end. For instance, not finding a decent job is a modern life reality, but also presents one major source for our rising paranoia and insecurity about the whole structure of life, including the socioeconomic aspects of it.

Our genetic flaws in combination with the rising social havoc infect our personality and dampen our spirit severely. Although the levels of personal intelligence and potentialities are important genetic factors for building a proactive personality, a variety of simple flaws can make us impatient, biased, or unable to focus and persevere for achieving certain worthwhile objectives. Yet, we do not wish to recognize these common bottlenecks and make some adjustments in our attitudes and thoughts. We just flow with the current and hope to survive financially and emotionally.

We move on from one project to another and never complete any of them as they soon feel boring or futile. We lose our sense of judgment and self-image due to our inability to embrace 'self' driven thoughts and incentives. This epidemic has ruined our chances for finding even a little peace and sanity, let alone the elusive success and happiness that everybody is so desperate to grasp. Even our philosophical thoughts and opinions are often for either hiding our failures or serving our rigid mentality and selfish desires. Accordingly, our inherent potentialities and thoughts do not transform into any kind of worthwhile and meaningful actions.

Many other forces hinder our ability to adjust our mentality and turn our significant thoughts into action. Our mere awareness of these inevitable life traps might at least help us a bit to subdue their effects and possibly alleviate our stress somewhat too. We might even learn to overcome our chronic resistance to act. For example, when we realize that our laziness or lack of perseverance stops us from implementing our plans or decisions, we may finally decide to do something about this self-imposed barrier before our whole identity and mind are shattered. With awareness and courage to acknowledge our weaknesses, we can prepare ourselves to act and find solutions instead of submitting to a substandard living helplessly and only whining.

The extreme harm we regularly cause one another with our vile actions is mostly due to our low characters and high frustration. We only blame other people's actions and attitude without giving even the slightest thought to the possibility of our own flaws contributing to the overall social mayhem. We always exonerate ourselves quickly and move on. Thus, everybody suffers the severe consequences of living randomly and acting selfishly according to our shoddy choices and decisions. Even when Self attempts to influence at least a bare minimum of our attitude and actions, e.g., by condemning our urge for revenge, we personally sabotage our chances with our childish habits. We seldom succeed to convince ourselves about the value of following a more tranquil life direction. Our shallow, selfish urges always interfere and cause more chaos, confusion, and mental distress for the whole society. Our rigid, demented personality does not allow us develop a solid foundation of thoughts and make life's important decisions more wisely and compassionately. The rising level of notorious actions and crimes, and the way they are spreading all over the world in all aspects of people's lives, demonstrate the demise of Self and the dominance of Ego and Model in modern societies.

Nevertheless, despite all the social hindrances around the glob and personal weaknesses maiming us, perhaps there is still hope for some people to develop the right mindsets, firm convictions, and real commitments to transform their profound and *practical* thoughts into worthy actions somehow. We could learn to develop a more 'self' driven life path. Accordingly, our new thoughts and goals for a simpler lifestyle would not only subdue our Ego and Model driven urges, but also help us cope easier with social demands. We can also take calculated risks according to our life philosophy. We do so by recognizing the rare opportunities that come around only in special stages of our lives, and most likely only once in a lifetime. However, we must also be prepared to accept the unforeseeable outcome of our decisions and actions, e.g., for deciding to pursue some means of self-employment, possibly in hopes of avoiding the hassles of working for others.

Changes and Adjustments

We are by nature quite stubborn and rigid with respect to our opinions and thoughts that have been carved in our minds due to genetics and early life experiences. Once we are conditioned and consequently develop our three aspects of personality, we usually do not want to see things differently. We resist ideas that are unfamiliar to us and sound threatening to our psyche and thought processes. We resist any suggestion that does not match our mental perception of those things. We block any communication that contradicts those perceptions. And we often stop others aggressively from expressing their personal viewpoints, because they sound so ridiculous to us; their viewpoints threaten our mental stability around our crooked values. Therefore, as a rule, we should not expect ourselves or others to change. Fast and fundamental changes in our mentality, personality, or life outlook are rare. With this knowledge of human nature, we appear too naive when we expect people understand their inner needs and the value of a 'self'-driven attitude, and then also adjust their minds to adopt new ideas and lifestyles. Especially, to the younger generation, ideas outside their limited frame of mind seem absurd and meaningless, in particular the idea of forward thinking and understanding the priorities and thoughts in the third phase of one's life.

On the other hand, we might change gradually rather smoothly, too, as we age and learn more about the vanity, or our purposes, of living. In some rare instances, people change fast and unexpectedly for the better or worse for all kinds of personal and psychological reasons. Depending on our life experiences, priorities, personal preferences and tastes, psychological defects, and social pressures, we might change intentionally or unconsciously to bring ourselves in line with new demands, values, and ideas.

In such cases, a person's high motivation and determination for change fuel him with adequate force, as he is convinced that change is necessary, logical, and fruitful for his physical and mental health. However, for the majority of us with little motivation to change, an alternative approach is needed to help us adapt. That is, instead of getting too uptight about our inability to change, the second best option is to make simple *adjustments* that would have almost the same effects of changing our personalities. Sometimes, we feel the pressure to make these adjustments. And sometimes, we feel the *desire* and *motivation* to do so for improving our relationships in society and reducing our stress too. Therefore, we make adjustments in three ways:

1) We adjust our *thoughts* in order to challenge our defective ideas and perhaps revise our life outlook gradually. Despite our high opinion of our ideas or addiction to a certain lifestyle, we may now suddenly realize that a more sensible lifestyle or idea is worth entertaining. We now sincerely want to at least nurture these thoughts in our head. This is the *adjustment of thoughts.* We try to become less dogmatic.

2) When our thoughts and beliefs are in disagreement with general norms, or due to adjustment of our thoughts, we may need to adjust our attitudes. With major changes, such as converting to a 'self'-control individual, there is always a great risk of not being understood or appreciated by family, friends, and society as a whole. Therefore, we adjust our attitude to cope with the reality of being, and being seen as, different from the majority, and even the possibility of being rejected. We have to adjust our attitude for our own sake, to get along with family and people despite our peculiar thoughts and beliefs. This is *the adjustment of attitudes.*

3) Sometimes, we feel dissatisfied with the outcome of our actions and decisions, regardless of the ingenuity of our convictions and thoughts supporting them. Therefore, we adjust our subsequent actions or decisions to correct the matter, at least for similar actions and decisions in the future. Sometimes, we may have to adjust our situation, e.g., our lifestyle or environment, because it has not turned out the way we expected it to be, or it is simply unbearable. This is the *adjustment of actions or situations.*

We may make these three types of adjustments separately, or in some combination, because we cannot change our personality or fundamental beliefs. Adjustments make our lives and encounters easier without losing our integrity and values. The above noted three types of adjustments could also be considered complementary in the sense that if we have problems in one area, we can make adjustment in the other one(s) in order to create a balance. For example, let us say we are involved in a relationship that does not seem to work because of partners' differences in personality and values, etc. If we assume that separation is not a viable option, for this instance, the 'situation' is nonadjustable. Also, partners cannot realistically adjust their principles and foundations of thoughts to accommodate each other. If a person has a profound foundation of thoughts, s/he does not wish to compromise his/her values or convince him/herself to think contrary to his/her beliefs. Therefore, the only possibility to continue this relationship would be to adjust his/her attitude, which is something s/he can learn to do if s/he really wants to save his/her relationships. Now, if one or both partners in a relationship cannot adjust their attitudes, the option of separation would have to force itself to *adjust the situation* at whatever cost.

We must adjust in at least one of these areas in order to make life experiences partially bearable. Otherwise, we would clash with ideas and people constantly, and hurt ourselves for people's lack of understanding. Without the ability and knowledge of continuous adjustments and flexibility, we would be in danger of extinction by various waves of opposition and disagreements. However, it is important to know which one of the three types of adjustments is most viable in different occasions. We would adjust our thoughts only when we are convinced that new thoughts are prominent and superior to the older ones. We cannot, and should never, do it because somebody, e.g., our partner, is demanding it. Normally, we adjust situations and our actions first, if we can, in order to prevent future and further mistakes. However, if there are good reasons to try to maintain an otherwise not very satisfactory situation, we should attempt to adjust our attitudes. We can think about the best combination of adjustments that can work for correcting a matter or instance. If it still does not work, we can try another combination of adjustments and test it. In the process, we learn a lot about ourselves and gain worthwhile life experiences. We learn a lot about compromise and teamwork as well. Nonetheless, there is need for being aware of why and what adjustments are necessary and undertaken. We should adjust to stop stalemate and our continuous doubts about our options.

Learning to adjust is an important life lesson and a major life decision, but we normally resent flexibility, especially in the earlier phases of our lives. We prefer to be stubborn and supposedly protect our pride and standards. However, stubbornness is usually a sign of naivety. We are often wrong about those issues we feel too certain about. There are usually ways to make life easier for ourselves and others by choosing some kind of practical adjustments in our approaches toward people and situations. Instead, we suffer a lot because of our stubbornness and false pride. Adjustment is different from changing, while they are complementary principles. Especially, knowing that we cannot readily 'change,' our second best choice is to know what and how we can adjust to compensate for our inability or unwillingness to change. Accepting the principles noted above, (i.e., that we can learn to adjust without changing), is a form of change by itself. We should introduce this concept in the foundation of our thoughts as a valuable life routine and philosophy.

In the earlier phases of life, we do not envision how restricted our actions and possibilities of adjustments would become when we move into the second and third phases of life. We assume innocently and naively that we can make adjustments as freely and easily throughout life the same way we did when we were young and free of responsibilities. We do not realize that, as we move up into the future phases of life, we get trapped within the consequences of our earlier decisions and actions, and it would become gradually more and more difficult, and often impossible, to make adjustments to our situations and actions. We do not wish to adjust the foundation of our thoughts either, as it would be like losing our identity and integrity altogether. As an example, we all strive to take on a special role in the family as a caring parent or spouse. Soon we become an adjusted person formed merely to fit our family's needs, to do certain work (that we might even resent), to maintain particular friends, and pursue a superficial lifestyle. This would become part of our identity. The fitted form and identity become fixed marks of our existence—and it remains mostly nonadjustable. For example, we cannot change or adjust our children because their attitudes seem offensive to us, and we cannot lose the love and companionship that we exchange with each member of the family. We have the options of adjusting our thoughts and/or attitudes to some extent in order to make our lives tolerable, but not our situation or the nature of things or activities around us.

We can say that many of our sufferings in life come from our naivety to assume that we would remain in charge of our actions and situations throughout our lives and that we can make adjustments to them easily when necessary. The reality is that we would not have the luxury of reversing or adjusting our situations as much as we desire once we reach the latter phases of life. We get trapped. We can and should make adjustment to the situations in these latter phases of life *only if* absolutely necessary, but there would most likely be a high risk involved and a big price to pay for it. If we cannot make adjustments in 'situations' to escape life traps, fortunately we can adjust our 'attitudes,' and perhaps even our 'thoughts' in some extreme circumstances, to mitigate the pressures of nonadjustable situations and our inability to act upon them.

CHAPTER TWELVE
'Forward Thinking' Philosophy

Forward thinking is a philosophical notion to set our life priorities and outlook according to the three fundamental questions everybody faces in the three life phases. The idea is to view life's essentialities based on our future wisdom after years of living and experiencing all aspects of life. Logically, the information content and value of our experiences are cumulative and thus our wisdom increases with age. Especially, our mentality, priorities, and outlook on life improve. (This is a plausible assumption for most people, as long as one's mental health is intact and before aging ruins a person's sense of judgment and reasoning.) Overall, we may assume that our wisdom in the third phase of life is more valuable and reliable than the one we have in the earlier phases. Yet, we believe to be the smartest person in the world during adolescence. We are usually most arrogant and stubborn about our viewpoints when we are least experienced, most impatient, too passionate, and quite vulnerable. In a way, we can say that almost all our helplessness and sufferings in life are the price we end up paying for our stubbornness and naivety during the earlier phases of our lives, especially the first one.

The wisdom and insight at each phase of life depends on person's intelligence and thought processes. Yet, by the third phase of our lives, we have faced almost all the doubts and decisions of life, made many mistakes and adjustments to our thoughts and attitudes, experienced the pleasures of life, and perhaps learned something about our spirituality and actualization needs. We are more realistic about our dreams and have leaned more toward our Self, since Ego and Model cannot serve us as much as before. We finally realize the value of Self for bringing us peace and tranquility. We grow deeper insight about life's essentialities and meaning. We learn to come to terms with ourselves and reach for our souls instead of pursuing many superficial goals. Unless our life outlook and values are too negative and dark due to severe life hardships and failures, a normal person learns objectivity and gains wisdom as s/he ages.

Our intention for forward thinking is to listen to the depth of the messages that people in their third phase of life convey about life by thinking or asking the question of, 'What was it all about?' There is no specific advice in this phrase, but only a fundamental and philosophical expression about life in line with a better understanding of our social values' vanity. All we need is attention and basic trust in the messages that come from the simple phrase, 'What was it all about?' However, if it is the wisdom in the third phase of life that we want to 'forward-think,' we must also adjust our misperception of old people and their wisdom. We must actually gain the capacity to imagine ourselves as an old person very soon and asking the same question.

As a young person, however, we dissociate ourselves from older people and their values. We cannot even grasp the concept of getting old and fragile ourselves consciously. Ironically, even people in their middle or old ages put a distance between elderly and themselves, desperately hoping to come across young and alert. Youths are too proud of their fresh and youthful values and outlook on life to even listen to any elderly wisdom. Our subconscious fear of death also makes us feel anxious around older people. All that traditional respect for the wisdom of the elderly has been eradicated in the new eras due to the fast rise of arrogance and superficiality. Obviously, some of the general perceptions about the values and viewpoints of older people is valid, since with old age come senility, depression, and health issues. Often, these factors make an older person's judgments less trustworthy and more depressing than usual. However, while they still have their senses intact, old people's question of, 'What was it all about?' is a reliable conclusion about the frailty and shallowness of life. Unfortunately, most people, especially elderly, cannot articulate their feelings and wisdom. However, they are all thinking the points noted in this chapter, at least subconsciously. We can see it in their faces anyway.

The three fundamental questions people ask themselves in the three phases of their lives have passed the test of history and would remain valid forever, because the overall human nature would not change anyway. We like to make life miserable for one another and we are not made to get along for a long time. Therefore, hardships, exploitations, and agonies of life would continue forever and the three fundamental questions in the three phases of life would stay intact. We can be certain that these three questions become even more pertinent in the future while societies continue to deteriorate so fast. We could verify the validity of these questions in any era by talking to people in different phases of their lives and capable of speaking intelligently and honestly. We can expect the same outcome even though we might believe that time has changed, we are more modern, and we are wiser.

Of course, nobody should rely on the wisdom of one person or group for building his/her life philosophy, anyway. While a specific individual's wisdom is valuable if we trust his/her faculty, our interest is mainly in uniform messages of a large group of thoughtful people in the third phase of their lives who have proven their high intelligence and impartiality, perhaps as scholars and philosophers. Meanwhile, we can also check with normal people in the latter phases of their lives and see how prevalent the main life messages are among the public at all levels of intelligence and lifestyles.

Forward thinking is mainly a hypothetical thought at this point. Maybe someday—in the 50th century perhaps—humans develop some magical techniques to foretell their future thoughts and states of mind. However, for now, we may use this hypothetical idea only to enhance our awareness, and to inject some doubts in our minds about the essentialities of life as we see them nowadays in our *presumably modern* cultures. We cannot realistically expect youth to think like their parents, let alone their grandparents, or really feel and understand the wisdom that comes only from actual experiences. All we can do, as intended here too, is to open their thought horizons to give a benefit of a doubt to the collective wisdom of people who all ask the same question, 'What was it all about?'

When we are young in the first phase of our lives, we are full of ambitions, plans, and need for pleasures. This is a natural attitude and expectation to the extent it corresponds with our instincts and basic needs. Beyond this primary intuition, our attitudes and thoughts reflect the conditioning norms, materialistic standards, and pleasure-seeking priorities of the modern society that we learn to imitate. We have turned into robots who follow the crowd and social trends with very little 'self'-control on the process and direction of our lives, although we strongly believe that we are independent and in charge. In this phase of life, as a young person, we are both naive and proud. We want to try our own ways and values, but at the same time, deep down in our unconscious, we feel committed to follow some standard life plans. We usually allow these standards and plans direct the path of our lives. We have some ideas about independence and breaking away, but at the same time, the criteria of success and the fake essentialities of life keep us trapped within a preset structure of life. They are the same values that all generations seem to adopt at each phase of life—the kind of mentality that keeps them totally dependent on their superficial habits and pretentious people around them—except that shallowness is increasing fast with every generation. In the first life phase, we are optimistic about future, sometimes even despite our cynicism about life. We think that we are smart and capable of making things happen for us, money, love, and fame, and everything else that we accept and admire as the criteria of success.

The main characteristic of this phase is the attitude of forward looking (not 'forward thinking') and wondering *what our lives would be like*. The essentialities of life are set with the same criteria that we have used to delineate the formula of success. In fact, in our minds, success and happiness are synonymous. Most likely, we do not even dwell on happiness and the factors leading to it, because we imagine that success brings happiness automatically—a major assumption that proves to be wrong in the second and third phases of our lives. Meanwhile, we fill our lives with short-term pleasures just to keep ourselves amused, and because everybody else is doing the same stuff. The path of life in the eyes of youth is quite clear. It consists of having more pleasures (for replicating happiness) while striving for, and looking forward to, more future success.

Our cultures define 'success' only in terms of materialistic criteria. Our immediate perception of the word 'success' is money, luxuries, power, fame, sexuality, and extravagance. What we do to get to this point does not matter, and what we feel even when we are there still does not matter. All we are used to perceive and measure is one's level of wealth and fame as valid ends all by themselves. Automatically, we associate these symbols of success directly to an absolute definition of success and conclude quickly about a person's degree of success and happiness. In fact, we have become so naive and conditioned that when we are told that an individual is not happy despite his wealth and fame, we get extremely surprised.

Strangely enough, we reject the idea that a person is actually not successful because he is not happy (despite his money and power). That is, we assume readily that if somebody is successful, according to our cultural interpretation, he should be happy, but not the opposite (as noted in the previous sentence). Naively, we insist that this person is really successful, but unable to appreciate it or be happy. Facing such a perceptually untenable and paradoxical situation, we then struggle to change our position and assume that happiness is something that we can buy with our success, rather than being an inherent state of satisfaction erupting from 'real' success. We try idiotically to redefine the relationship between success and happiness. So, even in our minds and perceptions, we are inconsistent in relating happiness and success. Although 'success' and 'happiness' are synonym in our common perceptions, we readily refute their relationship when someone's happiness does not materialize despite his success. Therefore, the only justification we offer to reconcile this inconsistency is that he does not know how to buy happiness with his success.

Success, as defined and recognized through various social symbols, and in the way we have imposed it upon ourselves in our cultures, is in fact more synonymous with suffering than happiness. We suffer a lot emotionally and physically by working so many hours and worrying about our profits and competitions, and at the end, all we can show for it is stress, loneliness, and defeated Egos. Even when we achieve our objectives of winning the competitions and making our wealth at any cost, we find our success to be at best only a business target; once we reach that target we have to shoot for a higher one. In the midst of all these struggles for success (higher targets), we become increasingly ignorant about the real meanings and sources of happiness, while hypnotically believe that we are happy or it would happen soon.

In all, we have spread a major misperception in our culture about success. Accordingly, we have conditioned ourselves, particularly in the earlier phases of our lives, to follow bizarre objectives and lifestyles for becoming successful and happy. Forward thinking is for reassessing these old habits and crooked social values regarding success and happiness. We should adjust our thoughts on this important issue.

Three important points must be clarified here:
1. Throughout the three phases of life, we all seek various forms of pleasure to mitigate our sufferings temporarily. This may even turn into an addiction if we believe that worrying, planning, or thinking about life is not a worthwhile strategy. We strive to 'live in the now' as much as possible. Building this type of easygoing mentality and a sense of irresponsibility is not the intention of 'forward thinking' philosophy.
2. Although 'Forward Thinking' messages discussed in this chapter might initially sound negative and depressing, their ultimate intention is to increase our chance for happiness (or at least contentment) by seeing life in a more realistic perspective. This important point is further explained below.
3. A young person who feels the futility of life must realize that s/he is in a special state of mind that could happen to anybody at any age or phase of life. These feelings are unrelated (or sometimes only auxiliary) to the main theme of 'forward thinking' and philosophical thoughts that majority of us hold in each phase of life. The point is that our outlook on life, e.g., its futility in the context of present socioeconomic systems, must be based on philosophical thoughts and wisdom, and not out of laziness, habit, or even intense suffering.

Phase Three Reference

The ultimate question of 'What was this life all about?' strikes us harshly in the third phase of our lives. Thus, the idea behind the simple philosophy of 'forward thinking' is to familiarize ourselves with this inevitable late discovery at the beginning of our lives. Then we may consider adjusting our mentality and plans according to this cruel reality. There are many profound messages in this ultimate question, such as:
- We would all face and sense the question of, 'What was it all about?' when we reach the third phase of our lives.

- We would feel disappointment, and doubt our wisdom all along, throughout previous stages of our lives, regarding our futile worries and struggles for success.
- Life is indeed too short, even shorter than what we keep hearing and imagining.
- Our criteria of success and its outcome do not prove useful and meaningful, but rather quite irrelevant for reaching even a relative sense of happiness.
- The outcome of our plans often turns out differently.
- Our judgments about life and people change.
- We sense the absurdity of positive thinking.
- We realize our naïveté to trust certain values, thoughts, and criteria of success and happiness.
- We feel major regrets, helplessness, and sadness for the loss of an otherwise beautiful life.
- We feel the ultimate below—that there is no hope of escape from our present trap or much left to do.
- We finally accept that we are alone in this life regardless of all the friends and family surrounding us.
- We throw in the towel and accept our eventual resignation, defeat, and desperation.

Obviously, these messages are in fact too harsh to adopt as a reality of life, especially for young people who are just blooming with all kinds of optimism and enthusiasm. How can we tell them about the sad reality that would prove to be the *truth*, but sounds too depressing and negative? And even if we tried, how can we expect them to understand the depth of the messages wholeheartedly without giving up on life? The intention of the messages is most likely not even clear to us. It is easy to misinterpret these messages and believe that they are intended to portray the futility of life and our struggles to succeed. However, this is not the intention.

The real purpose of exposing ourselves to these messages is only to raise our awareness. In fact, the purpose is to see the futility of wasting our lives on those petty things and plans that we have learned to consider essential for success. The ultimate purpose is to obtain the highest level of satisfaction from life, find the real means of achieving happiness, and see the beauty of the real world. The interpretation of the messages must be based on an initial understanding of the purpose of 'forward thinking.' The main idea is to prepare ourselves for the inevitable shocks in life and thus sail through this journey as smoothly as possible with minimum scars, regrets, and expectations. Furthermore, the idea is not to encourage 'living in the now' more actively. On the contrary, a main objective of forward thinking is to plan our lives diligently by identifying and monitoring life's essentialities every single day.

The messages must motivate us to adjust our thoughts, attitudes, and actions to abandon the phony values and hollow lifestyles in the perceived world. Initially, the messages may appear counterproductive for setting the right values for our life challenges and struggles. They may create even greater doubts about the purpose of living and keeping ourselves amused with work, all kinds of pleasures, etc. We would probably get confused when no substantive joys and goals seem to come from following the forward thinking messages. What should our new values be if we now must consider social norms and values unimportant or at least questionable? These are legitimate concerns. However, we can overcome these hurdles if we contemplate the forward thinking messages along with the fundamental notions within the foundation of our thoughts, our philosophy, and primary wisdom. With the help of our foundation of thoughts, we replace any old and unessential value with more meaningful convictions and experiences. The process of adjusting our thoughts, attitudes, and actions is for the sake of a smooth transition from the old way of living and acting to the new ones. How we can make youth interested in this type of mentality—to abandon at least the excessive aspects of their pleasure-seeking desires—is an extremely tough job, though, if possible at all! The idea is not to abandon our social values and ways completely, but only adjust them for a more meaningful path of life.

Many other aspects of the 'forward thinking' can also be studied. For example, the messages of forward thinking reflect that all of our struggles and efforts to boost our Ego would prove futile and funny. At the end, our fat Ego would burst and we would see the emptiness of it all, not to mention our sense of stupidity. Therefore, once we adjust our attitudes, we learn to remain indifferent to suggestions or offences that our Ego usually would not tolerate, like somebody telling us that we are 'wrong' about something. Under normal condition, we spend a lot of energy and time to fight back and prove that we are not 'wrong.' We learn that, in the final analysis, from the viewpoint of forward thinking, it does not really matter whether somebody thinks we are right or wrong as long as we maintain an objective view of our thoughts and deeds. Only our objectivity and integrity matter in life, not other people's opinions. Our only goal is to find the means of staying objective, which is mainly useful for keeping our sanity and peace of mind.

With forward thinking, we would find it much easier to curb our fears and insecurities about the love we do not receive, the jobs we cannot find or promotions we do not get, the wealth we have not accumulated, etc. We can better control our anger about losing our spouse who proves to be extremely insensitive and ignorant, and when we realize how s/he disregards or misunderstands our love, etc. We can witness and withstand our kids' wickedness, cruelty, and apathy. We can see that our shallow senses of success, even when achieved, do not give us mental satisfaction and true happiness, i.e., peace of mind. We realize that not only those accomplishments are not the essentialities of life to be overly concerned about or lose our energies on, but also we realize how such alleged essentialities only heighten our fears and entrapments. Instead, we seek our sensible beliefs and real essentialities of life by setting better priorities and building our foundation of thoughts.

Phase Two Reference

The question, 'What is this (life about)?', which hits us in the second phase of life, also provides some great messages. The question implies that we are right in the middle of a mess and feel trapped. However, in this phase of life we are still hopeful and believe to be clever enough to escape the traps. We still believe there are ways to get out of this situation and things would eventually start to make sense. We think we might have done something wrong that could be corrected, e.g., by getting a divorce and finding a new spouse. We are still assuming that the same criteria and foundation of thoughts that we have followed so far are good enough to rescue us from our present entrapments. We still think of success and happiness in the same way and according to the same criteria. The question of, 'What is this?' contains the following messages:

- We are facing a major flaw in our plans and perceptions of life, as we had envisioned and eagerly adopted in the first phase of our lives.
- We are truly surprised to face such harsh outcomes at the prime of our lives.
- We feel the mess we are in and our entrapments in a serious way.
- We become anxious and frustrated, and do not understand why our plans, logic, and common sense do not work.
- We doubt the validity of our criteria of success, and thus the presumed automatic happiness.
- We notice the social chaos and people's hypocrisy more clearly and feel sad about the whole situation.
- We are still confused about the meaning of our experiences and remain doubtful regarding the real sources of our prob-

lems. Yet, we do not seem to have any other options open to us. So, we feel obliged to follow the same path and values to rectify the issues.
- At the same time, we blame our past mistakes and wonder whether we could find a way to correct them.
- We also blame others and bad luck for our failures, but we sometimes feel our naivety and dip into self-pity.
- We question our lifestyles with deeper doubts about the meaning and purpose of everything happening around us.
- The lingering sense of questioning things and reflecting— 'What is this'—keeps intensifying. We do not know who to trust and where to turn for guidance.
- While we look for alternatives to get out of this mess, we seem helpless, as our dilemmas feel quite serious and overwhelming.
- We have all kinds of doubts about our future and our options, while none of those options seems viable. Still we force ourselves to push forward and we hope for a more manageable future. (It is only in the third phase of our lives that we lose our doubts and hopes, and finally believe in the frailty and shallowness of our dreams altogether.)
- We face the biggest doubt of our lives and keep asking ourselves: 'Is this what life supposed to be?'
- Yet, we still try to remain somewhat optimistic and keep looking for a solution despite our cynicism about the bizarre manifestation of life.
- We just get deeper in the same old habits, e.g., working harder and seeking more pleasures, for dealing with the tough dilemmas erupting in this life phase.

The question, 'What is this?', in the phase two of life shows that a big part of the optimism and enthusiasm of phase one diminishes and a sense of reality kicks in. We face the walls of resistance, disappointments, and discouragements. Definitely, some beautiful experiences of life keep us going. Some moments and experiences of happiness and pleasures partly make up for our depressions, delusions, and confusions. However, we realize on a grand scale how those perceptions of happy life and success have been a deceiving mirage. They only look promising and satisfying from a distance when we are in Phase One, but are empty and elusive when we actually reach them and touch them in Phase Two. They are boring at best.

The main, shocking finding in Phase Two is about our view of success and happiness. We realize that we have no realistic set of criteria outside the conditioning and restricted social norms. We realize that happiness does not come automatically from success according to our naïve initial imagination and expectation during Phase I. In fact, we might realize that we inflict sufferings upon ourselves in pursuit of that elusive 'success,' and that our struggles for success only add to our pains and stress. We feel that our present mentality and approach have created a large variety of entrapments. We suffer for the lack of a meaningful sense of success, despite our incessant struggles for it, and, even when we have captured all the symbols of success. Thus, we imagine, there should be something wrong with the present definition of success. So now, we like to rediscover the meaning, and means, of 'success,' before it is too late and we get completely old and useless.

We find out in Phase Two that we have been misled to assume we can direct and shape our lives any way we desire. We understand that following the values we have learned and practiced keeps us at the mercy of external forces and other individuals as our sources of satisfaction—but also the main causes of our sufferings. The consequences of our erroneous major life decisions, e.g., a bad career or marriage, are haunting us. We now realize how we have missed our life opportunities due to those wrong decisions. We may find out that our real needs and happiness are not achievable within the crude standards and lifestyles that everybody follows rather blindly. We might at least imagine the possibility of a more meaningful life, question everything we have been doing so far, and perhaps find some motivation to seek other options that could give us freedom, wisdom, 'self'-control, and peace. Whether we act upon our findings and seek a different lifestyle, or at least make some adjustments, is a different matter. However, most often, people do not or cannot make a tangible adjustment.

When we are in our second life phase and ask the question of, 'What is this?', we should remember that, by following the same life routine, the next question awaiting us would be, 'What was it?'; and that in fact would come around very soon. A motivated person may be able to turn his situation around by adjusting his foundation of thoughts, attitude, and actions, once he truly grasps the messages of the forward thinking. He can redeem himself just by pausing his routine life long enough to internalize these awakening messages.

By forward thinking during the second phase of our lives, we want to sensitize our mentality and build up our resilience and wisdom. We also want to reassess our foundation of thoughts and personal life philosophy in hopes of detecting the causes of our failure so far. We hope to find a better philosophy of life in order to avoid getting trapped into the questions of, 'What is this?' and 'What was it?' for the rest of our lives.

But we must also beware of the pitfalls of making drastic changes before establishing our foundation of thoughts and knowing the new criteria for success. So many of us take drastic actions to relieve ourselves from the agony of the question, 'What is this?, when our jobs or marriages do not seem to work. We call it mid-life crisis. However, quitting our jobs or divorcing our spouses and still following the old criteria for finding a new job or spouse would only lead to more frustration and failures. Seeking more pleasure or losing sight of our responsibilities would not solve the problem either, but in fact makes us even more susceptible to the ultimate blow in the third phase.

Phase One Reference

We ask the question 'What my life will be like?' in the first phase of our lives. In the 'forward thinking' domain, this question would take a different meaning and form. If we have established our foundation of thoughts and life based on the awakening messages of forward thinking, asking this question would be redundant in any phase of one's life. In that circumstance, the essentialities of life would not change from one phase to another except that they feel more profound and true. Therefore, looking forward to future outcomes and consequences are meaningless in the way we would normally plan them in the perceived world. In the real world, only our understanding grows while real values remain consistent—cold. The truth does not change; it only becomes clearer and harsher to us with time. Therefore, we learn to become more flexible in our minds and attitude to withstand the sad truth and life's unchangeable rigidity. We do not see success and its criteria in the way we normally do nowadays, and therefore, it cannot be measured now or in the future. In the real world, the only interpretation of success would be 'self'-control, from which true peace and happiness emerge, not sufferings. The test of success is only when we have a decent response for the question of 'What was it?' when we are ready to die.

In all, forward thinking in the first life phase is only for increasing our level of awareness about each circumstance and each thought that would prevail in the future phases of life. If we understand even partially, in Phase One, some of the forward thinking messages, then perhaps we would be mentally prepared to deal with these disappointing facts when they actually hit us. Furthermore, if we could really adjust our thoughts, attitudes, actions, and the criteria of success in the lower phases of life, we increase the possibility of peace, fulfilment, passion, enjoyment, and true happiness in the following life phases.

Forward thinking could trigger a mild state of awakening. We could remain in this domain for a tangible amount of time to attain the real sense of it, rather than passing through it quickly as a tentative awareness. We could reach for a high platform of awareness by absorbing these questions truly and grasping the meanings of those subtle messages. We could reach out for a state of permanent and full awareness, which would lead to deep awakening and the path of wisdom.

A parallel question that emerges during forward thinking is, 'What becomes of my soul (after my earthly life)?' And we already know that perhaps only a few individuals (saints) may have known the answer to this bizarre question, if at all. The question about the future of our souls would remain unanswered forever, as the greatest doubt and mystery of our lives, perhaps even if we were at the summit of the path of wisdom. The existence of a lasting soul, if at all, would surely not be the same type of life experience and feeling as we envision and talk about our spirits now. Most likely, it would be so isolated and different from our earthly life that cannot have any relation to our senses, present existence, naïve contemplations, or be viewed as a continuation of our being. Soul is probably a form of energy teeming around, if that, and then released from, a contained mass we call human existence.

The whole process of life remains full of mysteries, doubts, and decisions. Despite our initial exposure to forward thinking ideas or similar thoughts or experiences, we remain doubtful and cynical about our viable life options. We can neither convince ourselves, nor find the courage, to break away from the norms that so conveniently accommodate our conditioned minds. We do not seem to become really aware of the messages that are in front of us. We simply forget or send them to our unconscious. How many times have we felt our vulnerability and nothingness and soon forgotten them and returned to our expressions and feelings of superiority and Ego domination? How many times have we promised our spirit to change our ways of life when we visited a cemetery, went to the funeral of our young friend, witnessed the miserable life of crippled and helpless people, and saw pictures of masses of children dying in millions from hunger, wars, and neglect? How quickly we lose our compassion and awareness and return to our deep-rooted greed and self-serving thoughts and attitudes!

How soon we forget is no wonder. How our rowdy doubts control the whole domain of our thoughts and render us helpless is no wonder. What is of tremendous wonder is our inability (and unwillingness) to retain a state of self-awareness on a more regular basis! If only we learn to internalize our single and simple awareness experiences, we might eventually find a basic path of wisdom, to make the rest of our lives somewhat easier to go through. What is of tremendous wonder is our inability to let 'forward thinking' rejuvenate our spirits and the foundation of our thoughts!

Epilogue

In the Prologue, I mentioned that the main point for writing this trilogy was to communicate better with my children about the main facts of life and perhaps help them think and live healthier. I also noted that I failed to raise their interest to read the first draft of the book for many reasons. For one thing, most of the points in this trilogy sounded odd or contrary to the mentality that kids develop nowadays. My wife's disagreement with my opinions and outlook on life restricted my influence over my kids too. Her way was, of course, in line with the common approach in society, i.e., a perception of an ideal world revolving around materialism, egotism, individualism, competition, superficiality, etc. The appeal of the modern lifestyles and the support that people give one another in propagating those values made the points in this trilogy look bizarre and ludicrous. How could I tell my kids that they were being spoiled or argue constantly with my wife about it? How could I convince them that they were filling their brains with values that would cause them only confusion and stress all their lives? I tried not to alienate my children with my messages that contradicted their mother's as well as the whole society's viewpoints. So, I kept quiet a lot and hid the book in a corner.

Fifteen years later, I found the manuscript and read it again. I felt that over this period, I have become even more sceptical about social affairs, the waning state of humans' self-awareness, and the misery we are inflicting upon ourselves. I was glad that my rather moderate opinions were not printed, because now I am even more cynical about people's communication (especially between parents and their children) and the possibility of finding peace of mind in our modern societies. In the first draft of the book, I had tried to show my children that life is mainly a process of adaptation for survival, which includes a great deal of compliance and conformation. Now I feel even less eager to encourage anybody to adapt or comply if they can learn to live as independently as possible, both financially and emotionally. Unfortunately, adaptation and compliance are still necessary to some extent. However, I suggest more resistance toward norms, values, and lifestyles that are destroying our health and humanness. With our solid foundations of thoughts, convictions, and awareness, we must play a role in changing social norms and mentality, e.g., by curbing our craving for materialism, superficialities, and pleasures. We might develop all the right thoughts and make the right choices, but more importantly, we need the right attitude to live productively in society, although we continue to resist the temptations and group pressures to pursue their values.

It will be helpful, I believe, to develop a 'social sickness' index that indicates the overall health of society based on its citizens' level of stress, failure in their relationships, job dissatisfaction, phoniness, wasteful consumerism, etc. It would not be difficult to create such an index scientifically. We only need to be honest in terms of measuring the causes and effects of our crooked lifestyles and the impact of capitalism. Developing this index is easy if only we knew the public really cared about such information, but more importantly, we were convinced that some responsible authority would take on the task of collecting the relevant data and doing this vital measurement probably once a year. This index can reflect our success or failure in developing our foundation of thoughts and certain fundamentals to provide a more liveable environment for citizens. It is time to put less emphasis on measuring societies based on their level of wealth and employment, etc.—which by the way only confirms how miserably our capitalistic systems and mentality have failed. Now, we must measure the extent of social sickness that is getting out of hand.

If the author were asked to provide a subjective rating of this (social sickness) index at this point, he would suggest 7 on a scale of 1 to 10, where ten would be a picture of total social madness. If we can learn to become better people and less selfish, it would probably be possible to bring down the index of social sickness to around 4 in about three centuries, which would be an extraordinary accomplishment. But this is only another imagination by this naïve author. We will never stop screwing up one another until we are all totally insane, phony, and dysfunctional. We are fast moving toward 8-9-10 in not so distant future.

A philosophical question raised in this trilogy is, 'Why live when life has become so meaningless and full of suffering?' This topic was partially tackled in Chapter One, but it is important to reiterate that living might eventually give us an opportunity to laugh or feel fulfilled, or maybe even help bring the sickness index down to 6 or lower. Dying eliminates these chances, especially the ambitious goal of lowering the social sickness index. Besides, what we think and feel today (about living—as Shakespeare was eager to sort out too) is least likely the way we think or feel in the future, especially if we learn to pursue a path of self-awareness and see a bit of the *real world* without any travelling. Of course, when suffering becomes intolerable for some people, they could decide to end their miseries, hopefully after considering this option as calmly as they can in their state of mind, instead of acting hastily in a moment of emotional setback. Anytime we doubt the purpose of living, we must remember that living is only for getting those small victories now and then, at the cost of the never-ending struggles and unavoidable hardships. We may even succeed to realize that life is still a privilege despite the agony of living it.

Yet, often life hardships are of our making when we insist on living in our imaginary worlds. We are personally responsible for the way we have confused ourselves by insisting to live in this weird perceived world. We are personally responsible for creating such hurtful and meaningless values by making a world revolving around our naïve impressions, ideals, ambitions, laziness, ignorance, and self-pity. It is our crooked genes and lifestyles that cause our suffering, as they push us to follow certain life routines, like helpless addicts. We just cannot avoid the same selfish, greed-ridden thoughts for more power and pleasures. Our mindless pursuit of materialism not only obstructs our chance of building a solid foundation for decision-making and managing our doubts, but it is also too exhausting and stressful.

As a primary conclusion, we discover that humans' natural qualities do not match their common (idealistic) perception of themselves, and that this mental incongruity accounts for most of our personal and interpersonal problems. In addition, the characteristics of the environments we have gradually built around ourselves make it impossible for us to converge with either our natural or idealistic view of a human. Nevertheless, it seems as if we must face the same old cliché, 'Who are we?' even more seriously now, in order to detect the origin of our personal and social problems. Our findings would then make us wonder with even more surprise, 'Why have we become this way?'

Under the present circumstances, it is quite difficult for parents to advise their children about life. They are doomed if they support them to follow their shallow dreams, as they often turn out to be too fanciful and frustrating for them. And parents are doomed also if they try to push their children a bit toward a more practical and simpler lifestyles in hopes of curbing their rising expectations from life and relationships every year. We get blamed for both not letting them live freely and warning them about their phony ideals. How can we tell our kids that all their dreams nowadays, including fame, love, trust, dependence, and all the rest of all those good imaginations are only sure ways of losing more chunks of their independence, identity, and integrity?

Of course, there is a lot of fun living in the 'perceived world' according to our fantasies, as if we had gone to the movies to relax our busy minds for a short while. However, the danger is that our permanent existence in the 'perceived world' has overwhelmed our whole being and identity and thus obscured our senses and judgments. This submission to our phony identities and lifestyles causes our chronic depression and stress, all due to the prevalent features of social living nowadays.

Like everybody else, I personally live in a dream world occasionally, too, although I have learned how to enjoy it without getting too serious or uptight about its capacity and meaning. I dream mainly about peace of mind for my children and all the people in the world. I dream of people changing their mentalities someday and embracing more meaningful norms for our societies. I dream about my books making sense to at least a small group of people, who would in turn advocate practical ways of living in peace toward a healthier society. These dreams and writings keep me occupied and alive and they are my ways of thanking my creator.

Yes, I believe in God or the creator, which somehow exists in a form and format not comprehensible to us now or ever. My private sense comes merely from a general appreciation for an imaginary concept of the 'real world,' contrary to religious ideologies. I believe everybody can have a similar relationship with his/her creator without resorting to religions, which are at best absurd imaginations about a specific entity called God and the fake truth they wish to force about supernatural. We have used this concept of God, and invented all types of perceptions and ideologies around it, to fulfil certain social needs and perhaps induce some morality. However, we have failed to create even a uniform God to bring us together or enhance morality. Instead, we worship too many kinds of Gods and we fight one another forever over whose God is a better one and which one has sent us the right messages. That is exactly what Arabs did with their wooden idols and forced the emergence of Islam.

Anyway, returning to my personal objective for writing this trilogy, it does not seem like ever happening. My hopes for a deeper and more effective communication with my children through this trilogy have not yet borne fruits. Only my naïveté has been proven to me again, in assuming that youth may find it in their interests to be more thoughtful for handling their doubts and decisions. They all seem eager to make their own mistakes by following the alluring features of the modern world. In addition, genetics and parents' erratic viewpoints and lifestyles hinder the development of a uniform learning environment for children, especially when one or both parents wish to spoil their kids, as it has become customary in the new era. The competition in society to give children all the privileges they supposedly deserve and more is too stiff to allow any one parent teach the reality of life and its hardships to his/her children. Instead, they grow up to believe that life is a place to find happiness, which they also imagine comes from pleasures, sexuality, wealth, and arrogance.

Anyhow, there is not much we parents can do, but wait and hope our kids would find their relative happiness. As a tortured father, sometimes I spell the biggest curse on my kids when I say, "I hope you have many children of your own." On the other hand, I feel guilty that my innocent curse would also affect my grandchildren who must live in a horribly chaotic world in the years to come. I believe my kids get the gist of my sarcasm. To be sure, however, I have advised them a few times openly to not have any kids even if they are lucky enough to find a compatible companion. The heartbreak of loving your kids so much, while watching their agony in society nowadays, is too much. There is no point creating more souls that must endure so much disappointments and hardships anyway. I ask my kids to be wise and less selfish on this regard at least, although I really like to have a dozen grandchildren.

Nonetheless, I hope my children and many other youth get a chance to read this trilogy patiently and do their own objective thinking too. Volume II discusses various topics for building our spirits realistically instead of trusting positive thinking blindly. It talks also about the task of finding our personal sense of spirituality. Volume III covers many points about the structure of human life and the importance of dealing with a bunch of major decisions and doubts for living—i.e., 'life' decisions. Before closing this volume and after all the general issues raised in this book, I would like to offer the following direct points in summary as my final (futile) advice:

1. Any person over the age of twelve, with a healthy body and mind, must be capable and responsible for his/her own actions and decisions.
2. Seeking advice and help from people, parents, or even God, is good only for strengthening your information base and self-confidence. However, the final decision and subsequent blames and victories are all yours.
3. Everybody, especially youth, has enormous level of doubts about many things, and many of your decisions have high levels of risks. Yet you must weigh all the risks, make a decision, and move forward.
4. Despite all your efforts to make the best choices and decisions, you would often feel that life and the whole universe is running erratically, mostly against your needs and objectives.
5. Your tangible achievements seem to depend on other people's judgment and approval, but if you wish their acceptance, you must often become a lot like them, speak their phony language, and thus sacrifice your identity and creativity in the process.
6. Do not argue when people express a different perspective about issues. Encourage them to open up, just to give yourself a chance to learn more stuff about life and people in general.

7. The effects of genetics and the limited mental capacity of people and yourself cannot be helped. Deal with them.
8. Luck and destiny play a large role in everybody's life. But good things may happen to you too. Therefore, you do not want to be held back by many personal weaknesses, including your health and relationships, when luck finally knocks on your door.
9. Others would often misjudge and mistreat you. This includes your spouse, children, friends, bosses, colleagues, neighbours, etc. Only if you can live merely by your own judgments and convictions, you can ignore other people's perceptions and viewpoints. Otherwise, find the means of balancing all these judgments—yours and theirs—no matter how ridiculous and unfair they appear to you.
10. Life is not supposed to be fair and, in fact, fairness is only a fantasy.
11. The modern society and people are mostly corrupt or damaged and thus incapable of showing compassion, responding to your needs, or even understanding your basic thoughts and logic.
12. Nobody really knows who he or she is, let alone knowing or caring about who you are. You cannot understand others either.
13. You can never make people change or even see the need for it. You would not change yourself either unless you go through a long process of self-awareness and develop a deep desire to become a selfless and needless person merely for your own sake.
14. However, you can adjust your attitude, thoughts, or environment in order to cope with the rest of the world a little easier and in harmony.
15. Your basic need for a companion turns into a hurtful struggle all your life due to people's rising arrogance, narrow minds, and shallow lifestyles. People are no longer capable of relating or living harmoniously. Accordingly, despite their life-

long search for a soul mate, their chances of finding one are getting slimmer every year.
16. Therefore, not finding a reliable companion should never surprise or distress you.
17. Yet, it helps to look for someone to share your lives together, while always viewing all relationships a temporary, instable arrangement that demand constant monitoring and nourishing as much as possible. And still maintain your strength to live alone and independently, because separation and solitude are becoming the real facts of the 21st century.
18. Working for others, particularly in organizations, is stressful and often against a normal person's sense of independence and integrity. Therefore, learn the means of coping in such environments to minimize the chance of losing your identity and self-respect.
19. Always be careful about your health. Cherish your body and mind, as they are your best friends and assets. We all forget them until they are gone and never return.
20. Always enjoy, and be thankful for, your passions and creativity, because they are your second best assets, after health, and the only tools that may soothe your soul and keep you going in life.
21. Without passion and creativity, you would always feel lonely and desolate no matter how many friends and acquaintances surround you.
22. Staying practical is as important as using your potentialities for both 'self'-actualization and maintaining a simple life. So be prepared for adaptation and losing some of your freedom, passion, and time for creativity.
23. Plan your life to be independent, but also remain flexible and compassionate toward others. Despite the social corruption and humans' inherent impurity, maintaining some degree of social attachment is useful for keeping your mind and spirit intact.

24. Most people must do undesirable work for their subsistence. Take it as neither a burden nor a serious objective of your life. Merely consider it a necessity, an acceptable background or nuisance, while following your real dreams in life.
25. Life is made only of hardships, aside from the times of creativity, with some occasional chance for joy and pleasures along the way, if you are lucky.
26. Always live within your means so that you are never a slave for money or eager for extravagance.
27. Control your habit of buying things for fad or boosting your spirit.
28. Do not use credit to purchase things unless you can pay it off at the end of the month.
29. Of course, the credit to purchase your home is necessary, as long as it is at most only 70 percent of the property value, and if your mortgage payments are not more than 1/3 of your monthly net income. Repay it as fast as possible too and stay debt free and thus less needy.
30. The most important and rewarding challenge in life is to learn to become a good human despite our crooked nature.

www.ingramcontent.com/pod-product-compliance
Lightning Source LLC
Chambersburg PA
CBHW071237160426
43196CB00009B/1095